FAR SIDE OF THE MOON

FAR SIDE OF THE MOON

Apollo 8 Commander Frank Borman and the Woman Who Gave Him Wings

LIISA JORGENSEN

CHICAGO
REVIEW
PRESS

Copyright © 2022 by Myth Merchant Films Inc.
All rights reserved
Published by Chicago Review Press Incorporated
814 North Franklin Street
Chicago, Illinois 60610
ISBN 978-1-64160-606-6

Library of Congress Control Number: 2021944683

Typesetting: Nord Compo

Printed in the United States of America
5 4 3 2 1

This is a book about heroes. About some who are
known to us already but especially about
the ones who are unknown.
They are the ones who give us thrust.
We could not leave the ground without them.
This is for Colonel Frank Borman—thank you for
being a hero who actually lived up to the word.
Thank you for trusting me with your most precious memories.
And for Susan Borman, whose voice I have heard the whole
time I was writing this, thank you for the inspiration.
You are my Wonder Woman.
And to the rest of the astronauts' wives and their children.

You are all warriors.

CONTENTS

AUTHOR'S NOTE

THIS BOOK is based on countless hours of in-person and telephone interviews with Frank Borman and many others mentioned in the acknowledgments, conducted over a two-year period from March 2019 to January 2021.

Those who knew Frank Borman in the past or have written about him will recall him as a serious, pragmatic, stubborn, tough-as-nails professional in everything he did. But when it comes to his beloved wife, Susan, the joy and pain associated with their love story brought this larger-than-life man to tears.

Frank never wavered in his recounting of the moments I'm certain he would rather forget. On my first visit, I met with Frank in his modest home in Billings, Montana. There were no personal mementos that would tell you anything about his life in the US Air Force, NASA, or Eastern Airlines or any of the many trips he took around the world to represent his country. The only thing that hinted at his past life was hanging on a hook on the back of the garage door: the flight suit and baseball cap he uses when he goes flying at the age of ninety-two. It's still in his blood to get in the air.

The only photos displayed in his home are those of Susan and their family, and his most cherished memento is the last card Susan was able to write to him, which he keeps tucked away in the top drawer of his desk and showed me on one of my visits.

When I met Susan in the spring of 2019, she had already lost the ability to speak due to Alzheimer's, but I feel I was able to hear her voice in some way—thanks to the candid interviews I conducted with Frank and her friends and family.

During one of my visits Frank pulled out two watertight plastic containers with decades of cards and letters that Susan and he shared over their lifetime. Among Frank's letters to Susan was one he wrote to her and the boys the night before Apollo 8 left for the Moon. It was something he'd not seen since he penned it in the late hours of December 20, 1968.

Although the Bormans' story unfolded in an analog world, the digital world has preserved much of their personal and professional lives. Courtesy of NASA, I was very fortunate to have access to a variety of films and printed materials, from the Gemini and Apollo flight plans and voice recordings to detailed mission transcripts. I have deep gratitude to the many writers and filmmakers that preceded me who captured the context and historical elements that are the backdrop to the Bormans' story. Unless otherwise noted, all of Frank's and Susan's quotes and information about them are theirs.

PROLOGUE

Since humans first gazed into the heavens, the Moon has fascinated our collective imaginations.

When Apollo 8 commander Frank Borman first saw the far side of the Moon, it was like nothing ever seen on Earth. Nothing was that desolate. It was a harsh place with no color—just shades of gray everywhere you looked. This was the only time during that historic voyage that all communication was cut off from NASA and everything that connected him to home.

We have those times in life. Times when there is a "loss of signal" and we can't see anything but the void. For the crew of Apollo 8, that period of disconnection from the world they left behind in December 1968 lasted about forty-seven minutes every time they made the revolution around the Moon and were cut off from everything and everyone that they loved.

All the technology that got them there couldn't reach them in that place.

For those of us who experience that disconnection in our own lives, the abyss can last for much longer. It might seem that the loss of signal is permanent. But it never is.

After we finally come around to the other side and see the light, we look back and realize how sometimes the desolation can be beautiful. We can see what it taught us, what we learned.

As we gaze ahead to the brilliant colors in front of us—beautiful Earth—we appreciate it even more for having lost it for a while.

This is not a story about an astronaut who accomplishes the impossible.

This is a story about love and how it becomes the gravity that brings us back into the light.

1

"YOU KILLED YOUR FATHER"

Susan Borman was lying in bed on the night of December 28, 1972. She had just hosted a dinner party of some of the top executives of Eastern Airlines with her husband, former astronaut Colonel Frank Borman, who was now the senior vice president of Eastern after retiring from NASA barely two years earlier. She had made their apartment in Miami as welcoming as possible, knowing what her role was in the new career her husband had taken on—to be the consummate hostess. She was used to adapting, after moving over nineteen times in their twenty-two-year marriage. The wife of an ambitious air force pilot turned astronaut, she was accustomed to almost everything that life could throw at a person.

But on this night, lying in the dark beside her sleeping husband, who had no idea what was really going on, she felt like she couldn't breathe again and knew that she was in for another sleepless night. She wanted another drink so badly. It was the only thing that helped.

Eastern Airlines Flight 401 was on its final approach into Miami International after midnight on what had just become

December 29, 1972. The airplane left New York on time, and it had been a normal, uneventful flight right up until the pilot attempted to lower the landing gear. An indicator light in the cockpit that confirmed the landing gear was down and locked didn't come on, and the pilot and crew had to figure out if it was a burnt-out light bulb or something more serious.

The pilot decided to check the issue out himself. He put the plane in autopilot, left the cockpit, and was trying to get to the bottom of the problem with a maintenance technician. Unbeknownst to him and everyone else, the copilot accidently bumped the control yoke and kicked it out of autopilot. The plane was gradually descending, and because the crew was fixated on figuring out what was wrong with the landing gear, no one realized it until it was too late. Investigators would uncover later that a burnt-out indicator light was responsible for the chain of events to follow.

In approach control at Miami International Airport, a ground controller was watching his radar screen, and the dot that represented Flight 401 seemed fine until the letters "CST" appeared, which stood for "coast or sea level." The controller started trying to contact the aircraft to see if the crew needed help. There was no reply.

"Eastern 401," the worried controller radioed, "We've lost you on the radar. . . . What altitude are you at? Come in, 401."

Flight 401 had just crashed into a remote swamp in the Everglades.

The phone rang loudly close to 1 AM at the Borman house, which was never a good sign.

Frank turned on the light, rubbed his eyes, and picked up the phone. "Frank Borman here," he said, already alert.

"Mr. Borman," the unsteady voice on the other end said. "I am calling from system control, and I think that we have lost a plane."

Frank leaped out of bed. "What?"

"Flight 401 went off of the radar screen on its final approach. We think it might have crashed somewhere in the Everglades."

Frank felt a huge surge of adrenaline race through his body and took a deep breath to steady himself. "I'm on my way," he said, already thinking ten steps ahead. "Get rescue crews assembled ASAP. It will be a huge challenge to get them safely into that area."

Susan knew something was very wrong just by looking at her husband's face and the half of the conversation that she overheard. At this point in her life she was very familiar with what crisis looked like and had been awake anyway.

"What is it, darling?" she asked when he hung up the phone.

"I don't know yet, but we may have lost an airplane. I have to go and find out what happened." He was frantically pulling on his clothes and completely distracted.

He was already out the door before she was able to say anything else. "I wish you would let me help. I need to feel useful again," she whispered to the empty room.

The crash of Flight 401 was not the first disaster that Frank Borman had dealt with in his life. Nor would it be the last.

He had no idea that something else was transpiring much closer to home.

Susan Bugbee was thirteen years old when her charmed life fell apart. Up until then, she had lived in a middle-to-upper-class bubble and was completely adored by her father, an orthopedic surgeon who would take her on his rounds in their hometown of Tucson, Arizona.

Susan was born in New Jersey where her father, Frederick, had a thriving practice until he developed tuberculosis and ended up losing a lung. They had to move to the desert for his respiratory health. And if losing a lung wasn't bad enough, Dr. Bugbee also had extreme asthma.

It was 1943, and Susan was "precocious, smart, and popular," according to her teachers. She could do no wrong, as far as her father was concerned. He tried to protect her from the fact that her mother, Ruth, had a dark side that he was never able to fathom and that, sadly, her older brother, Frank, struggled with learning disabilities and behavioral issues that were never properly diagnosed. She knew that she was loved by her daddy, and she worshipped him. He always tried to shield her from the dysfunction that was going on within their home.

One of Susan's favorite things to do was to accompany her father to the Indian reservation outside of Tucson, where he offered free medical care to anyone there who couldn't afford to pay. He was a big man who loved to laugh. As often as possible, he took Susan with him to the places that needed him the most. He believed in exposing her to environments that would hopefully instill compassion within her young heart and show her that not everyone had the advantages that she did.

Dr. Bugbee allowed her to roam around while he was working, and she always seemed to be drawn to the building where the artisans were creating the jewelry and art that they sold to tourists in a small shop near the road. They enjoyed the outgoing blonde girl who constantly pestered them with questions about what they were making.

Young Susan fell in love with the beautiful paintings of the isolated landscapes that were the backdrop of her childhood in the Arizona desert, but her favorite thing to look at was the silver and turquoise handcrafted jewelry.

"Susan . . . sweetheart, where are you?" she heard her father call.

"I'm here, Daddy," she shouted back from the artists' workshop.

Her father was smiling and shaking his head as he came through the door. "I should have known to find you where all of the pretty things are." He came over and gave her a quick hug.

"Daddy, look at this necklace and this bracelet! I would love so much to have them. Maybe for my birthday?" She smiled up at him and Dr. Bugbee knew that he would be back to get them for her. Saying no to this sweet girl had always been impossible.

His smile dimmed just a bit. "We better start heading home before your mother gets upset."

Susan nodded solemnly. "Yes, Daddy." She turned around and waved at everyone who had been so kind to her and silently wished that they could put off going home just a bit longer.

It was another hot and sunny Arizona day in August 1943, just a few days before Susan's birthday party that she had been looking forward to for weeks.

She had invited all her close friends, and her father promised to get her the biggest cake he could find at the bakery. She was smiling to herself as she opened the door to her house, only to find something out of her worst nightmares.

Her father was having a severe asthma attack, which wouldn't have been as alarming if he'd had two healthy lungs. Her mother screamed at her to run to the pharmacy, because the oxygen tank that was always supposed to be full and ready for him was empty. (The first metered-dose inhaler for asthma wouldn't be invented and approved until the 1950s.)

Susan's face turned white with fear. She ran as fast as she could and pleaded with the pharmacist to drive her back to get to her father as quickly as possible. The pharmacist knew the doctor well and didn't hesitate. He grabbed a full tank and ran with Susan to his car without even locking up the store. They sprinted into the Bugbee house with the full oxygen tank to find her mother slumped over her father's body. She looked up at her thirteen-year-old daughter with cold disdain and said, "You're too late. You killed your father."

Susan's life changed irrevocably that day, and at her young age, she had no way of processing all of the ways it would affect her. All she knew was that her beloved father was gone, and she was left with a woman who could barely stand her and blamed her for her father's death.

Susan's heart was completely shattered.

There are certain moments that shape us, that we never get over. We carry the wounds our whole life and they become a part of who we are and who we become. Susan never got over that—how could she? How could anyone? Trauma reshapes us, and you never see your life the same way again. It is more than a loss of innocence—it's the demise of the person you used to be.

But the person Susan became in spite of this horrible tragedy and the life she lived in the years that followed was extraordinary. In 1945, her sophomore year, she would meet the one person who would not only change her life in a big, some might say historical way—he would never, ever leave her. Not even when she forgot who he was.

Frank Borman was born in Gary, Indiana, on March 14, 1928, at a complex time in history. In 1929, shortly after Frank's first birthday, the Great Depression began when the stock market crashed and poverty swept across the nation. By the time Frank was five, thirteen million Americans were out of work. Countless families were uprooted and so began the largest internal migration in American history. A popular song of the time proclaimed, "The only place the Depression hadn't reached was heaven." For millions who had lost everything, most notably their dignity, their faith and hope were all they had. While Dust Bowl refugees fled drought-stricken farms and headed west for greener pastures, Edwin and Marjorie Borman packed up and headed south to the Arizona desert. Their five-year-old son Frank had been struck with extreme respiratory problems, and doctors warned the couple if they didn't get their only child to a dryer climate, they might risk losing him.

But it was in the Midwest that Frank's love affair with flying began when he went to visit his aunt on his mother's side in Dayton, Ohio. She worked at Wright Army Airfield and was dating an army pilot stationed there. His father, Edwin—whom everyone called "Rusty" because of his red hair—took his five-year-old son to the airfield and paid five dollars to go up with little Frank in an old biplane. He sat beside his dad in the front seat, with the pilot in the cockpit behind them, and was immediately captivated by the sense of freedom and the magic of being in the air.

Rusty was making a decent living in Gary as the owner of a successful auto garage at the time and had a very tough choice to make because of the dire situation the country was in. Finding work elsewhere would be almost impossible. But Frank's parents chose to sacrifice their way of life for their son's health, and in 1933 moved to Tucson, Arizona. They then had to scrounge for whatever work was available there. Frank's mother Marjorie took in boarders for extra money and his father was eventually able to get a lease on a Mobil service station in Tucson, but it was a challenge to say the least.

Rusty's mantra for life was: *Do not quit. Stay in there and pitch.* Even though economic times were extremely difficult, Frank had what he would later express as a "loving and ideal childhood."

He was described by his elementary school teachers as stubborn and headstrong, always wanting to be in charge. His parents were hardly surprised and fostered that independence instead of trying to stifle it. He was left to his own devices most of the time, so he was able to explore the Arizona desert and create a world that all boys crave, one of exploration and wonder. He was closest to his father and, as an only child, he got all his dad's attention. One of their favorite things to do together was to build wooden model airplanes in the living room on weeknights after homework and fly them on the weekends. No matter what complications Frank had with the latest model he was building, his father would never step in to fix them. He let his young son figure it out all on his own. That hobby turned into an obsession with airplanes that would last a lifetime, and when Frank was fifteen years old, he was determined to learn to fly.

At $9 an hour (the equivalent of $150 per hour today), the cost of the lessons was more than his parents could afford, so Frank worked before and after school doing any job that he could get to earn the money to pay for them. He took his flight lessons at Gilpin Airport outside of Tucson from a thirty-year-old female flight instructor named Bobbie Kroll.

The first day Frank met her she walked up to him with a big smile, wearing jeans and a T-shirt. Frank had never seen a woman wearing jeans before. Female pilots were rare at that time, and Frank couldn't have been happier to learn from her. She was always calm, and no matter what happened in the cockpit during a lesson, she never panicked. Bobbie realized that she had a gifted student almost immediately. Frank had his first solo flight after just eight lessons, and from then on flying was not just in his blood; he knew that it would be his destiny.

Frank started high school in 1942 in the middle of World War II. His subconscious was already being groomed to be a warrior.

You couldn't pick up a newspaper or turn on a radio without hearing about the sacrifices being made for America's freedom. He was a good but busy student. He then became the quarterback on his football team, the Badgers, and continued his flight training. Even with the multiple jobs he held down to pay for that, he still managed to get mostly As.

Frank looked up to his gruff, no-nonsense football coach, Rollin T. Gridley. Coach Gridley set strict rules for his players and always demanded maximum effort from them all, especially his quarterback. Frank was the smallest quarterback the Badgers ever had and got the position only because the starting quarterback was injured. He didn't have much of a throwing arm, but he was a born leader. Frank seemed to thrive in difficult circumstances, and the coach knew that was something you couldn't teach.

Coach Gridley would not abide discrimination within the team, and both the White and the Black players always ate and stayed together when they were on road trips, which was very progressive in the mid-1940s.

The discipline and work ethic learned from football and Coach Gridley would remain with Frank for the rest of his life.

As busy and conscientious a student as Frank was, he had only one distraction: girls. And there happened to be one in particular—a smart, beautiful blonde fifteen-year-old sophomore named Susan Bugbee. She caught his attention over and above anyone else. From the first moment he saw her walk into a high school dance while the Glenn Miller Band played in the background, he was infatuated. She was wearing a simple blue dress that just made her natural beauty stand out.

He saw her from across the gymnasium and his heart said, *Yes . . . that one.* Normally a very confident senior, Frank developed a case of apprehension mixed with a bit of cowardice. He desperately wanted to ask her out but was so sure she would reject him that he didn't have the guts. He took on a challenge only if he knew he would win.

Frank turned to his best buddy for the last ten years, Wayne Crutchfield, whose father was a high school teacher and lived in a house just behind the Bormans. The pair grew up playing in the desert, going to movies, and smuggling animals home that they thought needed to be taken care of. Frank's mother never knew what she would find after the two of them had been out together. At one point there were guinea pigs, rabbits, a goat, a Gila monster, and a tarantula. They started calling it the Borman Zoo. Since Frank was an only child, Wayne became the brother he never had.

"Please call her for me, Wayne," Frank pleaded. "Just say that you're me and ask her on a date."

Wayne looked annoyed as he incredulously shook his head. He thought Frank was crazy but knew that's what buddies did for each other, and he knew that Frank would do the same for him.

"Fine, Squarehead," Wayne said. Squarehead was Frank's nickname on the football field because his head was almost too big for his football helmet. "I'll call her, but I think you should man up and do it yourself."

Frank just stared at Wayne without blinking.

"All right, all right—I'll do it," Wayne muttered as he picked up the phone. He dialed the number on the crumpled piece of paper that Frank had clearly been carrying around for a while. Finally, someone answered, and Wayne cleared his throat nervously and said that he was Frank Borman calling for Susan Bugbee. When she got on the phone, he kept it short and sweet.

"Hi, Susan, it's Frank Borman. Would you like to go out with me?" There was a short pause, and then she replied, "Yes, I would like that."

Wayne mumbled something about Saturday night and picking her up, then hung up as quickly as he could.

"She said yes. Are you happy now?"

Frank nodded but would always regret that he didn't get to hear her say yes himself.

Susan Bugbee had her share of male admirers, even though she wasn't aware of it. She was one of those girls that just lit up everything around her. It didn't hurt that she was also a "looker," tall and slender with big blue eyes, blonde hair, and a smile that you couldn't help but return.

One of Susan's best girlfriends, Beverly Sargent, would go on double dates with her. They met in junior high at Mansfeld School after Susan transferred from a Catholic school in Tucson. They went to dances just about every weekend, and Beverly was a little jealous that Susan always had her choice of suitors.

Beverly was with her the first time that Susan ever saw Frank Borman on the field at a high school football game. Even though he was smaller than most of the other players, the quarterback had a determination that got Susan's attention. She couldn't help but be impressed by the way he led the team. He was fierce and relentless. Because of those traits, the Badgers were undefeated that year and went on to win the state championship. Everyone in the school knew who he was.

When she got "his" call to ask her out, she couldn't imagine why he might be interested in her. Her mother was always in her head, telling her she wasn't worth much, so being noticed by Frank Borman had her twisted up in knots. She knew in her gut that he was special.

Frank picked her up on that Saturday evening and took her to a movie at the Fox Tucson Theatre. He had his first meeting with Susan's mother, whom he had heard of because she was the first female dental hygienist in Arizona and had been in the newspaper. After introducing himself and enduring the disdainful way she looked at him, he promised himself to try to avoid talking to her whenever possible. So much for making a good impression.

Susan looked completely lovely when she walked to the door, and he couldn't wait to get away from her mother and have her to himself. He was too nervous to even hold her hand but knew when he dropped her off at home that he was even more smitten. It would be the first date of many more to come.

———————

Susan's mother, Ruth, was extremely strict with her two children, especially with Susan. Susan's brother, Frank, had health problems and struggled in school, as well as just about everywhere else. He would end up becoming a talented artist in his adult years, but unfortunately that gift wasn't recognized until close to his death.

Frank Bugbee was held back a year in school, which, according to her mother, ended up being Susan's fault because people paid her "too much attention." Susan was never able to connect with her brother, even though they were all each of them really had. Her mother had pitted them against one another ever since they were young and made Susan feel guilty for things coming easier to her. She was a "daddy's girl."

It was a twisted psychological game that would continue until Susan left home, but in spite of the dysfunction and bitterness that she lived with, Susan remained down to earth, kind, and unselfish.

Some people are just born with darkness inside of them, and Ruth Bugbee seemed to be one of those people. Susan felt she had to be perfect in everything that she did, and after her father died, she was no longer allowed to wear pretty things—Ruth forbade it. Susan was forced to wear ugly brown lace-up shoes and plain, drab clothes to school and to church.

"You will not draw attention to yourself, Susan," Ruth would say to her. "Just who do you think you are?"

Despite the head games and abuse at home, Susan was still popular at school and good to everyone that she came across. She had her father's heart.

She learned very young to keep her feelings and emotions to herself as well as her dreams, her grief, and the hopes and wishes that any teenage girl should have. She understood that she had to do whatever was necessary to survive. And she made sure that she did it with a big smile on her face so that no one ever knew how afraid she actually was. It would be a skill she would need for the years ahead. It would help her become the perfect military wife and mother. It would also contribute to making her very ill.

2

DUTY CALLS

SUSAN AND FRANK'S FIRST DATE at the Fox Theatre turned into a second and third, and they dated exclusively his senior year until his graduation in June 1946. They attended his football games and went to parties, and even though Frank had a very full plate, he always made time for her. He made sure that she knew she was a priority in his life.

Susan felt safe when she was with Frank, something she hadn't felt since her father died. She was only fifteen years old, but she had already given her heart to him. Frank Borman was focused, driven, and knew exactly what he wanted. Susan decided early on that she would be with him for the rest of her life.

Frank saw something in Susan that was different from other girls. She was beautiful and popular but also had a heart of gold. Unbeknownst to everyone who thought they knew her, there was a deep sorrow that had made her wise beyond her years. Frank instinctively saw a strength in her that comes when life hasn't been kind. This was a girl you hang on to—unless you believe in something that you think is more important than human love and devotion.

———

Duty called.

Frank's dream since he got his pilot's license at fifteen years old was to be a fighter pilot, so going to West Point was always the goal.

West Point is a world-renowned institution, America's most elite and prestigious military academy. The West Point mission is "to educate, train, and inspire the Corps of Cadets so that each graduate is a commissioned leader of character committed to the values of Duty, Honor, Country and prepared for a career of professional excellence and service to the Nation as an officer in the United States Armed Forces."

One of Frank's favorite books was *Fate Is the Hunter* by Ernest Gann. Believing that fate is responsible for the way things work out was a viewpoint he adhered to, and so he found himself disappointed but resigned to accepting that the deadline to apply to West Point had already passed for the year after he graduated high school.

About that same time, a judge from Tucson asked Frank to mentor his troubled teenage son. Judge Ross had seen Frank on the football field and recognized that this young man was a born leader and motivator—things he wanted his son to absorb.

Frank agreed to help the judge's son, and he and his new young charge started building model airplanes together. A friendship was forged. Frank finally confided to him how disappointed he was that he missed out on going to West Point.

After their next building session, Judge Ross asked Frank to come to his study. "Frank, my son told me that you want to get into West Point," he said.

"Yes, I do sir, but it's too late," Frank said in a resigned voice.

The judge looked at him and smiled. "I may have a solution, and if you are really interested, I'll talk to our congressman and try to pull some strings."

Frank was momentarily speechless. He finally thanked him but refused to get his hopes up. Frank already knew that there was a waiting list for the esteemed academy, and he wasn't on it.

Fate would end up having the last word. He got a phone call a couple of days later and was told to get to the air force base in Tucson to take a preliminary West Point physical. He couldn't believe it. There were other guys on the waiting list, ones who should have been chosen before him. He was nervous about the grueling physical but passed it with no problems, and from there he received orders to get himself to West Point as soon as possible to take the entrance exams. The tests were extremely challenging, and at the end of that harrowing week, a West Point officer called everyone into a formation outside and read out a long list of names and asked them to step forward.

Frank's name hadn't been called. He was devastated and in the middle of a silent pity party when the officer announced, "If you heard your name called and you stepped forward, I am sorry, but you didn't make it. If you are still in the line, congratulations!"

Frank Borman was no longer a civilian. He was now a West Point cadet.

Frank told Susan when he left to take the exams that he would be back in three weeks. He soon found out that he wouldn't be able to go back home for over a year. He had to get through the initiation of "Beast Barracks," an intense two-month period of extreme mental and physical pressure, before school started in September. The academy was already weeding out the weak ones.

Frank had to access all the will and desire he possessed to get through it. He was a plebe—a first-year cadet—and the upperclassmen in charge made life as miserable as they could. It was absolutely brutal, but for Frank it would always be honor and country above everything else.

It wasn't long into training before Susan got a breakup letter. Frank decided he wanted to call it off before she could. His fear of rejection was a big catalyst for the tenacity that he was known for, but it was also responsible for some of his worst decisions. Susan was no longer his mission. He had a new one. And like everything else that broke her heart, she pushed it deep down and no one knew that she had been totally shattered again. Another man she loved had left her—but this time by choice.

––––––––––

Susan finished high school in 1948, while also participating in drama club and musical performances at church. She wanted to stay in Tucson to go to college with her friends, but her mother insisted on sending her away to the University of Pennsylvania and its dental hygiene program, to follow in her footsteps. Susan in no way wanted to be a dental hygienist, but that didn't matter to Ruth Bugbee. For someone who'd lost the feeling of "home" and security at such a young age, leaving her friends and hometown was devastating for eighteen-year-old Susan.

To make things worse, her mother sent Susan to stay with a couple in New Jersey whom Susan had never met, two months before classes even started. It seemed her mother couldn't wait to get rid of her. There are some people who should never have children, and Susan would always believe that her mother was one of those people.

Susan got through the next year in Pennsylvania like the trouper that she was. She really had no choice. One weekend she was at a party when she was approached by a scout from the Ford modeling agency. The tall, willowy blonde with big blue eyes and a beautiful smile wore clothes effortlessly. Susan had become a thrift store aficionado and was somehow able to turn the bargains she found into fashion. It was a talent she cultivated after leaving home, finally away from her mother's critical eye.

The modeling agent offered Susan a contract on the spot and wanted her to come to New York, but she wouldn't even consider it. She knew that it would be just one more thing her mother would resent her for, and she turned the offer down immediately. All she wanted was to graduate and go home to be with her friends and what was familiar.

Fate seemed to be guiding Susan as well.

———————

Following the defeat of Nazi Germany in 1945, it didn't take long for the Russians and Americans to square off as the two superpowers representing democratic and communist ideologies.

By 1949, tensions between the former allies escalated dramatically. The Russians had detonated their first nuclear weapon from plans stolen from the Americans and were into their second year of blocking access of essential goods to sectors of Berlin under Western control.

The Berlin airlift finally ended in May, just before West Point sent Frank and a few of the academy's best cadets to West Germany in the summer of 1949 to see the front line of the new Cold War for themselves. The damage that communism had done to the East German people would never leave him.

Visiting the concentration camp at Dachau, near Munich, and imagining the horror of that place, embedded itself deep within. He believed more than ever in freedom and that America was the country that stepped up to defend those who couldn't defend themselves, and that meant defeating the Russians and their oppressive communist way of life.

When Frank got back to the States, he was missing Susan more than ever. He had one year left before he graduated, and he was starting to think about his future beyond the academy. He admitted to himself that he regretted letting Susan go almost immediately after he sent the breakup letter, but pride and duty to the program kept him from reaching out. He thought about her all the time. *How was she? Did she miss him? Was she dating anyone else?* So, his letter writing campaign began. He was determined to get her back.

Susan returned home to Tucson after she graduated from the University of Pennsylvania and asked her mother to permit her to attend the University of Arizona in September. She wanted to go more for the social aspect, to hang out with her closest friends, whom she missed desperately. Her mother refused, and Susan had to start working for a dentist doing a job that she never wanted to do, just to pay for classes when they started in the fall.

Susan would end up being selected from over seventy candidates to be Tucson's representative in Mexico at a Mardi Gras festival and was featured in the Tucson newspaper with a stunning photo of her wearing a silver and blue fur cape and custom silver and turquoise jewelry worth over a thousand dollars. It reminded her of the exquisite things that were created at the Indian reservation she'd gone to with her father. That beautiful Southwest style of jewelry and art would always remind her of him.

Frank's parents mailed him the newspaper clipping, and when he saw the article, sitting in his small room at the academy, it was another reminder of what he had lost. The reporter described Susan as "beautiful—with poise, personality, charm, and intellect."

Frank had been writing Susan letters almost every week, but she was dating someone else and let him know that when she finally responded. "I don't believe that you are serious about me,

Frank," she wrote. "You were very clear when you broke up with me that your mission to be an air force pilot is the most important thing to you, and always will be. Why should I believe that you want me now? What has changed?"

Susan instinctively understood that Frank didn't value something unless it was a challenge. If he wanted her back, he would have to work for it.

But Frank Borman did not deal with rejection well. Being in second place or failing in any way was intolerable, and so he made another bad decision: his knee-jerk reaction to Susan's legitimate questions was to start dating someone else. He then asked the woman to marry him, as if that would make the situation easier to bear.

But all it did was cause more pain. Frank soon realized that he was making a huge mistake, because his heart would always belong to someone else. In the midst of planning the wedding, he broke another woman's heart. Not exactly his finest hour.

Just after New Year's in 1950, Frank got a phone call at West Point from his father, Rusty, letting him know that his mother, Marjorie, was very sick and had been hospitalized. He was given emergency leave to go back to Tucson to be with them.

On Frank's second day back home, he was taking a break from visiting his mother at the hospital and decided to take a walk down memory lane. Frank strolled around town visiting all his favorite haunts when he ended up at Pat's Soda Shoppe. As he entered, the first person he saw was Susan, and he froze. He'd forgotten how beautiful and vibrant she was. It took awhile for her to notice him, and when she did, she looked shocked but finally smiled and waved. She was there with some friends, and as he walked toward her he knew he was walking toward his true destiny.

He approached her table with a big grin on his face. "Hello, Susan."

"Hello, Frank. . . . What are you doing here?" Susan asked, hoping she didn't sound as nervous as she felt. "Did you come because of your mother? I heard that she was in the hospital."

"Yes. It's really good to see you. You have no idea. Can I sit with you for a while?"

Susan looked a bit flushed. "Of course. We just got here." Frank said hi to the rest of the table as Susan slid over and made room for him. "How is your mother doing?"

"She's slowly getting better every day. Thank you for asking." Frank couldn't take his eyes off of her. "How are you?"

Susan smiled as she turned her body toward him. "I'm OK, taking courses and living at home, so that's not ideal. You know my mother," she said with a touch of sadness in her eyes.

"Yes, I do." Frank looked at her with quiet understanding. It wasn't a secret that Ruth never really liked Frank. He always felt he had to jump through multiple hoops just to spend time with Susan, and Ruth went out of her way to show her disapproval every time he came to pick up Susan.

The time rushed by as they sat in that booth catching up. Frank started to feel like they had never been apart. "Su Su, I want to keep writing you. Will you keep writing back?" he asked, with barely concealed hope.

"Yes, Frank, I would like that." Susan smiled and then leaned forward and said quietly, "But we can only be friends. I'm with someone else, and aren't you supposed to be getting married?" Frank thought he saw pain in her eyes, but she looked down right away and when she looked back up at him, it was gone. "You understand, right?"

Frank nodded. "Of course. I understand, and I am no longer getting married."

Susan looked surprised and maybe just a bit relieved. She stared at him, not able to reply. He took her hand and gave it a gentle squeeze. "Good-bye, Susan. I'll be in touch."

As he walked to the door of the soda shop, he started to smile. Susan Bugbee was going to be his girl again.

Susan watched Frank leave, and tried to stop her mind from racing. *When had he decided not to get married? Why was she so happy about that, even though it totally crushed her when she found out that he was going to marry someone else? Why did he have to look so infuriatingly strong and handsome? It just wasn't fair.*

She especially hoped that she hadn't let on how much she missed him in spite of all the hurt he had caused her or how she checked the mailbox every day hoping for another letter from him. Susan took a deep breath and pasted what she hoped was a believable smile on her face. She turned back to her friends at the table and tried to join into the conversation but couldn't stop thinking about the agonizing fact that Frank Borman still carried her heart with him.

Frank returned to West Point and graduated at the top of his class. He was eighth out of a class of over six hundred other cadets. The ceremony was beautiful, but it was bittersweet because Susan wasn't there. He missed her more than he ever believed he could miss someone. He had asked her to come just as a friend, but she'd said no.

Everywhere he looked he saw fellow classmates with their fiancées or girlfriends. The only consolation was knowing that he had his choice of commissions because of his impeccable grades and performance. He chose the coveted spot as a fighter pilot with the air force. He was that much closer to accomplishing what he set out to do, but as he looked around West Point's beautiful grounds at everyone celebrating, he vowed to get Susan back no matter what.

West Point was now behind him. He had a new mission.

3

"IT'S THAT KIND OF DATE"

SUSAN WAS STILL TAKING CLASSES at the University of Arizona but didn't really have any direction or vision as to what she wanted to do. She was working at the dental office to pay her tuition, because her mother wouldn't hear of Susan doing anything except what Ruth thought she should do. Susan hated it. Ruth refused to listen and insisted that she do as she was told. The only bright spot was that Susan could secretly buy clothes with her own money from the Junior League thrift store, just like she had in Pennsylvania.

She had always loved fashion and despised wearing the ugly shoes and the shapeless clothes that Ruth had made her put on when she was younger. She kept her new things hidden at the back of her closet like treasures and would wear them whenever she could leave the house without Ruth knowing. It was Susan's own quiet rebellion.

Since her father's death, Susan had never been allowed or encouraged to give a voice to anything that was locked inside and had no idea how to listen to her own heart. She stopped dreaming because, deep down, she didn't believe anyone really cared enough to support her dreams, so she became the supporter. She became the rock to anyone who needed her, even if it became the reason that she was sinking. But that's all Susan knew, and it's how she learned to survive in a home that replaced love with rules. If she'd had any aspirations, she'd silenced them long ago. It was just easier that way.

———————

Frank had sixty days' leave before he had to report for his flight training at Perrin Air Force Base in Sherman, Texas. He bought himself a blue Oldsmobile Rocket 88 stretch coupe with money he had been given as a graduation present and was very excited to finally have his own wheels. He decided to drive his mother and father home from West Point so they wouldn't have to spend the money to fly back to Tucson after attending his graduation.

Truth be told, Frank had an ulterior motive. He wanted to go back to Tucson, and he wasn't going to leave until he got what he had come for. He had $300 left of the $600 nest egg that he had saved up over four years. The other $300 was in a small box in his pocket—an engagement ring that he bought right after seeing Susan at Pat's Soda Shoppe. No one would ever accuse Frank Borman of entertaining the idea of failure once he set his mind on something.

Almost as soon as he arrived in Tucson, he called Susan to ask her to go to dinner with him. She was still dating Carl, a Catholic guy that Ruth absolutely detested, because there was no way that her daughter would ever end up with a Catholic. For once, Frank seemed like the better choice.

"Susan, the phone is for you," Ruth yelled. "I think it's Frank Borman, and if he's asking you out, say yes."

Susan came out of her room looking confused and a bit flustered. "Why would Frank be calling me for a date? He knows I'm dating someone else, and he's on his way to becoming an air force pilot."

"Well it's not like you will marry him or anything," Ruth whispered loudly as she rolled her eyes, "but I think you should be seeing other young men, preferably other young Christian men . . . as in someone that isn't a Catholic."

Ruth Bugbee had no idea how close Frank and Susan had become again thanks to the letters that had been going back and forth between them. She also had no idea that her daughter had been in love with Frank since she was fifteen years old.

Susan was both angry with and embarrassed by her mother as she took the phone. "Hi, this is Susan."

"Hi, Su Su, it's Frank, and I would really like to take you to dinner. I need to talk to you," Frank said in a rush. "Are you free tomorrow night?"

Frank had to wait for the longest few seconds of his life until Susan finally answered. "Yes, I think that I am," she said softly. She wished it wasn't so good to hear his voice.

"That's great!" Frank said excitedly. "I will pick you up at 6 PM, and I have already made the reservation."

"I'll be ready," she said. "It will be nice to catch up."

"I can't wait to see you, Su Su," Frank whispered. "Until tomorrow."

Frank hung up the phone and smiled as he patted the box in his pocket. Tomorrow couldn't come soon enough.

Frank was standing in front of his closet the next day confronted with a problem that he had never thought about before: *What should I wear?* he thought as he shook his head. *What do you wear to ask the love of your life to marry you? A suit is out of the question. That would be overkill.* Frank laughed out loud at the ridiculous conversation he was having in his mind. *Get it together, Borman. Just put something decent on.*

Frank finally decided on his new air force uniform—it was sharp, and he knew that ladies seemed to love a guy in uniform.

His shoes were perfectly polished (a habit ingrained at West Point), and he took one last look in the mirror to check and smooth his hair and then walked out of his room looking more confident than he actually felt.

"Bye, Mom and Dad," he yelled as he was walking down the stairs. "I'm probably going to be late tonight."

"You going to see some friends and catch up?" asked his dad as he walked toward Frank. "Wow, son, you look pretty spiffy," he smiled as he winked.

"I'm going to see Susan Bugbee, Dad," Frank said as he shuffled his feet. "I better go so that I'm not late."

"Where are you taking her?" his dad gently asked. He could tell Frank was nervous.

Frank turned a bit red. "I'm taking her to that small Italian restaurant outside of town."

"Wow, you're taking her to *that* restaurant? Isn't that the couples hangout?" His dad's eyebrows shot up and he smiled. "So, it's *that* kind of date, huh?"

"Yes, Dad," Frank looked up. "It's that kind of date."

"Good luck, son."

Frank got in his newly washed Oldsmobile that he couldn't wait for Susan to see and started rehearsing his speech in his head. Unfortunately, he got to her house faster than he intended, so he wasn't completely sure what he was actually going to say.

Come on, Borman, he mentally lectured himself. *You are making this too complicated. Get your ass to her front door and take it from there. . . . Besides, you still have to get past her mother.* He grinned to himself as he checked his pocket one last time and touched the ring box, like it had the power to help soothe his nerves.

Frank took a deep breath, got out of the car, made his way to Susan's front door, and knocked. The door opened and he took another deep breath and pasted a smile onto his face.

"Good evening, Mrs. Bugbee," Frank said as he prepared himself.

"So, Frank Borman. You are done with school?" Ruth looked down at him grimly. "I've heard that you are going to be a pilot in the army or some such thing."

"Yes, ma'am," Frank said. "Actually, it's the air force."

"Same difference," she said testily. "Are you still a Christian? You attend a Christian church?"

Frank looked bewildered. "Of course, ma'am."

Thankfully, Susan walked to the door just then, and Frank seemed to forget her mother was even there.

"Hi, you look really nice," Frank said as his eyes drank her in.

Susan blushed and smiled, "Thank you, so do you."

Ruth Bugbee cleared her throat loudly. "Don't be out too late, you two."

Frank finally tore his eyes away from Susan. "No, ma'am," he said to Ruth and gave her what he hoped was a reassuring smile. Frank held out his hand to help Susan down the stairs and guided her to the passenger side of his car.

"Is this new?" asked Susan. She hoped Frank couldn't tell she was nervous.

"Yeah, my parents and grandparents gave me some money for graduation, and I used it for this," Frank said proudly as he opened the door and helped her into the passenger side. "I ordered it right from the dealership."

"It's a great car, Frank," Susan said, looking around at the interior smiling. "It has a new-car smell."

Frank beamed. "It's pretty cool, and don't tell your mom, but it's fast, too!"

Susan giggled. "Any car that you would want would have to be fast." She looked at him with a mischievous grin. "And if there was a way to put wings on it, you would."

Frank's eyes softened. "You know me better than anyone, Susan." He closed the door and walked around to the driver's side.

It had been several years since their last date, but Frank felt like no time at all had passed between them.

As they were driving to the restaurant, Frank seemed a bit fidgety, which did not go unnoticed by Susan. She was anxious as well but wasn't used to seeing Frank like this.

"Frank, what's going on?" she asked. "You said that you wanted to talk to me about something." Frank didn't answer right away and kept staring straight ahead, so she asked, "Where are we going?"

Frank cleared his throat. "I thought I would take you to that Italian restaurant out of town. Wayne recommended it."

Susan looked out the window and smiled. "That's supposed to be a great place. I have never been there." Susan looked down and rubbed her damp palms.

Frank was focused as they made their way out of Tucson on a dark, dirt road to get there. The restaurant was a popular hangout for young couples because it was in the middle of nowhere, and you had to pass by a couple of great places to "park." He had already driven out there earlier in the day to make sure that he wouldn't get lost. This date needed to be perfect.

Frank looked over at Susan and smiled as he took her hand and held it the rest of the way, only letting go when they finally arrived at the almost deserted restaurant.

As he came around to help her out of the car, he couldn't help but think about how it seemed that nothing had ever come between them. The horrible breakup letter he sent, the years apart while they were both in college, the fact that they had both tried to get serious with other people. It was as though none of it had happened because it was always supposed to be Frank and Susan. He desperately hoped that she felt the same way.

As they were led by the owner to a small table near the back of the restaurant, he couldn't help but notice that the two of them couldn't take their eyes off of each other.

"Is it a special night, you two?" the older man grinned and asked.

Frank pulled out a chair for Susan and looked up beaming. "I just graduated from West Point, and I haven't seen this beautiful girl in a long time," he said as he looked at Susan tenderly before he sat down.

"Congratulations, son," the owner said as he clapped Frank on the back. "I will bring you something right away so that you can make a toast."

As he walked away, Susan leaned forward and whispered. "I'm not twenty-one yet, Frank," she said anxiously. "My mother will be furious if she knows I'm having alcohol."

"I'll tell him to just bring us some colas," he said with a soft laugh as he got up to catch the owner. Susan shook her head and laughed too and then noticed that the jukebox had started playing something dreamy and romantic.

"Dance with me, Frank?" she said when he got back to the table.

"I thought you would never ask," he replied as he led her to the tiny dance floor.

It was a magical night, full of music, good food, and talking for hours.

When they finally left the restaurant to make their way home, Frank pulled off the road and parked the car. The view in front of them was spectacular. The night was warm and the stars were just starting to appear. It was like a hazy desert scene from the Southwest paintings that Susan loved so much.

Frank turned to her and took her hand. He brought it up and kissed it and then put it over his heart. He closed his eyes for a moment and took a deep breath. "Susan, I know you are seeing someone else and that I almost married someone else. I know that I hurt you. I know that I broke your heart when I chose my career goals over you. There are so many things that I wish that I could change, but I can't." He paused for a moment to get his emotions under control.

"All I know is that I don't want to leave for my flight training without you," he said with more feeling than she had ever heard from him before. "I never want to be without you ever again. Marry me, Susan?" She could barely breathe. She could feel Frank's heart racing almost as fast as hers was.

Frank started to fidget again because Susan wasn't saying anything. She just stared at him. He didn't know what she was thinking.

"Susan?"

She turned her head to look out the window for a few seconds, and as she turned back, she had a big smile on her face.

"Yes, Frank, I will marry you," she beamed, and then covered her face with hands that were shaking just a little. "I've always loved you . . . even when I tried to stop," she said as she looked up with tears in her eyes.

The only time that Frank had felt this sure of something was when he did his first solo flight years ago and knew in his soul that he was meant to be a pilot. He couldn't speak because he didn't want to make a fool of himself by getting completely choked up, so he just leaned over and kissed her.

When he finally sat back, he touched her cheek. "Thank you. You have made me so happy. We are going to have an amazing life together," he said as he reached into the pocket of his jacket and pulled out a small box. "I have been carrying this around with me for a while."

Susan took the box and her fingers trembled a bit as she opened it. Inside was a perfect ring—perfect for her. Frank got the ring out of the box and gently took her hand and slid it on. His eyes twinkled as she wiped at a tear that had escaped.

Her mind was reeling. She knew in her heart that she had made the right choice, but it was so fast. She tried to act like she was listening intently to Frank talk about getting married as soon as possible before he had to report for flight training. She couldn't help but think of how much she would regret that her father couldn't walk her down the aisle, how much she would miss his presence on such an important day, and that of course Frank would ask for her mother's blessing out of respect, even though Susan knew he couldn't care less about getting it.

Frank kept talking excitedly about the adventure that was waiting for them. He was always so sure of what he wanted and where he was going. Susan always envied him that. What would it be like to have that kind of conviction about who you were supposed to be? She had no idea what that felt like, but she was absolutely sure about one thing: she loved Frank Borman. But Susan didn't have a clue about what the future held or what this life she had just chosen would ask of her. It was the gift of youthful optimism and a big dose of naïveté.

As they were driving home enveloped in the romance of the evening, Susan suddenly grabbed Frank's arm.

Frank almost stopped the car. "What is it, Susan?"

"I'm so embarrassed that I just thought of this, but I am still in a relationship with Carl!" she said, looking genuinely upset. "We've been dating for quite a while now, and I owe it to him to break things off before I say yes to you."

Frank immediately got the determined look on his face that Susan knew well. "Leave it to me, Susan. I'll let him know that you are mine now. We are getting married, and that is that." Frank's tone indicated the discussion was over.

"But, Frank . . ."

"No, from now on I will take care of you. I don't want you to have to do anything that will upset you. Let me deal with this, OK?"

Susan turned in her seat to face him. "Frank Borman, I need you to look at me right now." Frank knew that he better do exactly that, so he pulled the car over and slowly turned to look at her. "Carl is my responsibility, not yours," she said firmly. "I will call him in the morning and explain the situation, OK?"

Frank reluctantly nodded. Susan had grown up since they had dated in high school. She was stronger and definitely knew her own mind. He would not only always admire that but also rely on it for years to come.

He slowly smiled, took her hand, and kissed it. "OK, Susan, you are right. I'm sorry if I overstepped. But I don't want you to worry about your mother . . . let me handle her at least," he said, knowing that she would probably make things as difficult as possible.

Susan nodded and smiled and then sat back and let the lights of the city soothe her as she looked out the window and Frank pulled back onto the road. She would worry about her mother and her guilt over Carl later. She smiled as she let herself start to think about the wedding, letting herself dream for the first time in a very long while. Susan closed her eyes and saw a girl in a pretty white dress walking toward a handsome man in a military uniform. She saw love.

They say that ignorance is bliss, which was a blessing for Susan in the weeks leading up to the wedding, because she was completely unaware of what Frank and the rest of the world would end up demanding of her one day.

Frank dropped Susan off at her house with a long kiss and a promise to come over the next day to get her mother's blessing. It was not something he was looking forward to, but it was the right thing to do and Frank Borman always did the right thing—no matter how tedious or challenging.

He was too excited to go right home, so he took a drive out to the little airfield where it all began, the obsession to fly and to be able to defend his beloved country.

Everything was perfect in that moment. He was going to be an air force pilot, and he was taking with him the only thing he cared about besides being in the air. Susan. Life was grand.

4

THE ARMY WIFE

THE NEXT MORNING SUSAN SLEPT IN, something she hardly ever did, but she had barely gotten any sleep the night before. What would her mother say? How would Carl take it? He had been hinting at marriage the last few months. She wondered now if she had gone out with him to rebel against her mother because he was a Catholic or to make Frank jealous. *Maybe a little of both?* she thought. Either way, she felt bad. Carl really was a good guy. She had to call him right away.

Susan finally got up and dressed quickly and snuck down the stairs to try to use the phone privately. Thankfully, her mother was nowhere to be seen, and she quickly dialed Carl's number.

"Hi, Carl," she said with a touch of dread in her voice when he came to the phone. "There is something important I need to talk to you about."

"Hi, Susan!" he said excitedly. "It's always great to hear from you."

Susan paused for a moment, trying to find the words to make this as painless as possible. "Carl . . . It's been really nice spending time with you, and you're such a great guy, but I have accepted Frank Borman's marriage proposal. I am going to marry him."

Susan held her breath hoping that he would accept it gracefully. "Carl?" she finally asked.

"So," he said, "you are trying to tell me that the guy that's been gone for the last four years and then just shows up . . . you are now getting married to him?"

"We have actually been writing letters to each other for a while," Susan said quietly.

"This is bullshit," Carl said, and with that parting comment, he hung up.

Susan closed her eyes. *That went well*, she thought.

She made her way to the kitchen.

"You got in late last night," her mother said from the kitchen table as she looked Susan up and down. "Just where did that Borman boy take you?"

Before Susan could answer, there was a knock at the door.

Ruth looked irritated, but then she usually did. She huffed and got out of her chair to answer it. Susan was frozen to the spot on the kitchen floor where she was standing.

"Hello, Mrs. Bugbee," she heard Frank say. He sounded a bit nervous but resolved. "May I come in to speak with you?"

Ruth raised her eyebrows and responded, "Back so soon? I was just asking Susan why she came home so late last night. Maybe you can enlighten me," she quipped sarcastically as she moved back to let Frank in.

Susan slowly walked into the hallway. Frank's eyes lit up. "Good morning, Susan," he said and smiled.

"Good morning, Frank." Susan blushed and started playing with her new ring that her mother hadn't noticed yet.

Ruth looked back and forth between them and shook her head. "Let's get on with it, Frank," Ruth said. "What do you need to talk to me about?"

"Well ma'am, I'll get right to the point." Frank squared his shoulders and looked her in the eye. "I asked Susan to marry me last night and she said yes, but I would like to get your blessing."

Susan stopped breathing as she watched her mother stare Frank down. She had no doubt who would win this silent battle. She would bet on Frank every time.

"Well, Frank Borman, you sure don't waste any—" but before Ruth could finish, there was a screech of brakes and a car door being slammed outside the house.

"Frank Borman," someone yelled, "I know you are in there and I want you to come outside right now!"

Susan put her hand over her mouth. "Oh no, it's Carl," she said in a strangled whisper.

Frank's eyes got bigger as he looked at Mrs. Bugbee and then at Susan.

"I just called him not that long ago to explain," Susan said, looking frantically back and forth between her mother and Frank.

"I'll deal with this, ladies," he said with a confidence he didn't quite feel. Carl Miller had a few inches and about thirty pounds on him. "I'll be right back."

Susan just stood there staring at the door, then finally looked at her mother, dreading what she would see.

Ruth Bugbee never missed an opportunity to give her opinion, whether or not it was needed. She also never failed to put Susan "in her place." But for once, she seemed speechless. She had a small smile on her face as she moved to the front window and finally said something. "Well, Susan, we might as well watch the show," she said in a mocking tone. "It seems that you are the cause of another fuss."

Frank slowly approached Carl in the Bugbees' front yard, trying to figure out how to defuse the situation as quickly as possible. "Hey, Carl, Susan told me that she spoke with you this morning," Frank said quietly. "She is going to marry me."

"Fuck you, Borman," Carl yelled back. "Who the hell do you think you are? You have been gone for four years. You can't just show up and steal a guy's girl. I was going to ask her to marry *me*, you bastard."

Frank tried very hard to stay calm. "Listen, Carl, first of all, I didn't steal her. Second, we have been writing each other off and on the whole time I was away. So, please just leave and accept that I am the guy Susan chose."

"Accept this, Borman," Carl hissed as he made a fist and threw the first punch.

Frank wasn't a violent person, but he'd learned at a young age— and even more so at West Point—that there were times you had to defend you and yours. You never back down from something that's worth fighting for. Carl was going down.

It didn't take long. Frank didn't want to humiliate him; he just wanted to get this over with as quickly as possible. He was trying to get Ruth's blessing, and this wasn't going according to plan at all.

As Carl lay on the grass in the front yard with a bloody nose, Ruth slowly opened the door and came outside. "You have my blessing, Frank," she said with a smirk. "I see that the Christian God was with you today." And with that she went inside and left a bewildered Frank out in the yard trying to figure out what that meant.

Without her mother noticing, Susan quietly came out and walked over to the two young men who had just fought over her. Frank tried to stop her, but she turned toward him and gave him "the look." Frank receded into the background.

She walked over to where Carl was still lying on the grass. "I'm really sorry, Carl. . . . Everything happened so fast." Her face was flushed, and she looked down at the ring on her hand. "I love him . . . I always have." She paused and took a deep breath. "I'm sorry if I hurt you."

Carl stood up, wiped the blood from beneath his nose, shook his head in disgust, and got in his car without saying another word.

Frank and Susan watched him drive away, and then Frank turned to her with a big grin as he rubbed his sore knuckles. "So, is four weeks enough time to plan a wedding?"

On a beautiful day in Tucson on July 20, 1950, Susan Bugbee became Mrs. Frank Borman. Their wedding was organized by Susan's mother and was held at the Episcopal church that her father had taken her to as a girl. Ruth was a Presbyterian and had forced Susan to go to a different church after her father died, but Susan insisted on getting married in her father's church. It was the only way she could feel him somehow beside her, even though he couldn't walk her down the aisle. Ruth tried to change it, but on this Susan would not budge. She didn't stand up to her mother often, but this mattered too much.

Susan's brother, Frank, walked her down the aisle, and her best friend, Beverly, was her maid of honor. The groom's best friend, Wayne, was the best man. Marjorie and Rusty Borman beamed as they watched Susan walk down the aisle toward their only child. And even though Ruth had to control the rest of the wedding, right down to the dress that the bride wore, Susan really didn't care. She was going to be someone's wife. Someone who chose *her* over everyone else, someone whom she had loved since the moment she laid eyes on him at that football game.

She was saying good-bye to her controlling mother and would have her own home—her own life. She would finally be free.

Frank and Susan had one week for a quick honeymoon and made their way to the North Rim of the Grand Canyon—it would forever remain one of their favorite places in the world—and then on to Vegas. It was the first of many adventures to come for two young and idealistic people in love. Neither of them knew what living a military life would actually entail. They didn't know how difficult the many transfers and moves would be that came with being a brand-new second lieutenant. They didn't talk about the constant threat of death that a fighter pilot would face on a daily basis. There was only a giddy enthusiasm to start their married life together.

As they were heading back from their honeymoon to Frank's first air force training post in Texas, they stopped just outside of the Grand Canyon at the Navajo reservation she had been to many times with her father, to look at pieces of art and jewelry made by the Native Americans living there. Susan found herself immersed in memories that she hadn't thought about in years, and Frank could tell that there was something very special about this place for her.

Susan fell in love with a handmade silver and turquoise necklace, bracelet, and ring. They reminded her of the jewelry that she'd asked her father to get her for her birthday when she was a little girl. It was quite expensive for two young people just starting out, but Frank wanted to get a special wedding present for his new, lovely bride.

Susan had never actually owned anything so beautiful and begged Frank to take her back to Tucson before they left for Frank's flight training so that she could show her mother. Frank was anxious to get to the base, but he would do anything to keep Susan smiling, even though he suspected that she would be disappointed with her mother's reaction. Ruth Bugbee had never celebrated Susan in any way. He didn't believe that she would start now.

They pulled up to Ruth's house a week after they had left Tucson, and Susan checked herself in the car mirror. She had all her jewelry on and was excited to go into the house to show her mother. Frank wasn't nearly as keen to go in. He had tried to extend an olive branch to his mother-in-law at the wedding, but Ruth just looked at him like he was something she had to scrape off her shoe.

No one really understood why Ruth was such an angry and bitter woman. She had been that way even before her husband had died, and Frank was constantly perplexed as to how someone with a heart like Susan's could have been raised by someone like her.

"Frank, how do I look?" Susan asked, a bit nervously. She smoothed the new dress that she had found at the Junior League thrift store just before the wedding. "Doesn't this dress look nice with my beautiful jewelry?"

"You always look perfect, Su Su," Frank said with love in his eyes as he took her hand and kissed it. "We should go in so that we can get on the road. The sooner the better," Frank added under his breath as he got out of the car.

Ruth was just opening the door as they walked up. "What are you both doing here?" she said, annoyed. "Aren't you supposed to be in Texas?"

"Yes, ma'am," said Frank, already bracing himself. "Susan wanted to stop and tell you about our trip."

"I'm sure that I don't need to hear the details," she said in an impatient voice. "Susan, Frank needs to get to his post. Are you being difficult?"

"No, Mom," Susan said with an embarrassed flush. "I just wanted to tell you what a lovely time that we had and that we stopped at the Navajo reservation in Tuba City and Frank bought these beautiful pieces of jewelry for me!" she said excitedly. "Do you remember that I used go there with Daddy?"

Ruth crossed her arms and then looked away. When she finally looked back at Susan, she sneered, "Don't be so smug, young lady."

Susan's face fell, and it was all Frank could do to not say something to this cold and indifferent woman. "Susan, we should get going. We have a long drive," he said as he put his arm around her shoulders.

Susan looked totally defeated. "Yes, Frank," she said. "We should go now. Good-bye, Mom," she whispered brokenly.

Ruth just nodded.

Frank couldn't get them out of there fast enough. As they drove out of Tucson, he turned to Susan and grabbed her hand. "You have a new family now, sweetheart."

Susan laid her head on his shoulder and Frank had no idea that she was crying silently as they drove away. *Why do I do this to myself, over and over?* she thought. *Why do I think that she might ever be proud of me?*

———————

The next six months would race by for Frank and Susan at the Perrin base in Sherman, Texas. They rented a one-bedroom bungalow right away, and Susan found out she was pregnant within a couple of months of arriving. They were surrounded by quite a few of Frank's fellow classmates from West Point and their wives, so their social calendar was full.

Susan enjoyed the first blush of married life, and Frank was as determined as ever to master the flight simulator that was the beginning of his flight training. He couldn't wait to get up in the air.

On a particularly overcast day in November 1950, Susan was rushed to the hospital in Sherman. She had suffered a miscarriage and was kept there for three days. She was absolutely devastated but didn't want to burden Frank with it.

Susan had been given a "bible" to live by as soon as they arrived on the Perrin base. The book was called *The Army Wife* by Nancy Shea. Susan read it cover to cover and was determined to execute it perfectly. She willingly became part of "Team Borman" and was determined to be the model military wife and partner to Frank and his ambitions.

According to the book, army wives were not supposed to bother their husbands with anything domestic, and there should always be a smile on their face—real or not. Showing negative emotion of any kind was frowned upon. Susan had had a lot of practice with that thanks to living with her mother, and when she left the hospital, no one had any idea, including Frank, how much she was grieving.

———————

Frank was at the top of the class again when he finished at Perrin and had his choice of what branch of the air force he preferred. He picked fighter training. He was informed that he had to report to Williams Air Force Base in Chandler, Arizona, which was just outside of Phoenix.

Frank and Susan were about to get introduced to the downside of military life. There was a housing shortage in the area, and the only thing that the young couple could find in their price range was a run-down trailer with no air conditioning.

Susan found out she was pregnant again and was plagued with terrible morning sickness. She was overjoyed but anxious at the same time that she might lose another one. She was stuck in a stifling tin box with only her cocker spaniel, Cindy, for company—another thing that she had wanted her whole life.

Susan loved animals, especially dogs, so she got one as soon as she could after she was married. Her mother would never allow her to have one growing up.

Of course, like a good military wife she never uttered a word of complaint about the living conditions. Because they had only one car, Susan was left in the small mobile trailer most days and did everything she could to make it look like some kind of home, completely unaware of the challenges that lay just over the horizon.

5

"EVERY MAN A TIGER"

"IF YOU SCREW UP IN AN AIRPLANE, don't give me any crap about being distracted because your wife is pregnant or some other personal crisis—that's your problem, not mine. Take a good look around you, because chances are the guy next to you is either gonna wash out or die," said training commander Leon Gray on Frank's first day at Williams. "As far as I'm concerned, your wives are government property who should be turned in at each base and a brand-new one checked out at the next base. I don't give a damn about your personal lives."

Commander Gray was tough and callous, but he definitely knew his way around a fighter plane. He personified the USAF's unofficial motto: Every Man a Tiger.

And so began a career that would put Lieutenant Frank Borman in harm's way for the next two decades.

Frank graduated from flight training on August 4, 1951, which was also Susan's twenty-first birthday. She was now seven months pregnant. Susan was the only family that was there to see Frank cross the threshold to get his "wings." She could not have been prouder of him. As she pinned his wings onto his uniform and kissed his cheek, she knew that another transfer was coming. She looked away and closed her eyes as her hand rested on her stomach, praying that they would end up somewhere clean and safe for this new life that was about to show up. Even though Frank had been a pilot since he was fifteen years old, he felt like he finally got his wings when Susan put them onto his uniform because she was there with him.

Since Frank was at the top of the class yet again, he was given a month's leave to get settled at his next assignment for more fighter pilot training at Luke Air Force Base in Glendale, Arizona.

It was perfect timing, as their first baby was due very soon, and Frank was able to find a small apartment for them on the west side of Phoenix. Frank chose the location so that they would be closer to his parents when the baby was born. He knew that Susan would get nothing but grief from her mother and therefore wanted two people he knew he could rely upon to be near to help out. They bought some unpainted furniture and Susan busied herself with an urgent need to set up "the nest."

They had barely started to unpack when Frank came home from a quick trip to his new squadron at the Luke base to see if any of their mail had been forwarded. When he walked through the door, he looked quite upset.

"What's the matter, Frank?" Susan asked as she slowly made her way over to him. At over eight months pregnant, she was feeling like she had been blown up like a giant balloon.

"I made a huge mistake going to pick up our mail today," Frank said as he looked anxiously around the apartment that Susan had worked so hard to set up. "The sergeant on duty had orders to grab the first four lieutenants that came through the door this morning and assign them to Nellis Air Force Base in Las Vegas. I have to report in Monday morning by 7:00 AM."

Frank felt a bit helpless as he looked at Susan. "I know we just got here, and the baby could come any time. I told them that we were about to have a child right away, but the captain firmly reminded me that my job is to follow orders. I'm so sorry, hon," Frank said quietly as he looked down and shook his head.

Susan closed her eyes briefly and took a deep breath. She was getting yet another lesson on what it meant to be married to someone who had to do his duty regardless of how it affected his family.

"I think I should take you back to Tucson to stay with your mother until the baby comes," Frank said, clearly frustrated. He knew his parents' place was too small for Susan and a new baby.

"Absolutely not!" Susan insisted. The very idea was abhorrent to her. "I will go with you, and we will figure it out. I want us to stay together and do this as a team, Frank. I will not go back to my mother's house. I'd rather have this baby in the back of a car than stay there."

Susan looked determined but was clearly upset. Frank knew that wasn't good for her or the baby. "OK, OK. Don't worry, Su Su. We will stay together. If it's in my power, we will always be together."

Frank hugged her and ran his hand over her beautiful blonde hair to comfort her. "I have to go make arrangements for a U-Haul trailer, and we need to start packing up everything we just unpacked." He eased himself back and looked at her. "Are you sure you are up for this? I have no idea where we are going to live once we get there."

Frank was still reeling at how things had changed so dramatically in just a few hours. Susan tried to smile. "I'm going with you no matter what, so let's start packing."

Frank kissed her quickly and nodded. "All right. That's all I need to know," he said in the resolute way he always approached an obstacle. He was about to leave but then stopped at the door and turned back with a grim smile. "Maybe you could say a prayer or two? We could use a little help with this one." And without waiting for an answer, he walked out of the apartment that they had rented just days before.

Frank left the apartment complex after telling the manager, who was none too happy, that he had been transferred. There were a thousand thoughts racing through his head. He had a lot to do with no time to do it. His partner in all of this was just about to give birth to his first child, and he was at a complete loss as to how to make sure that she would have everything that she needed.

Shit, he thought suddenly, *I have to get a hold of her doctor here to transfer her records to a doctor in Las Vegas.* He quickly booked the U-Haul and came back to see Susan frantically packing up everything they had just bought for the baby.

"Susan, we need to call your doctor to let him know that you are leaving," Frank said gently as he walked up and placed his arm around her. It was quite clear that she was stressed. "Can you give me the number?"

Susan started to look for her address book. "I was thinking the same thing, but I know he will be opposed to this, Frank. It doesn't matter, though. I am going with you no matter what he says."

They hadn't hooked up a home phone yet, so Frank had to go down the street to use the pay phone again. "Hello, this is Lieutenant Frank Borman, and I have just been transferred to the Nellis Air Force Base outside of Las Vegas. My wife is Susan Borman, and she is over eight months pregnant. Can I please speak with Dr. Carter? It's an emergency." Frank knew that was the only way to get him on the phone. Frank waited for what seemed like hours but was actually only a few minutes.

"Hello, this is Dr. Carter."

"Dr. Carter, it's Frank Borman, and as you know I am in the air force. I have just been transferred to Nellis, and I need my wife's records so that we can give them to a doctor in Las Vegas," Frank said in what he hoped was an authoritative voice.

"What?" Dr. Carter exclaimed incredulously. "Your wife is over eight months pregnant. No one in their right mind would move her anywhere right now. She needs to stay here!"

Frank closed his eyes and prayed for patience. "Sir, I would really appreciate you helping us out. My hands are tied, I am following orders, and my wife refuses to stay behind. Please, can you refer us to a doctor in Las Vegas?"

"Not in good conscience, no," the doctor said. "It is completely unsafe for her to leave. I will not help you put her in harm's way." Dr. Carter hung up the phone with a disgusted snort.

Frank took another deep breath, asked whoever was listening for patience again, and called his squadron. The same squadron that had just thrown a major curveball into his life.

"Hello, this is Lieutenant Frank Borman. I need the number of someone who can help me find my wife a doctor at Nellis. She is over eight months pregnant and we have to leave right away."

Whoever answered must have had some empathy. "Let me find the number for you at the Nellis base hospital, Lieutenant Borman," they said.

Frank got the number and called the hospital. Providence was in his corner, because he was actually able to get through to someone in charge there. Frank quickly told him what was going on.

"Don't worry, Lieutenant. I give you my word that your wife will be taken care of. We will make sure she has everything she needs and that her health records get sent here."

Frank finally felt like he could breathe a bit easier as he hung up the phone. He looked up. "Thank you," he whispered.

Frank showed up at the apartment with the U-Haul after he had to surrender the lease on their new apartment, which meant losing the damage deposit, a big blow to their meager bank account. Late that same night, Susan and Frank were on their way to Las Vegas.

Frank made a bed in the small backseat of the coupe for his understandably exhausted wife, and just before six o'clock the next morning they arrived in Vegas. He found a small motel right away and checked them in, got Susan settled, and then found a newspaper. He pored over the ads for apartments, and there was only one in their price range. Frank was so determined to get it that he woke the owner up early that morning and just said, "I'll take the apartment."

The woman on the other end of the phone was a bit surprised and still half asleep. "You're sure that you don't need to see it first?" she asked.

Frank chuckled softly as he rubbed his tired face, "No ma'am, I really don't have a choice. I need to move in today."

Frank took Susan to see it as soon as she could get going, and they were both so grateful that it was clean as well as furnished. They unpacked as much as they could, and Frank and Susan thanked whoever was looking out for them again.

In less than twelve hours, Frank had to report to Nellis. Another adventure had begun.

The training schedule at Nellis was challenging and frantic. Knowing that Susan didn't need to have anything else added to her plate, Frank didn't tell her how many new pilots were getting hurt or killed at Nellis on a weekly basis. The Las Vegas base had the highest accident and death rate in the air force, and they were losing more pilots in training than any pilots killed in combat in the same amount of time during the Korean War. Over the Labor Day weekend in September 1951, six pilots were killed in training accidents. The intense schedule continued at the base in spite of the death toll.

Frank tried to carpool so that Susan wouldn't be stranded, but she was left alone most of the time knowing she could go into labor at any moment.

She never complained. Susan Borman was going to be the perfect military wife. It was the one thing that she was determined to excel at. She might not be driven to succeed no matter the cost, like Frank, but she could do this. She had always been good at most things but never *great* at anything, so she made a pact with herself that she would be great at this life that she chose. She would raise their baby with love and support. She would be the mother that her own never was. She made the new little apartment in Las Vegas into a home as best as she could for their new addition, knowing in the back of her mind that Frank was supposed to be transferred to Korea in a few months and that they would be moving again.

Fortunately, Susan went into labor early in the morning on October 4, 1951, and Frank was able to take her to the hospital.

Their son Frederick Borman was born strong and healthy. Frank was able to see him for just a moment before leaving for two more training exercises that day. It was just another aspect of military life to get used to. No one stopped for personal tragedies or triumphs. The mission was everything—no exceptions.

Susan's mother, Ruth, came to Las Vegas, without an actual invitation from either Susan or Frank, to meet her first grandson and to supposedly help her daughter settle in with the new baby. She walked into Susan's hospital room on the base and called it a "veterinary clinic." She was so disruptive and obnoxious to everyone that Frank asked her to leave almost as soon as she arrived. He understood how much Susan needed to feel supported after delivering their first child and would protect her no matter what—even from her own mother. Ruth would hold that grudge against him forever.

Susan was enormously relieved to have her mother gone and tried to convince Frank that she didn't need any help. Frank knew that he would hardly be around, so he called and asked his mother, Marjorie, to come to Las Vegas. She was beyond pleased to be there for her first grandchild and was more than happy to help. She gave Susan all the support that a new grandmother should. Susan developed a close and loving relationship with her mother-in-law during that time that would last the rest of their lives.

———————

Just two months after Frederick was born, on December 4, Frank graduated with top honors from the flight training program at Nellis and had a short time to wait before he was sent to Korea. As dogged as ever, he was determined to be the best pilot possible and took an F-80 up to practice dive-bombing. He had a bad head cold, but no "Tiger" took time off for something like that.

Frank was going into his first dive in the jet when he heard a big popping sound and then couldn't hear anything at all in his left ear. He started to feel lightheaded and got the airplane safely back on the ground as quickly as possible. He then went directly to the flight surgeon on the base, who did some tests immediately. The surgeon finally came back into the room and looked at him for a moment with compassion before he said, "You have ruptured your eardrum, Lieutenant Borman. You are officially grounded for at least six weeks—maybe more."

Frank felt like he had been gut-punched. *Grounded?* No, not possible.

———————

Susan knew that something was very wrong with her husband. He had never been a great communicator, but she always seemed to know how to read him. He kept shrugging off the broken eardrum, yet she could tell that he wasn't coping well with what he perceived as a weakness that he couldn't fix or control. His orders were now completely up in the air. Korea was off the table, and he was told that he might have to go to the Philippines for more training but had to go by ship because of his injury. Any flying at all was out of the question, as it might damage his eardrum further.

Frank was sent to the base in San Francisco to await orders as to his next post, while Susan packed again to leave Vegas. Unfortunately, the only place for her to go was back to her mother's in Tucson. Frank's parents just had no room for her and the baby. The very idea of returning home was horrifying to Susan, especially since her mother had been told to leave a few weeks earlier. She was dreading having to take her new baby back to the very place she was so desperate to escape, but Susan refused to burden her husband with anything else, so she kept silent.

They arrived in Tucson just a couple of weeks before Christmas 1951, and Frank had to report back to the base in San Francisco no later than December 19. He didn't get the Christmas leave that he had requested and couldn't bear to leave Susan and little Frederick a second before he had to. He could tell that Susan was having a very hard time being back at her mother's. It was quite tense in the Bugbee household, and Ruth would barely acknowledge Frank's presence.

"I'm so sorry I have to leave you here, sweetheart," Frank said as he was packing his bag to leave. He could feel how anxious and upset she was.

"It's OK, Frank, just get your ear healed so that you can fly again. I know you won't be happy until that happens. Your son and I will be fine," she said with a strained smile. She had Fred in her arms and was gently bouncing him to settle him down while trying to hide her anguish.

Frank looked at both of them and could hardly believe how emotional he felt about having to leave them. He was supposed to take the bus to the base, but because he wanted to stay with them as long as absolutely possible, he secretly had booked a seat on an unpressurized commercial flight. By the time he arrived in

San Francisco, he had damaged his eardrum even more. When he finally got to the base, he found out that he would definitely be going to the Philippines instead of Korea.

On December 20, 1951, Frank boarded a transport ship called the USS *Ainsworth* feeling lonelier than he ever had in his young life, with a busted eardrum and a flying career that was possibly over before it had begun.

It would take twenty-one days to get to Manila. The *Ainsworth* docked in Hawaii on December 24 for four hours ashore. The only thing Frank cared about was getting to a phone and calling Susan to wish her and little Fred a Merry Christmas. It would be the last time he would be able to speak to her for a very long time.

Frank knew of one hotel in the area—the Royal Hawaiian Hotel. Lobbies in most of the bigger hotels had public pay phones, so he made his way there as fast as he could. Spying a phone that was not being used, he was so anxious to make the call that he rushed in and left the door of the booth wide open.

"Hello, I would like to place a person-to-person call to Tucson, Arizona, please," Frank said in a rush to the operator.

"I'm sorry, sir, but the calls for Christmas Eve to the mainland have been reserved for months now. There is no way that you will be able to get through."

"I have about four hours to wait. I won't leave this phone for a second," Frank assured her.

"Sir, again I am sorry, but you would need to wait about four weeks," she responded.

Frank hung up the phone and dropped his head for a moment to try to deal with all of the emotion and frustration he was feeling. He looked completely devastated as he walked out of the phone booth and was about to leave the hotel when a well-dressed man came over and put his hand on Frank's shoulder.

"Is everything OK, soldier?" he asked in a quiet voice.

It wasn't in Frank's nature to unburden himself to a complete stranger, but there was something about this man that made him just blurt everything out.

"No sir, I am not OK. I have just over three more hours of leave left before heading to Manila on a transport ship, and all I wanted to do was wish my wife and new baby son 'Merry Christmas,'" Frank said despondently. "There are no public phone lines available. There is no way for me to get through to them."

The man nodded in understanding and then smiled. "I happen to be the manager of this hotel, and I am going to see what I can do. Don't move."

Frank closed his eyes and prayed that there would be some way to hear Susan's voice. It was the only Christmas present that he wanted.

The manager came back about five minutes later and handed Frank a key. "Here you go. Just head up to this room, and you can use the private phone in there to talk as long as you want." The man patted his shoulder again and turned to go.

"Wait, sir," Frank said with tears in his eyes. "I can't thank you enough. You have no idea what this means to me. Please let me pay you something."

"No—that won't be necessary, and you are most welcome. *Thank you* for your service. Merry Christmas," he said.

"Merry Christmas, sir," Frank whispered, trying to keep his emotions in check as he held the key tightly in his hand.

Frank took the stairs two at a time as he bounded up to the third floor. He opened the door and didn't look at anything in the room except the phone on the desk. He dialed the number he had known by heart since high school.

"Hello," Susan answered, sounding tired.

"Hello, Su Su."

"Frank? Frank . . . how are you able to call me?" she said excitedly.

"Someone was looking out for me," Frank said gratefully as he looked up and smiled. "Merry Christmas, sweetheart."

He could hear the emotion in Susan's voice as she answered.

"Merry Christmas, darling. I miss you so much. Every day . . . every hour."

Frank closed his eyes and smiled for the first time since he'd gotten on the airplane to leave his family. They spent the next two hours talking about little Frederick and everything that he had missed since he left. He kept it all tucked away so that when the nights ahead became too solitary, he would remember the sound of her sweet voice.

When they finally had to say good-bye because Frank needed to get back to the *Ainsworth*, Susan hung up the phone and put her head down on the table. She would have given anything to be with Frank right now, regardless of the conditions. Living with her mother had always been extremely challenging, but it was almost impossible now. Susan would realize later in life how she enabled the dysfunctional relationship with her mother by not standing up to her, but as a twenty-one-year-old new mother, she just slipped back into the pattern of trying to survive.

Ruth was constantly criticizing her when it came to anything about her son. Susan couldn't seem to do anything right as a new mother, and most days she was made to feel like an unwanted guest in her childhood home. "I have to get through this," she whispered to herself. "For Frank and my little boy, I will do anything."

She slowly got up, wiped the tears away, and took a deep breath. She pasted on the feigned smile that had become second nature and walked out of the room to celebrate her son's first Christmas.

6

THE DEATH OF A DREAM

FRANK GOT OFF THE BOAT when they finally arrived in Manila with four other pilots. Everyone else he traveled with was going to Okinawa and elsewhere in Japan. He was ordered to go to the Clark Air Base on Luzon Island in the Philippines and report to one of the most remarkable officers he would ever meet in his military career, one whom he would always respect: Major Charles McGee.

McGee had served in World War II with a squadron called the Tuskegee Airmen, who fought bravely and with distinction. Named after the Tuskegee Army Air Field in Alabama, where they trained, the Tuskegee Airmen were the first Black aviators in the US Army Air Corps—what later became the US Air Force. Their extraordinary courage during the more than fifteen thousand missions they flew throughout the war earned them over 150 Distinguished Flying Crosses. They were an integral part of winning the war against Germany and Hitler. (Charles McGee would be promoted to the rank of general at a ceremony in Washington, DC, just after he turned 100 years old in 2019.)

"I'm glad to have you here," Major McGee said as he introduced himself to Frank and the rest of the young pilots after they had all reported in and were assigned to their quarters.

"You may have heard the saying, 'You play ball with me, and I'll play ball with you.' Well, gentlemen, that's not how it's done here. I have my own personal saying: 'You play ball with me or I'll ram a bat up your ass.'" Frank kept a straight face but thought to himself that his new commander was a man after his own heart.

Second Lieutenant Borman was determined to get back up in the air as soon as possible, so McGee gave him permission to go see the flight surgeon right away. Frank made the appointment, and the doctor took a look inside his ear and shook his head.

"This is the worst eardrum that I have ever seen. I am sorry to tell you this, but you will never fly again."

Frank had many skills, but dealing with the death of a dream he had worked toward since he was a child was beyond him. He felt totally destroyed. He couldn't talk to his best friend and partner in life about it, so he did the only thing he could: he took action to get transferred somewhere else, anywhere that didn't require riding a desk.

He asked for a transfer to the army and got rejected. He petitioned to be a forward air controller in Korea and was rejected. Every transfer he requested was denied. So, the skilled fighter pilot who had no chance of getting back into an airplane was put in charge of the facilities squadron that took care of maintenance at the Clark Air Base for the next nine months.

Frank decided to direct his frustration and intensity toward investigating some serious negligence in regard to the equipment that he oversaw and demanded that the captain responsible be court-martialed. He noticed that the captain had plenty of time to golf but not actually to do his job. When Frank brought his concerns forward, he was patted on the head and told to mind his own business. Not exactly his strong suit.

The only thing he had to look forward to was being able to talk to Susan on the shortwave radio periodically. He spent most of his free time trying to get a place for the three of them to live on base, knowing how badly she needed to get out of her mother's house. He felt as alone and lost as he had ever been in his young life.

He finally found something, but it would go to someone else if she didn't get there as quickly as possible. The government would foot the bill for her to come by transport ship but wouldn't pay for a flight.

"Susan, can you hear me?" Frank said loudly into the radio the day that he had secured a place for them.

"Yes, darling, I can," she said, not sounding like herself at all.

"I found us a place, but you need to get on the transport ship as soon as you can and get here so I don't lose it," he said excitedly.

"Frank, I have to tell you something. Our little Frederick has been quite sick, and he needs to get an operation. He has a hernia, and the doctor told me that it was quite serious." Her voice trembled slightly. "I am really worried about him, Frank. You know how badly I want to come to be with you, but I need to make sure that he is going to be OK."

Frank felt like he had failed in every way. He ruined his chances of being a career air force pilot, and now when his family could use some support, he was halfway across the world. "Honey, you just take care of our boy. I'll see what I can do to try and hold on to this place a little longer." He put the radio back on the cradle, held his head in his hands, and said a prayer.

He needed them. They needed each other.

Susan was at a very low point. The thought of her baby getting an operation petrified her. She really had no one to rely on. Her mother was a liability at best, constantly berating her and making both her and little Fred feel like a burden.

Susan would have done anything no matter how difficult to get to Frank, but it seemed impossible in that moment. "Please, God," she whispered, standing over Fred's crib and looking down at his flushed face. "Get us both to Frank. I don't want to complain, but I am dying a little bit every day here. Please."

She leaned over and kissed her boy on the forehead. "Don't worry, angel. Everything is going to be all right."

Fred finally got his operation, which was successful, but the doctor told her that he would need time to heal and that there was no way that she could take him to the Philippines, especially by boat. There was a high risk of infection on dirty transport ships that didn't account for a sick child.

When Frank was able to reach her again to ask how Fred was, Susan told him in a devastated voice that she wouldn't be able to come—she couldn't take her baby on an unclean transport boat for three weeks. There was hardly any money in the bank and they had only one possession of any worth: their car.

"Honey, sell the car and buy two tickets on a good airline," Frank told her over the radio. "I have the house on the base for a little while longer, but if you don't get here, they will give it to another family."

So, a twenty-one-year-old new mother with a baby who just had major surgery began the process of selling a car that she had no details about, and then had to get to Los Angeles from Arizona to obtain the passports she needed to fly overseas with her three-month-old son. She also had to arrange storage for the few things they had through the air force base at Tucson. She did it all without any assistance—her mother, of course, was totally against the move and refused to help in any way.

When she was finally able to get to the Oldsmobile dealership in Tucson, she explained her situation. The owner listened to her story without interrupting and then looked at her sympathetically once she was finished. "How much are the airplane tickets going to be, Mrs. Borman?" he asked.

Susan was holding Fred while rocking him. He was still a bit feverish from the surgery. "Well, sir, it is $1,500 for my baby and me to fly from Tucson to the Philippines."

The owner looked away for a moment and then finally nodded and gave her a quick wink. "OK, Mrs. Borman. I will give you $1,500 for your car," which was more than it was worth.

Susan's eyes welled up as she smiled and nodded back in gratitude. "Thank you. Thank you so much."

Susan left from Los Angeles on Pan American Airlines. She was understandably anxious because Fred was still recovering from his surgery and was therefore fussy and uncomfortable. Their first layover was scheduled to be in Honolulu. But halfway to Hawaii, the airplane lost two engines on one of its wings and the plane was in serious trouble. Everyone on board started to panic while a terrified Susan held Fred on her lap, trying to stay as calm as possible, whispering to him that everything would be OK.

The plane was able to make an emergency landing on the Big Island of Hawaii at the airport outside of Kona but had to get people out through the emergency exits. A stewardess frantically strapped little Fred onto Susan's chest before they exited down the slide and onto the runway.

The airline got the passengers to another plane as quickly as they could and finally landed in Honolulu. Susan and Fred were completely exhausted, but she still had to get enough formula to last for the rest of the trip, as everything she had brought was still on the crippled plane in Kona. She did her shopping in Honolulu, all while caring for a sick and fussy baby.

When they finally boarded the plane to the Philippines the next morning, Susan was just about at the end of her rope. Unfortunately, the new plane had engine problems as well and had to turn back twice for repairs. They were stuck on that airplane for hours longer than they should have been.

Frank had been waiting at the airport in the Philippines, pacing back and forth. He could barely deal with the impatience and excitement of seeing his wife and son again. When Susan got off the plane and saw Frank's face, she smiled for the first time in months. He looked so relieved when he saw her coming toward him and hugged her and little Fred in a way he never had before. He couldn't seem to let go.

As Susan rested in Frank's strong arms, she could feel something wasn't quite right with him. She would figure it out in time, but for now she just needed to lock herself away with the only real family she'd had since her father had died. She was finally home, because Frank was her home.

The quarters that Frank had secured were nicer than Susan expected, and she started to settle in right away. After living with her mother again, she realized how much she needed her own space and made a vow to never, ever go back. She could finally take care of her son without second-guessing herself constantly as a result of the daily criticism she faced there. She could finally breathe.

Frank felt better than he'd had since the heartbreaking day he got on the ship to come to Manila. His little family was with him at last, and he had just been promoted to first lieutenant. The only black cloud hovering overhead was his flying status—or what could legitimately be called his "non-flying" status.

Not long after Susan and Fred started to settle into their new home, Frank came home in a particularly dark mood after seeing the flight surgeon. He had been going off of the base to get an experimental treatment that involved putting radium in his ear once a week to get the eardrum to heal the damaged tissue. It seemed to be working. Even so, the surgeon on base believed he shouldn't ever fly again.

"I'm going to quit, Susan," Frank said quietly. He looked completely despondent. "It's no use. They will never clear me to fly, and that is the only thing that I want to do. It's all I have ever wanted to do." He shook his head in defeat. "I'll transfer to ground crew until my time is up, and then I will get a job as an engineer somewhere. God knows our life would be easier."

Susan looked at him with compassion but knew that he needed a serious pep talk. "That is very true, darling, but you can't quit. You can't walk away from something that you love, something that you have worked so hard for. There has to be a way."

Frank just stared at her with a combination of irritation and esteem. Didn't she know how hard he had been trying? But also, how did he get so lucky to be with someone who understood him so well?

He finally answered. "What do I do?"

Susan came over, put her hands on his face, and took a moment to silently convey her love for him before she said firmly, "You are going to go and talk to Major McGee, and you are going to convince him to let you fly. If your eardrum bursts again while you are up there, then we will have our answer. You will never forgive yourself if you don't try."

Frank immediately went to Major McGee to plead his case. "Sir, you know what I have been through and how hard I have worked to get my flight status back. The surgeon still won't sign off. But, sir, I really need to get up in an airplane. I truly believe that I can do this."

McGee looked at him for what seemed an eternity, and just when Frank thought it was all over, McGee gave him a brief nod, "All right, Borman, let's get you up in the air and see where we are at."

Frank almost fell to his knees in gratitude.

The men went up in the T-33 trainer three times just to be sure that the eardrum would stay intact, and then McGee let the surgeon know that First Lieutenant Borman was ready to get his wings back.

Because his commander followed his gut and bent the rules a little, and his partner and wife wouldn't let him accept defeat, Frank was airborne once again.

7

"I NEED TO TEACH YOU HOW TO SHOOT A GUN"

FRANK WAS DETERMINED TO GET COMBAT EXPERIENCE as soon as possible now that he was flying again and tried relentlessly to get transferred to Korea. After the fourth futile attempt, he had to accept that maybe it just wasn't meant to be and for the time being chose to be satisfied with flying reconditioned F-80s from Japan back to Clark Air Base in the Philippines. When he found out that Susan was expecting their second child, he knew that it was best for his family to stay where he was. He'd had a couple of close calls while flying those reconditioned planes, which he kept from Susan. He made a pact with himself after she lost their first baby that he would never make her worry needlessly.

All in all, it was a peaceful time for the Borman family. As soon as Susan found out that she was expecting again, her nesting urge kicked in with a vengeance. She got busy making their quarters as snug and cozy as possible. She found some beautiful rattan furniture while shopping in Manila and located a used crib. She was incredibly relieved that Fred was doing so well in their new home and seemed to have no side effects whatsoever from his condition and surgery.

Most of the officers at Clark Air Base had housekeepers. A great many of them were mothers who had to be separated from their families to do the cooking and cleaning for the officers and their wives. The housekeepers had to stay in a dormitory on the base.

Susan would never treat anyone differently because of his or her ethnicity or social standing, so naturally their housekeeper became family. Her name was Francie, and her home and family were a few hours' drive away from the base. She was a lovely young woman who, despite her small stature, seemed to do the work of two people. She was also quite shy, but because of Susan's way of making everyone around her feel appreciated, Francie started to open up.

One day Francie showed up for work at the Bormans' looking pale and unwell. She was trying to hide her condition, but Susan noticed right away that something wasn't right with her.

"Francie, why are you here? You are obviously sick, my dear," Susan said, looking concerned. "You need to go back to your quarters and take a hot shower and go back to bed."

"Oh no, ma'am! Please, I will get in trouble if I do that, and none of us house girls have hot water in our bathrooms," Francie said in a scratchy voice, struggling just to stay upright.

"Oh, Francie, I had no idea!" Susan answered. "From now on you will use our bathroom to shower, and I want you to go in there right now and then straight to bed. You will not get in trouble. I will make sure of that."

"Thank you, ma'am," Francie said quietly. "I am so glad that you are the one that I work for."

Susan bustled her into the bathroom and told her to take her time. She shook her head as she closed the door and wondered why the air force would supply hot water for them and not for their domestic workers. It was wrong. She didn't want to bother Frank about it now that he was flying again, but at least she could make sure Francie was as comfortable as possible.

Frank came home a few nights later and told her that he had to go to Japan for two weeks and was concerned about a string of burglaries that were happening on base. He was worried about leaving his pregnant wife with no protection, since the felons had not been apprehended yet.

"Susan, I need you to get dressed in something that you can get dirty. I am taking you to the gun range. I need to teach you how to shoot a gun," Frank said as he started to pack up the guns and ammo they needed.

Susan thought he must be joking. When she realized that he wasn't, she shook her head emphatically and looked at her husband like he had grown another head. There was no way she was going. "Absolutely not, Frank. I am perfectly safe here, and I am not learning to shoot a gun while I'm pregnant."

"That is why I need you to do this for me. It's not just protection for you. It's for Fred and whoever we have showing up soon," Frank implored as he took her hand. He knew that she would do anything to protect their children.

Susan looked down for a moment and closed her eyes. When she finally opened them, she looked resigned but determined. "OK, Frank, I'll get changed and be right back."

That is how Mrs. Frank Borman learned how to handle a gun. She may have been six months pregnant and totally opposed to the idea, but she did it anyway, because that is what a good military wife and mother would do. You dealt with what was in front of you whether you liked it or not.

———

Edwin Borman was born on July 20, 1953, on Susan and Frank's third anniversary, just as the Korean War was ending. As soon as she went into labor, Susan was taken to a group of Quonset huts that had been turned into Clark Air Base's hospital. The labor room and delivery room were in separate huts, so when the doctor believed that it was time, Susan was put in a wheelchair and taken to another hut to give birth.

She barely made it to the delivery room before Edwin, who was named after Frank's father, made his appearance. The couple hadn't told anyone back home in the States that she was pregnant, so the birth was kept quiet as well. Susan didn't want to talk to her mother if she didn't have to.

Edwin Borman was born a happy, healthy boy, and mom and son got back to their own quarters as soon as they could. Things were calm at the base for the next few weeks, but Frank and Susan both knew that change was on the horizon. Frank's tour in the Philippines was almost over, and in just a few months they would have to go back to the United States.

Frank was staying true to his intense, dogged nature and challenged a fellow officer over a report that had been filed. Although Frank was in the right and won the argument among their superiors, that same officer was in charge of the transportation for any officers finishing their tours who were going back to the States. He was definitely holding a grudge, because when it came time to leave, all the officers and their families traveled by air. Not the Bormans. They were assigned to a troop ship, which was a horrible way to travel for anyone, let alone a family with two small children. Frank was given troop duty on board for the twenty-one days it would take to get to the United States. They were put in a small cabin with two tiny bunk beds for a baby, a toddler, and two adults.

There were very limited laundry facilities on the ship, so Susan had to wash all the diapers and everything else by hand in a small washbasin. She had tried to use the one onboard laundry room soon after they arrived on the ship but got yelled at by one of the ship's officers for blocking the hallway with her laundry basket.

She came back to their tiny cabin, where Frank was watching the boys. He noticed right away that she was upset.

"What's going on, Su Su?" Frank asked impatiently. He was still irritated at being put on another boat instead of flying home.

Susan sniffed and turned so that Frank couldn't see her face. "It's nothing . . . really," she said too quickly.

"Susan, tell me. I thought you would be gone for a while." Frank walked over and gently turned her around. "What happened?"

Susan tried to keep the frustration out of her voice. "I was told that I was blocking the hallway outside of the laundry room and that I needed to leave. I was told to 'Get the hell out of the way.'" Susan looked at Frank with tired eyes. Neither of them was getting much sleep in the tiny room.

Frank's body tensed up and got very still. "Who yelled at you?"

Susan tried to assure him it wasn't a big deal. She would wash everything by hand.

"Susan, who was it?"

She knew he wasn't going to let it go. She finally relented. "It was the civilian liaison, OK?"

Frank stalked to the door. "I'll deal with it."

"Frank . . . wait!" Susan knew it was pointless as she heard the door slam.

"Hey! You goddamn son-of-a-bitch . . . yes, you." Frank's voice was booming through the narrow hallway. The man in question slowly turned around to watch an irate Lieutenant Borman come toward him. "Did you just yell at my wife and humiliate her for trying to do some laundry?" Frank shouted. "For trying to wash my two baby sons' clothes and diapers?"

The civilian liaison just stood there smugly without saying anything.

Frank grabbed him by the shirt and was a little gratified to see him look a bit fearful. "If you think about saying even one more word to her, I will fucking throw you off of this boat into the ocean, you piece of shit." Frank let go of him with a shove and stormed off, barely listening to him sputter something about reporting him. Frank couldn't care less. Nobody messed with his family.

When Frank was called in to talk to the commanding officer on the ship, he told him what happened. His superior was silent for a moment and then leaned forward on his desk and told Frank that if that son of a bitch bothered him again, he would help Frank toss him overboard.

The rest of the trip home was challenging for obvious reasons, but Susan handled it all with grace and never complained. Frank never saw her be anything but cheerful, even though he was completely miserable being stuck on a boat again. He reminded himself that it was much better than the first ship he was on all by himself. At least the Borman family was all together.

"... SUBJECT OFFICER IS TO REPORT TO MOODY AFB, VALDOSTA, GEORGIA, TO TEACH INSTRUMENT FLYING. HOUSING AT THIS BASE IS UNAVAILABLE TO PERSONNEL WITH FAMILIES AND HOUSING IN VALDOSTA IS VERY LIMITED SO IT IS RECOMMENDED THAT SAID OFFICER TRAVEL WITHOUT HIS FAMILY."

Frank finished reading the telegram to Susan as he looked at her with concern. They had only been back on American soil for a couple of days, and because Susan's mother was completely livid that Susan did not inform her about their second child, they were staying with Frank's parents in their tiny house. Apparently being angry and self-righteous was more important to Ruth Bugbee than meeting her new grandchild.

In Susan's mind there was nothing to consider. She was staying with Frank. Full stop. "We're going with you, Frank.

We will figure something out. We always do," said Susan with a confidence she didn't necessarily feel but desperately needed to believe. She would put up with anything not to have to live with her mother again.

Frank looked at her and nodded. He didn't want to leave them behind, and he knew how stubborn Susan could be when she set her mind on something. "OK, sweetheart. Let's start packing up the car."

Frank's father had found him a used Oldsmobile, and after loading a few of their things and putting the rest in storage, the Borman family set off for Georgia. They checked into a cheap motel and for the next few weeks tried to find a place to live. When their money ran out, they ended up in a run-down, sleazy tourist camp with one central toilet and shower for the whole facility.

They had to stay there for a month. Frank was gone every day to the base, working two shifts most days, and Susan was stuck in that filthy place with two small kids and no vehicle to use. It was yet another example of the challenges of military life, and like everything else that came her way, Susan made it work.

Frank finally found an overpriced, run-down prefab home on the edge of a swamp. Most landlords in the area were known to take advantage of servicemen, and this one was no exception. The rent was way too high, but Frank knew there was no other alternative. The small trailer had no air conditioning to help alleviate the blistering, humid Georgia weather and barely any room for the boys to roam around. Because of the proximity to the swamp that was full of poisonous snakes, the kids couldn't safely play outside.

It was another difficult situation that Susan managed without a complaint, and she kept the boys occupied without ever bothering her husband. It was something that was drilled into every military wife.

No man likes to clutter his mind with such details, and little irritations are your problem, not his.

—*The Army Wife* by Nancy Shea

———————

It took over three months for Frank and Susan to find a home more suitable for a young family, but they finally found something with a backyard that was actually safe for the boys to play in, and Frank added a screened porch himself that looked out over the cornfield beside them.

Valdosta, Georgia, in 1953 was what one would describe as very "redneck," and unfortunately typical of the Deep South at that time. The segregated Black school was disgraceful and unsafe for the children who had to go there, so Susan and some of the other wives from Moody Air Force Base got together to try and fix it up. The local White community in Valdosta were very displeased and let the wives from the base know it every chance that they got. The women did it anyway.

Because Frank had missed so many flying hours when he was grounded, he kept accepting double shifts to catch up and would become one of the best fighter jet instrument instructors the base ever had. The elephant in the room was the fact that many of the pilots were dying for reasons that the air force never seemed to investigate. It almost seemed like they were disposable, but every fighter pilot knew the risks going in, and it didn't dissuade them.

Susan was coming out of the base commissary one morning and saw two planes collide head-on right above her. Only three parachutes came down when there should have been four, and she knew that Frank had just taken off minutes before to fly an overnight mission. She drove as fast as she could to the field, where she saw the parachutes land and got out of her car to run toward them.

A man in uniform who seemed to come out of nowhere grabbed her arm to hold her back. "Lady," said the officer from the base. "You can't be here. You need to leave now."

Susan tried to argue, to no avail, and finally walked numbly back to the car and drove straight to Frank's commanding officer's home. His wife answered the door.

"Shirley, I just saw two planes from our squadron in a midair crash. I need to know if Frank was one of them," Susan said in a rush, visibly shaken. "I know you have been through this before." Susan looked at her with tortured eyes.

"Yes, I have, Susan, and there is nothing we can do. You have to wait," she said as she took Susan's hand.

So wait is what Susan did. When Frank finally called late that night after he arrived at his destination, he had no idea the agony that she had just been through. She didn't mention it until weeks later. They were a team, and she wanted him to succeed in every way. Frank took the risks—she absorbed the fear.

———————

Frank's favorite pastime when he was young was to build and fly model airplanes. It was what initially inspired him to want to fly himself. And not just fly but to understand how these amazing machines actually worked.

It had been so long since he'd had the time for anything that even resembled a hobby that when his schedule began to clear up and he wasn't having to do double shifts anymore, he started building them again. To spend more time with her husband, Susan got into it herself, and as much as Frank was loath to admit it, she was better than he was at flying them—at least flying them safely. The neighborhood kids would gather in their backyard to watch the two Borman planes fly around. Susan's always came back. Frank's didn't. The remote-controlled airplanes they were flying may have been brand-new technology for the time, but unfortunately they didn't handle like a fighter jet no matter how determined Frank was to fly his that way.

While still stationed at Moody, Frank applied for the prestigious Air Force Fighter Weapons School at Nellis in Las Vegas. He was accepted and wanted Susan and the boys close for the short time he would be taking the courses. They stored their things and rented their Georgia house to another air force family. They loaded up the Oldsmobile once again and made their way to Phoenix, where Susan and the boys would stay with Frank's parents while Frank was in Las Vegas training.

Susan adored Marjorie and Rusty and was grateful to be there. Even though their house was cramped and not set up for her and the boys, she was glad to be able to leave them with their adoring grandparents to go visit Frank when he had a bit of time off. It was a good period for all of them and a chance for Susan and the boys to live with people that knew what being a family actually meant.

Frank had also been trying for months to get transferred to Luke AFB—another base close to where his parents lived in Arizona. He was told that a new fighter weapons school was opening there and would need instructors.

The long-anticipated orders finally came, and the Bormans were off again in the summer of 1955 to Goodyear, Arizona, where they found a little house near the base. It was the nicest home they had lived in since they were married.

Twenty-seven-year-old Frank was quite enthusiastic to start his new assignment. He marched into the office of his new commander at Luke AFB and informed him that he was there to teach gunnery, to which his commander replied: "No, we need you to teach instruments again."

Frank was stunned for a moment and then got angry. "With all due—"

"Borman!" the commander barked. "I'm running this god-damned show, and you will teach what I tell you to teach!"

Frank went back to teaching instruments for the next three months before he finally got the assignment he desperately wanted—the fighter weapons school program instructing the best pilots the air force had to offer. He loved everything about it, and during that tour of duty made captain at twenty-seven years old. Frank and Susan were the happiest they had ever been.

The only thing that was consistent about military life is how quickly things can change without warning.

8

"YOU GAVE YOUR ASS
TO THE AIR FORCE"

WHEN THE TELEGRAM FROM WASHINGTON arrived in the late spring of 1956, Frank could not have been more surprised. The new captain who lived to fly was being transferred to a West Point classroom to teach fluid mechanics. He "only" had to acquire a master's degree as soon as possible in aeronautical engineering.

Frank took the telegram to his commander's office and showed it to him. His commander read it and then looked up at him and shrugged.

"Colonel," Frank said sharply, "I want no part of this, and I have decided to turn it down."

"What do you mean?" the colonel glared at him. "You don't get to make that decision, Borman. When you raised your hand all those years ago at West Point, you gave your ass to the air force."

Frank glared right back. "I don't want to teach, colonel. I want to fly fighters. That's what I am good at and what I trained for. I should be in the air."

"Nobody gives a damn what you want, Borman. You are paid to follow orders, and if the service wants to send you to West Point—start packing."

Frank opened his mouth to argue some more, but he was cut off. "Captain Borman, as far as I'm concerned, you are government issue and nothing more. If the government wants you to teach, then that's what you are going to do. Now get your ass out of here!"

When Frank got home and walked in the door, Susan knew right away by the look on his face that something was not right. She made sure the boys were occupied and then came to sit with him. "What's wrong, honey?" she asked as she scanned his face. "Was there another accident? Did someone get hurt?"

"I got transferred again, Susan. They want me to teach in a classroom at West Point now," Frank said tiredly as he rubbed his forehead. "I won't be back training and flying for a couple of years at least."

Susan held his hand, trying not to show her relief that her husband would be as safe as he had ever been since they got married. But she knew what flying meant to him—and as always put his needs first. "Did you already talk to the colonel?" she asked.

Frank looked at her glumly and nodded. "Well," she said, "I guess we are moving again."

Frank took a deep breath and let it out slowly. "If teaching in a classroom isn't bad enough, I have to get my master's degree first. I need to go in tomorrow to find out where I am doing that."

Susan put her head on his shoulder. "Let's just deal with one thing at a time, darling. We've been through this before, and as long as we're all together, it's going to be OK."

Frank walked to the kitchen window and looked up to the sky. *How am I going to stay on the ground?* he thought. He looked back at his troubled wife and gave her a sad smile. "You're right, Su Su. I'll go and find out tomorrow where I'll be going to school."

Susan came over and kissed his cheek. "I'll start packing," she said and gave him a smile that didn't quite reach her eyes. "Everything will work out, darling."

After Frank left the next morning to get the options for his master's program, Susan began the now familiar process of putting all their things in boxes. She felt Frank's pain like it was her own. She knew that flying was everything to him and couldn't help but wonder yet again what it was like to love doing something that much.

The only thing that she felt that way about was her family and whatever home they found themselves in. It was her job to make it a haven, and she really did love to make their space as beautiful as she could with the limited means that they had. She couldn't help but grieve a little every time they left a place that she had grown fond of. It was like each corner and room had a piece of her and Frank and of the boys' childhood, even if they were both too young to remember. She believed the memories would always be with her, but it was still difficult to leave. She wondered if it might ever get easier. It was one more thing she would never burden Frank with; she tucked it away just like the belongings she was packing up.

In the summer of 1956, the Bormans made their way to California. Frank was determined to get his master's degree in one year instead of two, and Cal Tech was the only place to offer that. He had no idea how challenging it would be. His only thought was to get it done as quickly as possible so that he could get through the tour of teaching and get back to flying.

They finally found a small place in Temple City not too far from the Cal Tech campus in Pasadena, and Frank began one of the most difficult years of his life in the military. Cal Tech was a highly competitive environment, and Frank had been out of school for over six years. He was never home. If he wasn't studying like a madman, he was begging to fly anything that he could at the nearest air force base. He used the excuse that he needed to keep up his flying hours so his license stayed current, but in truth he did it to stay sane. He would fly on weekends and family holidays, while Susan and the boys had to celebrate without him. Susan never said a word.

He finally finished that grueling year and graduated with his master's degree in June 1957, which qualified him for the teaching position. After the long drive from sunny California to West Point, New York, they found themselves with the last house on the post. It was a squalid, tiny apartment in a run-down eight-unit building. The other seven units had families, with thirty-two children combined. It was never quiet.

Susan had already moved seventeen times in the seven years since she had married Frank, and when they first arrived, he looked around the filthy, neglected space with regret in his eyes. Susan saw his anguish right away and walked up to him. "Look at me, darling. We don't put faith in bricks and mortar . . . but in each other." It was another one of those profound moments with this amazing woman that would stay with Frank for the rest of his life.

Susan got to work, and by the time she was done scrubbing and cleaning—adding her resourceful touches everywhere and creating beauty out of what seemed to be thin air—the place actually looked inviting.

She even made the rattan furniture that they had been dragging around since the Philippines work. The pieces didn't even look worn or outdated. It was a natural gift that she didn't realize she had, the ability to make things beautiful that shouldn't be. Frank added a portico off of the back of the small residence, and they settled into the next three years of their life.

Susan thrived at West Point. She had a reprieve from carrying the subconscious weight that comes with being the wife of a fighter pilot, and because of her kind and approachable nature, she made friends easily.

Not long after settling into the routine, Susan was chosen by the senior officers' wives to join the West Point Ladies' Reading Club, which was considered a huge honor, as Susan was the only junior officer's wife to have ever been asked to join.

There was a military hierarchy among the wives as well. The wives of senior officers didn't usually socialize with a lower-ranking officer's wife. It was a perfect way to get the women to push their husbands' military careers. With every promotion a husband got, the more power and respect a wife had on base.

The boys loved West Point as much as their mother did. There was an excellent school for children of personnel at the academy and countless facilities and activities for them to enjoy. Fred and Edwin would sneak away to watch the cadet formations as the soon-to-be officers drilled. It looked majestic through their young eyes, the flawless cadence and rhythm of the long line of gray uniforms. It was then that the dream of being a West Point grad was born for the two boys.

The tiny apartment that actually looked more like old World War II barracks would be the happiest and most stable home environment that the Borman family would ever know. Susan and the boys could have stayed there forever, but Frank was missing being in the air something fierce. Even though some weekends he was able to get his hands on a plane from the nearby Stewart Air Force Base, it wasn't the same as being on the front lines, pushing a fighter jet as far as it could go.

In October 1957, Susan was busy baking a cake for Fred's sixth birthday when the celebration was overshadowed by an event that would accelerate the Cold War and change the course of history—and the trajectory of the Borman family—forever. On the evening of October 4, Americans across the nation could look up and see the first man-made satellite streak across the sky.

It would have been a magical moment if it hadn't been launched by the Russians, who named it Sputnik 1. Compounding fears created by newspaper headlines and radio reports of Russia's technological achievement was the fact that for nearly a decade the Soviet Union had been growing its stockpile of nuclear weapons.

It didn't take long for the Bormans and the rest of the country to come to the same conclusion as the Pentagon. Without warning, Russia now had the technology to launch a rocket carrying a nuclear weapon and strike the United States in minutes. Fueled by the press and politicians alike, fear and paranoia swept across the country.

In his first year of school, while Fred and his classmates were learning the Pledge of Allegiance, they were also learning how to "duck and cover" under their desks, and families all over the nation were building fallout shelters in case Russia launched a nuclear attack.

One day after Frank was done teaching, a colleague of his let him know about a job offer for an aeronautical engineer with Convair, which built a number of advanced fighters and bombers for the air force. Frank decided to go for an interview just to see what they were all about, and once they met and spoke with him they wanted to hire him on the spot. Convair offered him three times more money than he was making as a captain in the air force, with plenty of benefits.

The job was in San Diego, one of the most beautiful areas of California, with an almost perfect climate. The interviewer was dangling the carrot of amazing schools for the boys as well as painting a picture of how great the city was for raising a family and assuring Frank that they would find a home for them.

Before he could finish his spiel, Frank cut him off. "I'm sorry," Frank said as he stood up, "I just realized that I'm wasting your time. I don't want to leave the air force yet."

Frank went home and told Susan about the interview and what they offered him. "I just don't think I can handle a civilian job right now, honey," Frank said a bit sheepishly. "I know it's a great opportunity."

"It's your life, darling," Susan said. "Whatever you decide, I'll support you." Susan got up and kissed him on the cheek and then went into the bathroom and dropped her forehead against the closed door, forcing the disappointment down. The job sounded like a dream come true—for the boys especially.

While Frank was teaching at West Point, he couldn't help but pay close attention to what was going on with Russia's space program. It was constantly being discussed within the engineering department, and no one could believe that Russia was beating the Americans with Sputnik. It was quite a blow to national pride. America looked at space travel as something from a sci-fi novel, but there was a rivalry becoming more intense between the two countries to possibly make it a reality.

Eighteen months after Russia launched Sputnik, President Dwight D. Eisenhower created the National Aeronautics and Space Administration on July 29, 1958. After a series of embarrassing launchpad failures, four months later NASA would launch its first satellite, Pioneer 1. The new agency was confident that it could surpass the Russians by putting the first human into space, but President Eisenhower was not convinced that this international showdown was a good use of America's resources. He was later quoted as saying, "Anybody who would spend $40 billion in a race to the Moon for national prestige is nuts."

Less than a year later, and with increasing political pressure to outmatch Russia, in April 1959, Eisenhower gave NASA the go-ahead to announce America's first group of astronauts for Project Mercury. Frank and Susan watched the evening news with the rest of the country as seven test pilots from the ranks of the air force, navy, and marines were paraded like preordained heroes in front of the press.

Chosen from over five hundred candidates, Group 1 became overnight celebrities. Although they hadn't flown in space yet, *Time* magazine was comparing them to icons like Christopher Columbus and the Wright brothers. Frank was surprised how the press was more interested in the astronauts' personal lives than their flying skills. As Susan listened to John Glenn wax on about God, country, and the unflinching support of his family, she couldn't help but wonder how she and the boys would be affected if Frank was chosen for such a high-profile mission.

While he was unsure what it would actually look like, Frank told Susan that space was going to be the new battleground in the Cold War. Frank was forever eager to get back to the job of being a fighter pilot, but for now orders were orders. Some days during lectures to his students, Frank would have to remind himself that teaching was just a short-term mission. But Susan was so grateful for their peaceful life at West Point and would have been happy to stay there forever.

Frank surprised Susan with an overnight trip to New York City in the fall of 1959. He had a short meeting there, and then they would be able to spend the rest of the time sightseeing and planned to spend some time alone. It had been a long while since they'd had a day together like this. As they were walking by Saks Fifth Avenue, Susan saw a dress in the window that caught her eye. It was like something from a dream. It was an off-white chiffon dress that fell just below the knees, with a matching jacket that had a small fur collar.

Frank saw the look in his wife's eyes and said, "Let's go in for a minute, OK? Just to look around."

Susan shook her head, "No, darling, it's all right. The prices in there are way more than we can afford." She started to pull him away from the window.

"Sweetheart, it won't hurt to look," he said. "I know how much you love fashion."

Susan just stared at him bewildered for a moment, then squeezed his hand. "OK, Frank," she said with a smile that was getting bigger as they started to walk through the entrance of the store. "Just a quick look."

Considering that Mrs. Borman had done most of her shopping at thrift stores her whole life, a place like Saks Fifth Avenue was a fantasy world. She was basking in all the beauty around her, while Frank was just trying not to bump into anything.

A well-dressed middle-aged woman approached them. "Hello, my name is Miss Ganzy. I work in the ladies clothing department. Can I help you find anything?" she asked, with a slight accent.

Frank spoke up before Susan could. "Yes ma'am, thank you. My wife would like to try on the dress in your window with the fur collar." Susan looked flustered for a moment, but Miss Ganzy answered before she could say anything.

"Oh . . . what a great choice." She looked at Susan and smiled, "What is your name?" Susan smiled back and extended her hand.

"My name is Susan Borman, and this is my husband, Captain Frank Borman."

Miss Ganzy stood up a bit straighter and extended her hand to Frank. "It's a pleasure to meet you, Captain, and can I thank you personally for your service? Have you served for long?"

"I joined the air force in 1950, ma'am," Frank told her with a touch of pride in his voice. "I am teaching at West Point right now."

"That's wonderful," Miss Ganzy replied. "And it seems that you have married a true lady who was born to wear most of the things that we sell here," she said.

Both Susan and Frank were instantly charmed by this down-to-earth woman in a place they hadn't expected to find one. Neither of them could know that she was a German Jew who had been rescued from a concentration camp in 1945 by American soldiers when she was twenty years old.

"Now," Miss Ganzy said. "Let's get you into that dress, shall we?" She took Susan's arm and led her to the beautiful changing rooms. Susan felt like royalty, and because of her pleasant, warm nature, all the employees on the ladies clothing floor started gathering around as she tried on a few things before the dress in the window was brought to her. No one was surprised that Susan looked like a *Vogue* model when she walked out in the dress and matching coat that seemed as if it were designed just for her tall and slender frame.

The other ladies who worked on the floor started gushing. "Oh, ma'am, that dress was made for you!" Frank was standing off to the side admiring this enchanting woman he was married to who was made to wear beautiful things but never once asked for them.

As Susan went back into the changing room, he pulled Miss Ganzy aside. "How much for the dress?" he asked.

She paused for a moment. "Captain Borman, please give me a moment. I think it might be on sale." She quickly made her way to the back of the store and when she returned, it was with the manager.

"Captain Borman, it's a pleasure to meet you," he said. "We have a special policy for military personnel. You receive fifty percent off of all of the merchandise that we sell here at Saks. And that is not just for today but for as long as you want to shop here."

Frank was visibly moved but just nodded. "Thank you very much," he said. "Please bring the dress to the front. We will be purchasing it."

The dress and matching coat cost $700 retail. Frank paid $350, which was more than half of his monthly military salary, knowing the experience for Susan was priceless. It was money well spent as far as he was concerned and was something that neither of them would ever forget. Susan was glowing as she walked out with the iconic bag that held the most beautiful clothing that she had ever owned.

The whole day had been like something out of a dream, and it was appreciated even more because she was reminded that even though her husband was gone or distracted so much of the time, he really did adore her.

While her trip to New York was a wonderful respite, Susan happily returned to West Point and her routine as a military wife and mother. But unfortunately she couldn't avoid the constant media reports or overhearing Frank talk with his air force buddies about the "Red menace" that threatened America's way of life. Regardless of what corner of the nation you lived in, the threat of nuclear war gave every American the feeling that the end of the world was imminent.

Susan opened the newspaper on the morning of October 7, 1959, to be greeted by another headline proclaiming Russia's technological supremacy and another first in the space race. Luna 3 was the latest in a series of Russian probes launched in 1959 to reach the Moon, but this time, the Soviets had coordinated the probe's arrival with the two-week cycle when the far side of the Moon was in full sunlight. Luna 3 captured the first photos of the mysterious unseen side of the lunar surface. The twenty-nine images that it beamed back to Earth were grainy, but it was quite obvious that the far side of the Moon looked nothing like the surface that was visible from Earth—it was far more rugged and ominous.

This was the second time in as many years that the Russian space program was overshadowing Fred's birthday, and while Susan knew it was ridiculous, she silently cursed the Soviets for interfering with another family celebration.

In the fifteen years that followed the end of World War II, the Cold War between the United States and Russia continued to escalate. Even though not a single shot had been exchanged between the superpowers, in the two-year period Frank would be at Edwards Air Force Base, the Cold War was starting to approach the threshold of nuclear war. The Russians were on every American's mind, especially within the military.

Frank knew that he had a lot more technical and academic training than most military pilots, and given that America wasn't at war currently, he believed he could contribute more to defeating Russia by flying experimental aircraft than by just playing fighter pilot. After talking it over with Susan, Frank decided to apply to the Air Force Flight Test Center located in the Mojave Desert, north of Los Angeles.

In 1947, Edwards Air Force Base had become a household name when Chuck Yeager broke the sound barrier in Bell's X-1 rocket plane. Adjacent to an ancient dry lake bed that doubled as a nearly endless runway, Edwards became the epicenter of aviation firsts where pilots and untested aircraft became legend. Edwards was the one place in the world where records were shattered and history was being made almost daily. The air force handpicked the "best of the best" to fly the hottest new aircraft. Despite the fact that testing an unproven design that traveled faster than a rifle bullet was incredibly risky, the air force had no end of aviators competing for a chance to attend the prestigious test pilot school.

Many of the nation's best pilots, like the base's namesake Glen Edwards, became legends only after being killed during a test flight. In June 1960, Frank and Susan pulled up stakes and moved to Edwards. Susan knew that this was the life that she had signed up for but was heartbroken to leave West Point.

A month before Frank was scheduled to report to Test Pilot School in California, on the morning of May 1, 1960, the Borman family arose to news that a U-2 spy plane flown by US Air Force pilot Francis Gary Powers had been shot down over the Soviet Union. The only thing greater than President Eisenhower's embarrassment was first secretary of Russia Nikita Khrushchev's anger. With Cold War tensions escalating, Captain Borman's skills were going to be needed more than ever.

To become an air force test pilot, you had to have an engineering degree as well as a great deal of fighter pilot training. The ones actually accepted to the program were the tip of the spear, and many of them didn't live very long.

In the remote high desert north of Los Angeles, where Edwards was located, the constant gusting hot winds felt like the devil himself had made his home there. Fifty miles from the nearest town, the base was isolated and devoid of anything green. The ancient lake bed it was built on was crawling with legions of snakes, scorpions, and baseball-sized spiders.

The Borman family made the long drive from New York to California and arrived at Edwards on a typical scorching day. Their 1960 Chevy had no air conditioning, and they could barely see anything through the windshield because of the dust and sand blowing all around them. Compared to the beautiful and lush greenery of West Point, this seemed like a wasteland.

They were given a small, dilapidated place that was as sparse as the desert outside. The windows didn't seal properly, so the sand would blow into the house every day. Susan spent her tenth wedding anniversary watching the dust devils spinning around outside of their tiny house, waiting for Frank to get home. *A **dry*** *lake bed. Well at least that's not false advertising,* Susan thought as she stared out of the dusty window.

She enrolled Fred and Edwin in the base school, and both boys began to make friends. Just like Frank had done when he was a boy, five-year-old Edwin created his own little zoo in the backyard composed of tortoises he had caught while dodging Mojave green rattlesnakes. The boys also enjoyed building model airplanes, which she helped them fly on the edge of the lake bed while the latest jets in the American arsenal streaked overhead.

By the fall of 1960, the Bormans had been at Edwards a little more than three months. Frank was busy all day, either in class or flying high above the expansive dried-up lake. Although Edwards had undergone improvements since it opened in 1933, the accommodations were nothing like at West Point.

One of the most difficult parts of being a military wife is having to start over every time you move. You have to make new friends, establish some kind of routine for your children, set up a home to create at least the illusion of stability—and you do this all on your own. Frank felt sorry for Susan sometimes but acknowledged that his career ambitions took precedence and probably always would. Edwards was the next wrung on the ladder. She would just have to deal with it.

Frank had been handpicked by legendary test pilot, and his new commander, Chuck Yeager. Aside from breaking the sound barrier, Captain Yeager had flown over sixty missions in Europe during World War II. In March 1944, Yeager was shot down over France but managed to escape over the Pyrenees mountains while carrying a fellow wounded airman over his shoulder. He was— and would remain for the next sixty years—one of Edwards's living legends.

Yeager was a hard-nosed pilot with an ego that could barely fit into the largest hangar on the base. He claimed that he was not only the best fighter pilot in the air force but its best test pilot. Yeager made it to clear to air force brass—and every aviator in the service—that he would consider only the top 1 percent of qualified pilots.

On a bitterly cold Friday in January 1961, John F. Kennedy became the thirty-fifth president of the United States after defeating Republican candidate Richard M. Nixon. Like Frank, former president Eisenhower was a West Point graduate who had also distinguished himself as supreme commander of the Allied forces during World War II. Frank was sad to see the "old warrior" retire, but the 1950s were over and new leadership was needed in Washington. JFK was young with fresh ideas and a manner that enchanted the country, but the optimism he brought to the nervous nation was short lived.

On March 23, 1961, the air force lost its first airmen in Southeast Asia. Seven of the eight servicemen aboard a C-47 transport plane were killed when they were shot down over Vietnam. With the threat of communism spreading at the hands of the Russians, the Kennedy administration saw Vietnam as the potential tipping point that might transform the Cold War into the next world war.

In April, as Frank was finishing his last few days at Test Pilot School, Russia launched cosmonaut Yuri Gagarin into space. Americans everywhere wondered, *How could a communist be the first human in space and the first to orbit the Earth?* That flight continued a string of firsts for the Soviets in space and sent even more cultural and existential shock waves across America. Ground zero was the Oval Office.

Five days after Gagarin's spacecraft parachuted safely to Earth, President Kennedy backed an invasion of Cuba. The Bay of Pigs was a failure for Cuban nationals in the United States and a catastrophic defeat for JFK, whose critics had warned that his youth and inexperience made him unqualified to lead the greatest democracy in the world.

Three weeks later, NASA helped America recover by putting Alan Shepard into space, but his short suborbital flight also served to underscore how far Russian technology was ahead of the United States.

By mid-1961, both the nation and the young president were having a crisis of confidence. In an effort to lift his administration out of its political quagmire, JFK made a bold and risky political move. Standing before Congress on May 25, the president made an announcement that would change the course of American history. Kennedy proposed that the United States "should commit itself to achieving the goal, before this decade is out, of landing a man on the Moon and returning him safely to the Earth."

The Apollo lunar program was a startling revelation. NASA had sent its first astronaut into space only three weeks earlier on a flight that had barely lasted fifteen minutes. The goal of creating the technologies and techniques of launching a manned mission to the Moon in less than nine years would be staggering. In subsequent speeches, JFK characterized space as the new frontier and emphasized American values of freedom and destiny. They were ideals Frank Borman believed in fiercely, and if space was the best way to defeat Russia, he wanted to be on the front line.

———

Frank graduated from test pilot school, earning top marks. He finished with other talented pilots, such as Michael Collins, whom he would meet again at NASA. Frank was one of five top students chosen by Yeager to spearhead a brand-new program called the Aerospace Research Pilot School.

With the promotion came better housing, and the Bormans were finally able to get rid of the rattan furniture they had carted around for years, after taking a much-needed shopping trip to Los Angeles to update their space.

That same spring, NASA asked the air force to submit the names of its best test pilots as candidates for the Group 2 selection of astronauts.

During the Mercury program, the air force was somewhat embarrassed when Virgil "Gus" Grissom's space capsule sank after splashing down in the Atlantic. Then Donald "Deke" Slayton, who should have flown the last Mercury mission, was grounded after being diagnosed with a heart murmur. The consolation prize was NASA appointing Deke head of the Astronaut Office, where his name would become synonymous with the space program.

Frank knew he was at a critical crossroads in his life and needed to talk it over with his biggest supporter. "Hell, if it wasn't for Susan pushing me to get back into the air while in the Philippines when I thought my flying days were over, I probably would've spent the rest of my life pushing paper," he admitted years later.

Frank went home to lay out his options to Susan. "I can stay at Edwards doing an important job with the space flight school we're building, or I can try and get into that program myself, as an astronaut. It's a chance to make history, but you have to understand it will involve unknown risks," he told her.

She looked at him in the solemn way that she always did when Frank's decisions would end up affecting the whole family. "Look, Frank . . . you have always pushed your career forward when you know that you'll succeed. I trust you, and I'll go along with whatever you decide."

Frank submitted his application to NASA, which was followed by a succession of physical and psychological exams. To increase the odds of their pilots being chosen, the air force brass sent Frank and several other candidates to "charm school." When she found out, Susan chuckled at the thought of her husband being told how to talk to the press and how to choose the proper utensils at dinner parties. She knew he would detest every minute of it.

But he did it anyway. Frank then returned to Edwards and put any thought of being an astronaut out of his mind by keeping busy getting the new undergraduate school ready.

Susan was as busy as ever making sure the boys were settled and happy with school and their extracurricular activities. It was a huge challenge for any mother, living so far away from anything that resembled civilization. She was stuck on the base most days, and the thing that no one talked about (especially at Edwards) was how many test pilots were killed during this time.

There was a black car that every military wife dreaded seeing and fervently hoped every time they did see it, that it would drive past. If it stopped at your driveway, you knew. The grim-faced administrator who got out of the vehicle didn't have to say a word. If you were lucky to have a good neighbor, she would come over to sit with you and hold your hand. Susan had to wear her black funeral dress way too often.

Every fighter pilot believed that it would always happen to the "other guy" but also had a very pragmatic approach to death. They refused to fear it, because fear made you weak. And like the warriors of old, if you gave your life to something you believe in, then it was worth it. No one thought about what it was actually like for the wives and children. They were told to be proud of the sacrifice instead of devastated and lost.

It's a sentiment that the US military was built upon—dying for the greater good. What a brilliant way to get the brightest and best to lay down their lives for the advances we all take for granted. Make it about triumph and heroism, and you'll have them lining up.

But what about those left behind? The women in their sand-filled, dusty houses were warriors too but didn't get any recognition. They never got to feel the adrenaline rush of going faster than the speed of sound, had no idea what it felt like to flirt with death every day and somehow escape it, and never knew the satisfaction of rising up in the ranks. They didn't get to experience what it was like to touch glory in some way but instead had to wait stoically and hope to God they never saw the black car pull up in their driveway. And if it did show up, they had to pick up the pieces, not only for themselves but also for their children. It was a massive price to pay, and there were so many who paid it.

One of Frank's new colleagues was a foreign fighter pilot from Italy. Frank figured that he must be missing his homeland and invited him over one night to have dinner. He called Susan to tell her and requested that she make the boys' favorite meal, her specialty for his new Italian comrade. It was something she had tried out a couple of years before that the boys went crazy over. When they asked her what it was, she informed them that it was called deep-dish pizza. The boys asked her to make it almost weekly.

Susan loved to have people over and was more than happy to make her special dish for the homesick pilot. When the two men showed up after a long day, the little house smelled amazing. "You are going to love my wife's deep-dish pizza, my friend," Frank said. "It's a favorite in this house."

As they all sat down at the table, Frank said a quick blessing over the food, and Susan placed the "pizza" on the table. Their guest looked confused and as graciously as possible asked, "Is this the pizza?"

Frank beamed and nodded. "You will love it!"

"I am very certain that I will, but in Italy and I believe here as well, we call this lasagna. It is made with the large pasta, no?" Susan turned red and nodded. That is when the Bormans found out that they didn't love deep-dish pizza as much as they thought . . . but they sure were big fans of lasagna.

Their new Italian friend was finally able to have his wife join him at Edwards. She couldn't speak a word of English, so Susan made sure that she introduced herself right away and did what she could to make her feel welcome. Not long after she arrived from Italy, her husband was ordered to go to South Carolina to check out a used F-104 airplane for Edwards and bring it back if possible. He was tragically killed there doing a routine flight check, and the ominous black car showed up at his quarters.

When Susan found out, her heart broke for the new widow. She was completely alone in a strange country and had no idea how to communicate. Susan rushed over to sit with her and comfort her in any way that she could. She immediately started making arrangements to have someone from the base assist her.

Frank was busy working on his latest assignment—the new curriculum—and had no idea what was going on with his now former colleague or his wife. He got an abrupt and unwelcome visit from the assistant commandant of the Test Pilot School, who proceeded to chew his ass out over the fact that Mrs. Frank Borman went to be with the new widow before the commanding officer's wife could get around to it. Frank just stared at him incredulously, and to get rid of the commandant, told him that he would talk to Susan about the breach of protocol.

When Frank got home, he explained to Susan that she caused a bit of a problem because she didn't follow the rules. He stopped in the middle of his speech, shook his head, and hugged her. She was understandably frustrated and upset.

"You did the right thing, Susan," Frank told her. "I hate military bureaucracy, so just forget it. You did the right thing."

"I just did for her what I would need if I was in a foreign country without family or friends," Susan said, exasperated. "They need to do better with how they handle things, Frank. The US military needs to do better." It was something no one wanted to talk about, not even Frank. The mission was all that mattered—collateral damage was part of the deal. Frank said nothing, and Susan knew in her heart that nothing would change.

———————

More than a year had passed since Frank had applied to NASA, but by the fall of 1962, he'd logged more than fifty-five hundred flying hours. With the exception of his commander, Chuck Yeager, it was clear to Frank and everyone at Edwards that the next battleground in the Cold War was going to be space.

Frank considered the consequences of letting down the air force and derailing his career by offering his "body and soul to NASA" when he applied to the agency. That all evaporated when Frank met General Curtis LeMay. The leathery faced, cigar-chomping general made spines stiffen when he entered the room, and his expression struck Frank as one of defiance.

"There's a lot of people who'll say you're deserting the air force if you're accepted into NASA," he barked through a cloud of smoke. "Well I'm the chief of the air force, and I want you to know I want you in this program. I want you to succeed in it, and that's your new air force mission!"

On September 17, 1962, NASA made the official announcement of the Group 2 astronauts. Major Frank Borman got the call informing him he was on his way to Houston.

Frank had one last task to perform before he left Edwards and his beloved air force, which he was dreading. He had to tell his cantankerous commander that he was leaving.

"Colonel Yeager, I just received great news," Frank said as he stood tall and prepared himself.

"What's your good news, Borman?" Yeager asked, already looking suspicious.

Frank took a deep breath and looked him right in the eye. "Deke Slayton just called me, and I've been accepted into the NASA program."

Yeager shook his head with barely concealed disgust. "Well, Borman, you can kiss your goddamned air force career good-bye!" he growled. Frank had a very short moment of doubt, but fate had guided him this far and he truly believed that his gut would never fail him. He walked away with a smile and couldn't wait to get home to tell Susan.

In keeping with a fighter pilot's predisposition for nicknames, NASA's Group 2 christened themselves the "New Nine." Frank and Jim McDivitt had been among the first graduates of the Aerospace Research Pilot School—the postgraduate, space-oriented course at Air Force Test Pilot School. Also selected was their instructor Tom Stafford along with former West Point graduate and air force test pilot Ed White. Group 2 also included navy pilots Pete Conrad, John Young, and Jim Lovell, along with NASA's two civilian test pilots, Elliot See and Neil Armstrong.

Susan was outwardly enthusiastic and supportive as always but had to give herself the usual pep talk by reciting *The Army Wife* manual: "Keep your fears and feelings to yourself." It was the mantra that Susan and many other astronaut wives would end up paying a high price for.

9

THE NEW NINE

SEPTEMBER 1962 BROUGHT another big change for the Bormans. After Frank had been chosen as one of the New Nine, the family left the California desert for the great state of Texas, only to arrive at a NASA that was in complete disarray, because the agency had just moved its headquarters from Virginia to Houston.

No one in the Borman family was prepared for their new celebrity status. The boys had no idea that their father had become famous overnight and thought they were just going to another air force base.

When they first arrived in Houston, Frank was told by NASA to take the family to the Shamrock Hilton because housing for them wasn't yet available. At the time it was considered one of the most glamorous and upscale hotels in the country. As they walked through the entrance and were surrounded by the elegant and stylish furnishings in the lobby, Frank started fidgeting and leaned over to whisper to Susan, "There is absolutely no way that we can afford to stay here."

They both looked overwhelmed and were soon approached by one of the NASA liaisons, who assured them that the hotel would provide a complimentary suite for as long as they needed to get settled into something more permanent in Houston—courtesy of the owner, Eric Hilton. It was the beginning of a completely new chapter for the Borman family, one that would challenge them all in different ways. For the next eight years they would be in the spotlight while the country followed their journey like it was their own.

———————

NASA's Mercury program was set to wrap up in eight months' time, in May 1963, followed by two-man Gemini flights ramping up to test and validate new technologies that would be essential for the Apollo lunar program that would follow.

All astronauts were given a specific subject matter in which to develop expertise. Frank was assigned to the Titan II booster, the critical part of the rocket that, if all went well, would get the astronauts safely into Earth orbit. In addition to classroom lectures, Frank was assigned to other areas of specialization. He was hardly ever home, completely focused on and consumed with his new job.

Frank and the other Group 2 astronauts were the latest kids on campus and were thrown into the mayhem as soon as they showed up. And the Mercury 7 astronauts made it quite clear to Frank and the others they weren't legitimate astronauts until they had flown in space.

As per standard operating procedure, Susan and the rest of the military-now-astronaut wives were on their own to deal with housing and anything else that required settling into yet another new place. The difference this time was that there was no on-base assistance. NASA was too new and hadn't established a support system. There was nothing to rent near the spacecraft center, so Susan and the other wives searched until they found some land in a brand-new development called El Lago located near a small town called Seabrook, about an hour's drive outside of Houston. They then had to hire a developer to build the houses for their families.

It was yet another challenge, but they did it with the panache that they would become famous for. They made it all work with forced smiles, wearing the cute outfits that were strongly suggested if not demanded by NASA, even though most of them had very little money to work with. These women were extremely resourceful and creative and, along with their husbands, became the face of a nation.

While the Bormans' new home in El Lago was being built, they had to rent a small place in Houston. Knowing the boys would have to switch schools as soon as their house was finished, Susan drove them to Seabrook every day from Houston so that they could get established in their new school, without having to worry about changing in the middle of the year. Fred was eleven years old and Edwin had just turned nine. It was an hour each way and just another example of the kind of mother that Susan was.

It was very important to her to make sure that her boys knew that they were never a burden and always loved. That they felt safe and secure. Everything she never felt growing up after she lost her father.

Susan was essentially a single parent, as were most of the other NASA wives. She organized a neighborhood committee to build a community swimming pool once they finally moved to Seabrook. El Lago was an undeveloped area and had nothing in the way of services, shopping, or community centers. The wives had to take charge of the things they desired to have in their new little neighborhood, and they wanted it to thrive, regardless of how long they would be there.

The boys came to Susan one day and pleaded with her to get them a canoe, so she enrolled in a canoe safety course for six weeks at the YWCA to make sure that she would be able to teach her sons everything they needed to know. She also taught Sunday school, worked in a hamburger stand at the boys' Little League games, and spoke at luncheons all across the country as a wife of one of the New Nine and on behalf of Field Enterprises, which sold encyclopedias and had a deal with NASA.

Susan seemed to handle everything so well that no one, not even her boys, had any idea of the demons that she was fighting inside. The thought of possibly losing her husband to a technology that was still in its infancy was a deep-seated trigger linked to her father that she wasn't actually conscious of.

Frank was away over 250 days that year, so it was up to Susan to carry the full load of everything else. Frank could find every knob and switch in the spacecraft with his eyes closed, but couldn't find a water glass at home because he didn't know where anything was kept. It didn't occur to NASA to prepare anyone for this major adjustment, and most of the men still had a fighter pilot's mentality and wouldn't dream of getting any kind of therapy or emotional support. They also expected the wives to bury any of their fears, and, whenever a news camera was pointed in their direction, to perform like a trained circus animal. It abolished any sense of privacy. The women and children were expected to look proud and brave in front of the media, when most of the time they were actually lonely and scared.

The reporters assigned to cover the space program didn't help matters. A good percentage of them were obnoxious and aggressive. Thankfully NASA made a deal with *Life* that gave the magazine exclusive rights to the "behind the scenes" personal lives of the astronauts and their families. Each of the new astronauts were given $16,000 a year to participate, which was a godsend to a group of people who were used to living on meager military pay—which for Frank, based on his rank and time served, was roughly $600 per month.

They would end up earning every penny and then some. Frank informed Susan that a reporter would essentially be living in the house and following her around. She begged Frank to say no, but he just dismissed her concerns and said, "Susan, this is good for the program. We are doing it." She looked at him with disappointment and walked away without saying a word. The only positive thing about *Life* having exclusive access to the astronauts and their families was that it kept other, more belligerent reporters at bay.

Another thing that none of the wives wanted to face was the fact that groupies threw themselves at their husbands on a continual basis. Between being away from home most of the time and the fame that was going to their heads, the now very famous astronauts had "Cape Cookies" in Florida.

The wives didn't want to acknowledge the fact that their husbands were the center of female attention nationwide and were likely fooling around. Susan had already witnessed the phenomenon on every air force base where Frank had been stationed. Fighter pilots had a massive gravitational pull when it came to the opposite sex. They didn't have to be the most handsome man in the room to score. The aviator persona and swagger attracted "party girls" like a fly to honey. Even married women weren't immune.

It was well known that most of the astronauts wore their machismo like their beloved flight jackets, and even if they didn't sleep with all the women they were rumored to have hooked up with, they didn't dispute the stories either. It played into the image that they were secretly proud of and liked to perpetuate. Most of them gave in to the temptation, repeatedly.

Frank was one of the exceptions and was called a fossil and "holier than thou" on more than one occasion. There were a few others in the "Straight Shooters Club"—Jim Lovell, Ed White, Bill Anders, and Neil Armstrong. These men genuinely loved their wives and children and refused to disrespect them that way, but it certainly didn't make them popular with their colleagues.

Although they didn't preach their moral code, they were a constant reminder that it was possible to remain faithful to the vows you made to one woman, even though the lure of temptation was everywhere. The astronauts would get wined and dined and invited to every party that was "the place to be." Before rock concerts became a banquet of sex, drugs, and rock 'n' roll, astronauts were the best show in town. They were basically tourist attractions. Ann Landers even did a column on the sex lives of the astronauts and "their desires." The public viewed many of NASA's celebrities as players.

The agency accepted the infidelity as part of the deal and did nothing to interfere but tried to encourage the press to keep the womanizing and partying quiet so as not to tarnish the "all-American image" they were selling to the nation.

In late 1962, chief of the Astronaut Office and NASA crew assignments Deke Slayton brought Frank and rest of the New Nine together for a briefing. He wanted to make damn sure that the men knew what was expected of them and what they had to lose. "As an astronaut, gifts and freebies of all sorts are going to be offered to you, but don't fall prey to the goodies! If you have any questions, just follow the old fighter pilot creed: anything you can eat, drink, or screw within twenty-four hours is acceptable; beyond that take a pass," he said.

Slayton realized later that he had underestimated how their celebrity status would become a problem in regard to the opposite sex, so when it was time to welcome the fourteen new astronauts from Group 3 a year later, he was far more blunt: "You are big boys, so I won't tell you how to behave. Hopefully most of you are smart enough to know that if you are going to screw around, you better be damn discreet about it. You are about to get a lot more attention, and whatever kept you out of trouble before, it won't help you here." He paused to look at everyone in the room, then continued, "We didn't bring you into this program to see your name spread all over the scandal sheets. If your extracurricular activities become more important than this job, we will replace you in a heartbeat." It was another reminder to all of them that not only were they expendable, but NASA owned them.

The agency dealt with the first astronaut divorce by backing up the threat that Deke Slayton made. Apollo 7's Donn Eisele hooked up with a "cookie" he met at the Cape during training. He then went and informed his wife Harriet that he was leaving her and his children while she was in a hospital room with their young son, who was dying of leukemia.

NASA and his fellow astronauts were appalled. It's one thing to leave your wife—but your dying son? They made things very uncomfortable for Eisele, who was strongly encouraged to resign six months later. He didn't exactly represent the image that NASA was selling, nor did any of his colleagues stick up for him. They all felt that leaving your family that way was completely without honor.

No one at the agency said it out loud, but the wives just weren't welcome at the Cape. It was an off-limits area full of vices, and Deke didn't want the headache of dealing with an enraged wife. If one of the men wanted to have his family visit, he had to give everyone a big heads-up, especially Deke. Sadly, most of the wives understood what they had to lose by making waves, and so any hint of adultery just wasn't discussed. It was one of the many reasons the cocktails and cigarettes were always flowing in someone's backyard in El Lago. Of the twenty-nine men who would end up flying in the Apollo program, nineteen of their marriages eventually ended in divorce, the majority of which occurred after Apollo ended in 1972.

It was a strange dichotomy, because NASA realized that being seen as a "rock star" was good for the astronauts' image and the program itself but not for their individual marriages. In other words, they saw these men and their families as commodities that were useful only until they weren't. In the end, the mission was all that mattered.

Susan hadn't been in Houston very long, but just as she'd done at all the other bases, she dove into her adopted community feet-first. She was quickly befriended by a kindred spirit, Marge Slayton, who was Deke's wife. Both women had seemingly boundless energy. Marge thought it was a good idea for all the wives to get to know each other better, so she and Susan created the Astronaut Wives Club in the fall of 1962.

Marge and Susan organized the first meeting of the club with a luncheon to welcome the New Nine wives at Alan and Louise Shepard's stylish Houston apartment in a building called the Mayfair. "Mother Marge," as the other ladies called her, was the social convener, and Susan was the organizer. Susan and Marge wanted their meetings to be as much about socializing and distracting themselves as it was a support group. They needed one another, even though they had to be very careful what they disclosed. No wife wanted anything to hurt her husband's chances of getting chosen for the next mission. Their futures were tied to their husbands' success.

Susan thought that one of the best and most honest descriptions of what it was really like to be married to a fighter pilot/astronaut came from Gene Cernan's wife, Barbara, during a public speech she had been asked to give. "Being an astronaut's wife means living alone most of the time," she said candidly. "He is gone all week, every week, and there are no such things as vacations to reconnect. It means putting away your own ego while you watch the world worship your man. It means learning to change your own tires, fix the plumbing, and deal with all of the money and domestic issues yourself. You deal with family emergencies without being able to consult your mate, and you wait by the phone every night just to hear his voice, because that is all you really have from him. You must put on a brave face for the cameras, no matter how scared you are, and endure the pain of seeing your dear friends at funerals who have just become widows. You must hide your emotions and never show any weakness." She then added, "You can only do this if you believe in the program as much as your husband does. You belong to a special club where the normal rules of life don't apply. You are part of a team, and you have to be as effective at your job as he is at his. That is the only way that it can work."

It was a moving speech and one that Barbara truly believed in. But not long after Gene Cernan became the last astronaut to walk on the Moon, Barbara told him just before she filed for divorce, "My name is not going to be in the history books for doing anything like yours will, but I know what I did." If you ask most of the astronauts from the 1960s, they would agree with Barbara Cernan. Every one of those extraordinary women should be in the history books right alongside their husbands.

In the summer of 1963, Deke Slayton started picking crews for the first Gemini flights. The Gemini program would be the critical forerunner to Apollo. Latin for "twins," Gemini would be crewed by two astronauts, and the sole purpose of the program was to prove the foundational techniques and procedures needed to put an American on the Moon and return him safely to the Earth. It was a challenging list of unknowns that included extravehicular activity, or EVA (space walks), rendezvous, docking, and the effects of long-duration zero gravity and radiation on the human body.

During the NASA press conference held to announce the New Nine, a reporter had asked the new recruits about their ambitions for the Moon, and Frank immediately declared to loud applause, "I'd like to be on the first team." It turned out that a few folks at the agency agreed with him. Deke Slayton announced Gemini 3 as the first flight scheduled for the spring of 1965, commanded by Mercury veteran Gus Grissom with Frank in the right seat as pilot.

Frank went to meet with Gus at his home, but Gus didn't warm to him at all.

"Frank thought that their time together was great, but Gus felt differently. Frank was rejected by Gus, so the pilot seat went to me," said John Young. "Frank Borman was very solemn and had leadership stamped all over him. Competence was never a question with Frank because he operated at a higher level than most of us . . . but he just wasn't one of the guys. Frank was born to lead, and that was a problem for Gus."

"The egos of Grissom and Borman were too big to fit into a single spacecraft," added Gene Cernan.

For the first long-duration flight, Slayton slid Frank into the command seat for Gemini 7 along with another astronaut from the New Nine, Jim Lovell. A former navy pilot, Lovell was known as a smooth, reliable operator in the cockpit, so it wasn't any wonder that the astronaut class clown Pete Conrad gave him the call sign "Shaky."

Most call signs were like nicknames. You didn't get to pick your own, and it was usually something ironic. Frank got "Happy." No explanation needed.

"Jim got along with everybody so that was a big help, because we were asking these two men to spend two weeks in a very small space that was equivalent to the front seat of a Volkswagen," said Slayton later in an interview. "I ended up choosing Frank Borman for one of the Gemini long-duration missions from the very beginning because of his tenacity—and Jim was a capable guy that got along with everyone that you could have assigned to any mission. . . . It was really interesting to me to see the difference between Jim and Frank," he said with a smile. "You could tell either one of them to take the hill. Jim would look things over and very carefully make a decision, and Frank would be out of the foxhole before you finished talking—but both of them would always take the hill."

Many of the prime and backup teams spent time together, but socializing with the other astronauts wasn't of much interest to Frank. "I was something of a loner anyway. I regarded the other astronauts more as professional comrades than as truly intimate friends . . . with one exception, Ed White. We lived near each other in El Lago and shared a philosophy that brought us together. Each of us were totally committed to our wives and children. We became quite close, and I don't know of any other astronaut who was more genuinely liked and admired."

Ed's first flight would be as pilot aboard Gemini 4 with Frank's old classmate from test pilot school, Jim McDivitt, as commander. NASA had given the go-ahead for White to perform the first extravehicular activity. On the third orbit of NASA's first multiday mission, the astronauts locked their helmets and depressurized the spacecraft. After some frustration struggling to unlock his overhead hatch, White was able to push it open to reveal the Hawaiian Islands more than a hundred miles below. Tethered to the spacecraft, he floated outside the vehicle for twenty minutes while McDivitt took photographs and provided color commentary back to Houston. McDivitt's photo of White floating in the vastness of space with the Earth below him made the cover of *Life* magazine and became one of the best-known images of the twentieth century.

Although there were some problems with voice communications, it was clear White found the spacewalk an emotional and awe-inspiring event. He loved it out there. With the dark side approaching, White climbed back into the spacecraft beside McDivitt and secured the hatch. As Gemini 4 slipped into darkness, White reported to Mission Control, "Having to come back inside the spacecraft is the saddest day of my life."

While the EVA had proven a future Apollo astronaut could exit the lunar module and get back in safely, the milestone was overshadowed by NASA's second-place finish—again. Four months earlier, the Russians had gotten the better of the United States when cosmonaut Alexei Leonov became the first human to walk in space. The "We'll get 'em next time" adage around NASA was starting to sound like the agency's unofficial motto.

The Bormans and Whites were spending more time together as couples, and so Susan was with Ed's wife Pat, a lovely petite blonde who always seemed to have a smile on her face, during the Gemini 4 launch. But, unfortunately, Pat White's exuberance couldn't make up for the nation's second-place finish and the media's harsh criticism of NASA. Pat basked in any attention that her husband received. Being married to an American hero was the closest thing that Pat ever had to feeling like she was "someone."

Over cocktails, Susan celebrated with her friend as the White children raced around the house, unaware of the magnitude of their father's accomplishment.

Susan was so happy to see Pat filled with a peace that seemed to vanquish the fears she expressed earlier over her husband's chosen profession. Pat was still elated weeks later when Ed returned home to El Lago for some well-deserved time off with her and the kids.

Meanwhile, Frank's training for his first flight was a "meat grinder schedule" that afforded little time for Susan and the boys. He'd arrive at the office by 7:00 AM for briefings and simulator training then spend his lunch hour lifting weights and jogging.

Frank had spent the better part of 1965 staying at the Ramada Inn in St. Louis, where his Gemini 7 capsule was being built by McDonnell Aircraft Corporation.

Back at home in El Lago, Susan was on her own to contend with the media, who'd pulled up stakes from the Whites' house to set up camp on the Bormans' front lawn for the upcoming launch of Gemini 7. Peeking out through the curtains, Fred and Edwin could see the infestation of reporters and photographers everywhere they looked.

Finally, their oldest son, Fred, broke down as he looked at the mob outside of their home. "Mom, why didn't you tell us that it would be like this?" he asked, clearly distressed. "I didn't know that it would be so hard."

The night before the launch, Frank barely slept. In the air force, he'd never feared piloting a new fighter jet or test flying an unproven aircraft; it was an accepted part of the job description. Tossing and turning, Frank watched the clock turn from the eve of the flight to launch day—December 4, 1965.

It was exactly fourteen years to the day since Frank had graduated from flight training at Nellis AFB, and although he was just about to make his first flight into space, he was consumed by an emotion he was not very familiar with. Major Borman had an "agonizing fear" for his wife and sons. "I didn't want to be a heroic casualty in man's conquest of space, and I was not oblivious to the hazards involved. I wanted to stay a living, breathing husband and father." Frank didn't want to even imagine the hardships and pain Susan and the boys would be forced to endure if they lost him.

The conflict was always there—mission versus family. NASA was built by former members of the US armed services, and the military culture came with them. "NASA astronauts were self-centered; they had to be," Frank admitted. "The mission had been pounded into your brain until it alone was in sharp focus, with everything else in your life obscured. But then the other image creeps into your thoughts—the family that damned well could be left, their dependency and their own world destroyed in a split second of disaster. The mission momentarily blurs and retreats, but I always opted for the mission." So Frank prayed that God would watch over Susan and the boys until his obligation was fulfilled.

Frank and Jim had launch-day breakfast with Deke and a few other astronauts, including his close friend Neil Armstrong. Inside the suit-up trailer adjacent to Launch Complex 19, Frank pulled on his one-of-a-kind lightweight suit, which the David Clark Company made for his and Jim's long flight. Frank's last order of business before he stepped out of the trailer to take the ride to the launchpad was to slip a small color photo of Susan into the shoulder pocket of his suit.

Frederick and Edwin devoured the lunch NASA had provided them, but food was the last thing on Susan's mind as she pushed it around her plate. Escorted by a small entourage from the Public Affairs Office, Susan and the boys were driven to the VIP area of Kennedy Space Center.

Susan sat with her eyes transfixed on Frank's four-ton spacecraft, which looked more like a corrugated tin can than a sophisticated flying machine meant to support life in the vacuum of space. The calming voice of NASA announcer Jack King seemed to distract her as he counted down the last few seconds before announcing, "Zero, ignition."

With the blast of the Titan's two main engines, Susan watched the 120-foot rocket loaded with one hundred thousand pounds of highly explosive fuel lift off from Pad 19. Billows of smoke and fire blasted the launchpad, and she could feel the ground shake beneath her. She kept the boys close and held them tight. Instinctively, she turned her head to look away just as a photographer captured her in that moment of fear as Gemini 7 blasted toward the heavens.

Of all the photos taken by the press of the launch, the one that made the front page was of Susan turning her head away in fear while holding the boys. It was a moment of extreme anxiety for her husband and best friend, and some at the agency as well as in the rest of the country were quick to criticize her for it once the photo was published. How dare she show any real emotion? How dare she be anything but proud and patriotic? "For heaven's sake, wipe your tears. You're ruining my morning coffee," one woman wrote in to the newspaper when she saw the photo.

Susan's rebuttal, a classy yet honest response that was so indicative of the gracious woman that she was, was published in newspapers around the country: "These past weeks I have worn my heart on my sleeve," she wrote. "Some people say that they were glad to see an astronaut's wife willing to admit that she was scared. Others were unhappy that I didn't maintain a stiff upper lip. At one time the criticism would have cut me deeply. I have since realized that you can't be all things to all people, so I decided not to pretend. I decided to be myself. I am just a woman who loves her husband and wants him to be safe."

10

"THAT IS WHY YOU TEST ON THE GROUND"

F RANK'S FIRST SPACEFLIGHT was anything but glamorous. He and Jim had the "honor" of proving the human body could endure a round-trip mission to the Moon. NASA had calculated a lunar mission would take no more than nine days, so it was decided Gemini 7 would exceed the maximum and orbit the Earth for fourteen days. From bowel movements, or lack thereof in Frank's case, to eating and sleeping, by Frank's calculation the NASA doctors had him and Jim "hooked up to more electrodes and other measuring devices than Frankenstein's monster." Some of the discomfort of the mission was alleviated by the beautiful and breathtaking view of Earth from two hundred miles high.

On day seven, Mission Control informed Frank and Jim, "We'd like to tell you congratulations on your halfway mark. You're now heading downhill. I see the Borman boys are here." Caught by surprise, Frank radioed back, "Hi, boys!"

Susan was standing by and told Frank that everything was fine at home, but that Edwin was quite worried his father "would be too tired to take them fishing when he got back." While small moments like this helped Frank feel a little closer to his family, it also amplified how far apart they actually were.

Never before had American astronauts been in space so long. The boredom of eating tasteless, freeze-dried food packaged and prepared for easy digestion was far from "culinary excellence" and did nothing to alleviate the lack of creature comforts found inside NASA's second generation of manned spacecraft.

Frank had been accused for most of his life of being quite "literal," so it was no surprise that the book he brought to help pass the time up there was titled *Roughing It*. It's a semi-autobiographical book of travel literature by Mark Twain. And Lovell's more epic *Drums Along the Mohawk* by Walter Edmonds did nothing to speed up the clock.

The novelty of orbiting the Earth in a phone booth–sized spacecraft had long since worn off. Without the ability to move, by day eleven Frank reported they were feeling a little "crummy" and he wasn't sleeping well at all.

With three days left to stare out the window, Frank and Jim were eager for the highlight of the mission to commence. NASA wanted to attempt the first-ever rendezvous of two spacecraft and put another check in the box for a future Apollo mission.

Even though the two Gemini spacecraft were not designed to dock in space, on December 15, Gemini 6—originally scheduled ahead of Gemini 7—launched with Mercury veteran Wally Schirra and Frank's former test pilot instructor from Edwards Tom Stafford.

Every fighter pilot worth his salt can fly in formation, but now Frank would be attempting to do that with another spacecraft two hundred miles above the Earth while traveling at more than three miles per second. After a few problems with radio communications, sixty-two miles out, Stafford radioed that he could see a bright star rushing toward them. He first thought it was Sirius, but in fact it was the docking lights of Gemini 7.

Just a little more than three football fields away, Gemini 6 came into full view of Frank and Jim and closed to within 130 feet. Like a sign from the heavens, as they neared the designated rendezvous point, the twin stars of Castor and Pollux in the Gemini constellation appeared in Frank's window. Mission Control erupted in cheers and lit up cigars as if they'd just become new fathers in celebration of the first manned spacecraft rendezvous and America's first victory of the space race.

It was also the first time four American astronauts had been in space at the same time. After flying in formation as close as one foot, on the fourth orbit Wally peeled Gemini 6 off for reentry. The adrenaline rush of the successful rendezvous was short lived as physical exhaustion and mental fatigue set in, with the stark realization that Gemini 7 had three more days left circling the planet.

One of the side effects of breathing a pure-oxygen environment is acute dehydration. Despite drinking volumes of water and fruit juice, Frank's skin and scalp were in a continual state of flaking. Unfortunately, having to keep very hydrated also meant excessive urinating, which involved a low-tech process that employed a condom attached to a bag with a line that vented into space. Most often it worked . . . but when it didn't, the astronauts chased droplets of urine that would float around the cabin. Luckily, getting rid of the waste from their bowel movements didn't pose the same problem since the doctors at NASA required them to store their fecal matter so it could be analyzed when they got back to Earth. If you combine the astronauts' washroom activity with the inevitable fact they didn't shower for two weeks, no description of the smell inside the cabin of Gemini 7 is required.

As much as Frank would have loved to have deorbited early, he knew he wouldn't be satisfied unless his first mission as commander was perfect.

Nineteen minutes after their 323rd hour in space, the official capsule communicator, or CapCom, radioed, "Gemini 7, you ready to come home now?" Frank's answer was immediate, short, and assertive. "Ready!" Plunging through the atmosphere in a fiery thirty-five-hundred-degree plasma tube, Gemini 7 hurtled toward the ocean off of the Florida coast where the aircraft carrier USS *Wasp* was on station awaiting their arrival.

At ten thousand feet, Frank released the peppermint-striped main parachute, and a few minutes later he and Jim were bobbing in the Atlantic. Peering out the window, Frank couldn't see the recovery helicopter from the USS *Wasp*. "Shit! We must have missed it by more than Wally did," he said to Jim in a disappointed voice, referring to his bet with Schirra that he'd make the most precise landing. Frank would soon find out that he'd beaten Schirra by landing nearly three thousand feet closer.

Frank and Jim had completed every one of the twenty experiments that were part of the trip and proved the human body could endure the time it would take for a lunar mission. Frank may have lost ten pounds, but the twenty different doctors who examined him all reported no ill effects. Gemini 7 had traveled more than 5.1 million miles and completed 206 orbits over 330 hours. The flight set four records: most orbits, distance covered, time in space, and the rendezvous of two manned spacecraft.

Frank Borman couldn't care less about records and firsts; what mattered most was that he'd completed the mission. He and Jim looked like scruffy hoboes when they were picked up and taken to the deck of the aircraft carrier, but all in all were in great spirits.

"Jim Lovell was an outstanding partner," Frank later recalled. "Like all the others in our group, he was bright and competent, but he was something else too—he had a marvelous sense of humor, was always positive, and had a cheerful outlook. I'll be forever grateful to Deke Slayton for having picked him as my pilot."

Except for needing a break from one another and a good night sleep, Frank's and Jim's minds were in great shape. But the muscle atrophy that had set in from being sedentary for so long made it difficult to stand.

Lovell was a former navy pilot, but Frank was the landlubber from the air force and there was "no goddamn way" he was going to let sailors carry him off the recovery helicopter in front of his navy rivals.

Calling on his stubbornness and tenacity, along with a healthy dose of adrenaline from three thousand cheering sailors, Frank willed his legs to work and walked unassisted with Lovell off the chopper and across the wooden flight deck of the *Wasp*. As they were being escorted to their postflight medical tests, someone put an envelope into Frank's hands. He recognized the handwriting immediately as he opened it.

> *My dearest Frank, I only wish that I could be the one to open the left hatch. This note is the next best thing to reach you as soon as possible. In our hearts we have been together these past two weeks—every moment. Our two boys have been a great comfort and hearing your voice literally made it bearable. My love and pride just can't be put into words. Knowing that you are safe and on your way home lets me know that God heard my prayers. All my love forever—Susan*

Inside the letter were two photos reminding him of what mattered the most—Susan and their boys. As he removed his spacesuit for the last time, he remembered the photo of Susan he had taken with him and removed it from the shoulder pocket. During his two weeks in space he never once removed it from his suit, worried it might distract him and take his focus off the mission.

Back in the States, Frank was awarded the NASA Exceptional Service Medal. Fifteen years earlier, Susan had pinned on his wings, and now the air force wasted little time promoting the thirty-seven-year-old to full bird colonel, the youngest in air force history. The navy promoted Jim Lovell to captain. The mission also marked America's first major victory against the Russians—the space flight had been longer than all previous Russian missions combined.

The minute all the hoopla surrounding Gemini 7 was done, Frank focused on fulfilling his promise. He loaded up the car with fishing gear, and the three Borman men went fishing.

The whole family returned to Tucson a few weeks later for a parade in Frank's honor. There was a big banner that his best friend, Wayne Crutchfield, was responsible for hanging off of one of the buildings on Main Avenue that said, WELCOME HOME SQUAREHEAD.

It was a touching tribute, and as Frank and Susan looked at each other from the backseat of the convertible that they were in while waving at everyone, they had a moment of, "Who would have ever dreamed this?" Ruth Bugbee was somewhere in the crowd, and Susan hoped that just for once her mother might actually be proud of her and the man she had chosen to marry.

Soon after the Gemini 7 mission and some of the craziness with the press started to abate, Frank got a telegram from West Point asking him to come back. Susan wanted to go. It was the one place she had felt truly at peace because Frank wasn't putting himself in danger on a daily basis. But the new colonel had one mission—to beat the Russians to the Moon and help win the Cold War. He was staying with NASA, and Susan kept her disappointment to herself.

The culture at NASA was very competitive among the astronauts, which also extended to their wives. The agency encouraged the competition, to get the absolute best out of these men and to control them to a certain extent. The public only saw the wives as a united front. They would smile and make sure to have their best dress on whenever they left the house in case they ran into a photographer. Most of them would admit that they liked the attention that their husbands received and the fame and favors that came with it.

That's where Susan was different. She had never been impressed with the swag. When all the wives of the New Nine were sent fur coats in a big fancy box from a high-class department store, Susan was the only one who sent hers back. She thanked the company in a note but informed them that she didn't need free clothes and that her husband would buy her one if she wanted it. So it was easy to understand how Susan's perceived strength, confidence, and beauty might be threatening to some of the other wives.

They would never say anything to her face but secretly felt that Susan thought she was somehow better than they were. That could not have been further from the truth. She just didn't trust that these things came with no strings attached. Her intuition was almost always right and would be something that Frank could count on for years to come.

Despite all the reasons that the NASA wives had to keep things to themselves, Susan still got very close to Pat White. They bonded initially because Frank and Ed became friends, and they liked to spend time together as families. Ed was a family man; it was just another reason Susan and Pat were so close—they were both married to good men. The Bormans and the Whites would escape the chaos for any weekend the men could get time off and take their kids fishing and boating. They became each other's extended family.

If NASA had a poster boy after John Glenn left NASA, it was Ed White. Tall, good-looking, and incredibly smart, he was exactly the image that they were selling to the public—a perfect representation of the all-American man attempting the impossible.

Ed had been Frank's backup for the Gemini 7 mission, but his next assignment was to be part of the three-man crew for the very first Apollo flight. Deke Slayton had also chosen Gus Grissom to be the Apollo 1 commander, along with a rookie astronaut named Roger Chaffee. Planned for a late 1966 launch, the program was delayed until early 1967 due to technical challenges with the new Apollo command module.

The last flight of the Gemini program was commanded by Jim Lovell with crewmate Edwin "Buzz" Aldrin. On December 22, 1966, NASA marked the official end of the Gemini program, and the agency's singular attention became Apollo and a Moon landing before the end of the decade.

Susan and Frank celebrated Christmas 1966 with the boys and rang in 1967. With less than three years to make JFK's deadline of walking on the Moon by 1970, Susan knew that she would see even less of Frank but was looking forward to the short vacation that he promised to take the family on as soon as he could get the time.

With the first Apollo flight now scheduled in January, the new three-man spacecraft would be flown into Earth orbit atop the Saturn 1B since technical issues with the Saturn V rocket delayed its first test flight until later that year.

NASA was still riding high in the battle to beat the Russians, but that was all about to change.

On Friday, January 20, 1967, the S-IVB, the third stage of the Saturn V, began its final acceptance test at the Douglas Aircraft facility in Sacramento, California. While the S-IVB made up only fifty-eight feet of the Apollo stack, its single J-2 engine would be responsible for getting Apollo into Earth orbit for a systems check. Then the J-2 would be restarted to accelerate the spacecraft to 23,200 mph to escape Earth's gravity.

Eleven seconds before the simulated liftoff, the third stage exploded without warning. While no one was injured, the detonation completely obliterated the test stand. The search for the problem revealed that a helium tank had ruptured and fractured a fuel line. To make matters worse, investigators found that the subcontractor, one of more than twenty thousand working on Apollo, had made the tank out of inferior material. Douglas and NASA wasted little time removing both the tank and its manufacturer from the program.

The agency reassured itself that its philosophy of rigorous ground testing would uncover any other flaws and significantly mitigate risks to manned flights, but the events of January 1967 and the tragedy to follow would jeopardize America's entire lunar program.

While the faulty tank was just one part, Apollo had 5.6 million parts. That meant if 99.9 percent of all the components of a single lunar mission worked flawlessly, the mission could potentially have fifty-six hundred failures. Frank understood that problems came with the territory, and part of his standard operating procedure had always been to never tell Susan anything that might worry her needlessly.

The week after the explosion, the Bormans finally got to sneak away for some much-needed family time. Frank had been working many long days without a break and knew that Susan and the boys were feeling left out. They went to a cabin that they stayed at with the Whites in the past, which was owned by their good friend Bill Elkins. Bill was a lawyer and the brother of another friend of Frank and Susan's whom they met at the church they attended in Houston. Jim and Bill Elkins were what one would describe as Houston "royalty." Jim was the chairman of the biggest bank in Houston at that time. They would both become lifelong friends of the Bormans.

Just as Frank, Susan, and the boys were sitting down to dinner after arriving at the cabin a few hours before, they heard a knock at the door. Frank got up and opened it to find a Texas Ranger standing on the porch with a grim look on his face. The cabin didn't have a listed phone number, so NASA had to track him down another way.

"Hello, can I help you? Is there something wrong?" Frank asked the young ranger.

"Sir, I'm sorry to disturb you, but the Space Center in Houston has been trying to reach you. There is an emergency, and they want you to phone them immediately." Frank nodded, quickly thanked him, and went directly to the phone inside the cabin.

Susan knew right away by the look on her husband's face that something wasn't right.

Frank called and was transferred to Deke Slayton immediately. He didn't bother with a greeting. "Frank, we had a really bad fire on Pad 34. Grissom, White, and one of the new guys, Roger Chaffee, are dead."

Frank closed his eyes as his stomach flipped. He cleared his throat. "What in the hell happened?"

"We have no idea yet, but we're organizing an investigation committee, and you are on it," Deke said in a tone that Frank had never heard from him before. He sounded like someone in extreme shock. "Just get to the Cape as soon as possible."

Frank rubbed his eyes. "Deke, I *have* to stop at Ed White's house first. Susan and Pat are close, and I think she'll need her right now."

"Fine with me," he responded gruffly. "I'll have an airplane waiting for you as soon as you are ready to leave." Frank hung up the phone and Susan came over quietly.

"Frank, what is it?"

Frank looked at her with tortured eyes. "Ed White is dead," he whispered in her ear as he pulled her into an embrace. "There was a fire, and Ed, Gus, and Roger Chaffee all died." Frank just held her for a moment, knowing that life was about to get even more intense for all of them.

"We need to go and see Pat." Susan pulled back and looked at him. She knew how upset Frank was and refused to cry in front of him, but it was like her worst fear had come true. Ed White was highly intelligent like Frank—but he was bigger, stronger, and seemed invincible. If this could happen to him, it could happen to her husband.

She couldn't stop the horrible, runaway thoughts that were going through her mind. She finally nodded jerkily. "I'll get ready right away," she said in a strangled whisper. She then went into the small bedroom of the cabin, closed the door, put her hand over her mouth, and silently screamed.

When Frank and Susan got to the Whites' home there were NASA officials already there, trying to pressure Pat into what they thought was best for Ed's funeral. Their only goal was to mitigate the bad press from the situation. Ed had told Pat years before, when they first got married, that he wanted to be buried at West Point like his father.

Pat was barely functioning and trying to get that across to the NASA representatives, but they weren't listening. NASA officially wanted all three men to have their ceremony at Arlington National Cemetery.

It was bureaucratic bullshit, and Frank wasn't going to stand for it. "Frank," Pat sobbed as Susan sat down beside her to offer whatever comfort she could, "They told me there would only be one ceremony, but I promised Ed that his funeral would be at West Point."

"That's nonsense," Frank told her as he took her hand. "We're going to do exactly what you and Ed would want, and I will take care of it." Frank squeezed her hand in reassurance and then got on the phone and started barking orders until he got in touch with someone high up the chain of command in Washington.

"Ed White's funeral will be at West Point, like he requested," Frank barked. "That's the way that it's going to be, so go ahead and arrange it." He hung up the phone before whoever he was speaking to could answer him. He knew it was the right thing to do, so everyone else had better get in line.

Frank left Susan with the grieving widow, got a few hours of disturbed sleep, and then jumped into a T-38 that Deke had commandeered for him. He actually felt lucky, albeit with a touch of guilt, because instead of having to deal with the crushing grief of losing someone he thought of as a brother, he was able to dive headfirst into an investigation that would provide a much-needed distraction from the devastating trauma.

Unbeknownst to him, he was leaving behind a wife who was taking the tragedy as if it had happened to her, and it would set off the unconscious belief that she was going to lose Frank, just like she had lost her father. Susan knew from Frank's time in the air force that it took only the malfunction of one part of an aircraft to take the life of a pilot. But she chose to believe that something like that could never happen to her husband, while Frank took every step necessary to shield his family from anything he hoped would never amount to a real concern.

"Failures happen up there," he would always say, "and that is why you test on the ground."

But it was a test on the ground that just claimed the life of his comrade.

11

"THERE'S MORE TO LIFE THAN LIVING"

FRANK AND SUSAN ALWAYS TALKED OF RETURNING to West Point one day, but neither of them could have imagined it would be to bury a beloved friend. The bereaved streamed into the historic old Chapel at West Point. No one spoke. Glances and handshakes were the best the mourners could manage. The only sounds that could be heard outside the Gothic cathedral were birds singing in the cool February air.

Pat White asked Frank and his Gemini 7 crewmate, Jim Lovell, to act as pallbearers for her husband. Both men had been chosen with Ed by NASA in the Group 2 astronaut selection of 1962. Frank considered the other astronauts more as professional comrades than intimate friends, with the exception of Ed. "I don't know of any astronaut who was more genuinely liked and admired than Ed. He's as close to NASA's image of the ideal astronaut as any man could be," Frank told Susan after meeting him for the first time five years earlier.

Frank looked across the casket at Jim, who was doing his best to fight back the tears. "There's more to life than living, Borman," Frank reminded himself as his white cotton gloves gripped the heavy brass handle of the casket. "If you believe in something bigger than yourself, you don't welcome death—but you're ready if it comes for you."

Frank was a trained soldier but had never lost anyone he'd cared so much for, and the feelings were overwhelming. Frank and Jim slowly shuffled from the hearse to lower their brother into his final resting place. Fate had claimed a cherished friend and the first of the New Nine astronauts.

Shrouded in a black veil, Pat White sat graveside surrounded by her family. The sky was clear as a missing man formation of air force jets streaked overhead. Fighting his emotions, Frank bent over to present Pat with the flag that had draped Ed's casket. No words could give this tragedy any meaning or ease the heartache and pain. Frank placed his hand on Pat's shoulder to comfort her and she placed her hand over his and gripped it tightly. Frank tried to move away and return to his place, but Pat couldn't seem to let go of his hand.

Susan had accompanied Frank to more funerals for fallen men than she could count, but Ed White's death wounded her husband in a way she'd never seen before. Filled with grief and anger over the needless loss of his friend, Frank finally had to tell himself that enough was enough, and it was time to get back in the fight.

Despite NASA's own philosophy of "Don't take anything for granted," in the "go fever" rush to the Moon they had done just that, and it cost lives. The agency was left to investigate the cause of the fire, and NASA leaders knew they needed to assign an astronaut who was not only technically proficient but, more important, would cut through all the red tape and bullshit to get to the cause so they could fix it. They needed to get back on schedule. When it came time to choose someone to find the cause of the Apollo 1 fire, everyone agreed there was only one choice: Frank Borman.

In the five years since Frank joined NASA, he'd earned a reputation as a highly skilled and tenacious problem solver. Mike Collins would later describe Frank as "aggressive and capable. Someone who makes decisions faster than anyone I've ever met with an amazingly good batting average . . . which would be even better if he slowed down a bit."

Frank would level anyone who got in his way of getting the job done. Aware of what was on the line, he felt the mission couldn't afford a single weak link. "I actually took exception to the few weaker astronauts in the program. I felt every man had to be well qualified in every respect, with no ifs, ands, or buts."

While some might criticize Frank for being cold, unemotional, and often abrasive, NASA believed his approach to a problem made him the best choice to be the only astronaut assigned to investigate the Apollo 1 fire. "I was always the impatient and outspoken one. If you can't do your job, get the hell out of the way so I can do mine. I wasn't the most popular astronaut for that very reason, but I didn't give a damn," said Frank in an interview later. Even knowing the investigation might jeopardize the Apollo lunar program, NASA director Bob Gilruth told Frank not to pull any punches, even if the blame led right back to him.

"A good move, given Frank's independence and complete honesty. He wasn't going to let anybody bullshit him," said astronaut Tom Stafford.

Frank attacked the investigation like an army of one. He didn't have to explain to Susan that the future of America's lunar program depended on his findings, but felt it was just as important to honor Ed, Gus, Roger, and their families. On numerous occasions Frank visited all three widows, offering to answer any questions they had about the events surrounding their husbands' deaths.

NASA had removed the bodies of the astronauts but left the spacecraft untouched until Frank arrived at the Cape. He was the first one inside the blackened spacecraft, and what he found was a pilot's worst nightmare.

The extreme heat had melted the seats in the capsule and fused all three of the astronauts together. The smell of the burnt flesh was horrendous. "I was no stranger to violent death and its aftermath, but nothing I had witnessed in the past came close to what I saw there at the Cape. I can't even begin to describe the chamber of horror," Frank admitted grimly.

Frank listened to the tape recordings over and over for clues. In the hours leading up to the fire, communication problems plagued the "plugs out" test of the Block I command module that the men sat in, mounted atop a Saturn IB rocket. In the hope of identifying the communication problem, ground control put a hold on the simulated launch at T minus ten minutes. One minute before the fire, a frustrated Gus Grissom barked to ground control, "How are we going to get to the Moon if we can't talk between two or three buildings?" As Frank listened further, it was clear that contrary to NASA's official press statements, his friends had not died quickly. The next transmissions were chilling.

GRISSOM: Flames!

CHAFFEE: We've got a fire in the cockpit!

A small television camera trained on Grissom's window captured the orange glow of flames and legs flailing in panic.

WHITE: We've got a bad fire!

CHAFFEE: Get us out of here now! We're burning up!

Final screams of pain were followed by a ball of fire and silence. Frank wanted to believe that NASA's press reports about how they died were for the benefit of their wives and children more than they were about spinning the truth to save the program.

Bolt by bolt, Frank and his team began to meticulously disassemble the charred Block I command module. As he started to dig further, Frank found that "North American [Aviation] was schizophrenic, populated by some conscientious men who knew what they were doing and at least an equal number who didn't know their asses from third base."

Three superbly talented pilots and astronauts, all family men, had died atop a stationary, unfueled rocket parked on the launchpad. Frank was angry and determined to find out why. "The more we probed for answers, the more depressed the people on the investigation got. They'd take downers to ease the pain of the guilt and uppers so they could face the next day," he admitted. Some of the engineers involved couldn't handle the weight of the guilt, ending up addicted to drugs and eventually having breakdowns.

This complex command module with fifteen miles of wiring filled with highly flammable materials in a pure-oxygen environment had turned into a death trap for three good men. The fact that it had happened during a routine training exercise was simply unacceptable. Frank took it upon himself to make sure it would never happen again. Not on his watch.

Some days, Frank found it difficult to stay detached, especially when it started coming to light that there were many mistakes that were, in his words, "negligent."

The death of the crew combined with the overwhelming stress of getting the program back on track plagued NASA and each of the four hundred thousand people involved in getting America to the Moon. The fire had changed everything.

The tragedy set off a chain reaction within the country as well. These men were reluctant celebrities, but celebrities nonetheless, and had become real-life superheroes to the American public. To lose three of them so senselessly was a huge shock, and if people weren't interested in the race to the Moon before, they started paying attention now. It was America's first reality show, and the press became more rabid than ever before.

While the men were at NASA trying to figure out what went wrong, their wives were left to deal with the media onslaught. They were expected to keep up appearances, but fear had spread through them. They couldn't turn to their husbands for support, so Dr. Charles Berry of NASA's medical department took it upon himself to keep them quiet by handing out Valium as if it were candy. The agency didn't care about what was going on with the domestic lives of their astronauts. It cared only that the wives get in line and show a brave face, regardless of whatever destructive behavior they had to participate in to do that. NASA knew if it lost the public, all the funding that it relied upon would vanish along with the hope of American footprints on the Moon.

Susan began to spend every evening that she could with Pat. She was there to be a support, to listen, and to try to help in any way. She would cook dinner for her teenage boys, make sure they had what they needed, and then go over to the Whites'. She was consoling Pat more and more—often accompanied by glasses of wine. It was the beginning of what would become an issue for Susan. She realized how much the alcohol really calmed her anxiety, and although no one, including Frank and the boys, would ever see her drunk, she started a habit that was going to be very hard to break.

One night while sitting with Pat as she cried, Susan put her arms around her friend, trying to be strong for her. Pat just kept repeating the same thing over and over as she sobbed, "Who am I, Susan? If I'm not Ed's wife anymore, then who am I? I've lost everything. It's all gone."

One of the other wives had described Pat this way: "She just worked at being Ed's wife, and she was wonderful at it, and that was all." NASA's unwritten rule regarding the wives was: "When you are in the program—you are in. When something happens to your husband—you are out." These women didn't just lose their husbands; they also lost a way of life that had become their own. Barbara Cernan later said to reporters, "If you think going to the Moon is hard, try staying home."

Susan refused to let Pat know how seeing her pain and anguish was affecting her, but she couldn't help but put herself in the same place. The despair and fear followed her when she went home, and she couldn't close her eyes without seeing Frank burning up and not being able to stop it. Susan had dealt with the deaths of Frank's fellow colleagues in the past the way he did. "It won't happen to me, Susan," he would say. "It might happen to another guy, but not me."

Ed's death was different. He was so physically strong—stronger than Frank—and yet he wasn't able to get the hatch of the spacecraft open to save himself. If this could happen to the strongest astronaut that NASA had, how was Frank supposed to stay safe? What guarantee was there that he would survive this highly experimental project that he had committed himself to? No one could guarantee that, and as a result Susan couldn't stop the thought that she would end up like Pat. Deep down, she started to believe that if Frank stayed with NASA and went up again that he wouldn't be coming home. Although she would never admit it out loud because she was too well trained for that, whatever faith she'd had in NASA had been totally shattered.

The astronauts as husbands and fathers were partly to blame as well. They just assumed that their families would adopt their "mission at all costs" philosophy, which was actually one of the reasons that the space program would end up succeeding. NASA needed them to think that way. They needed the fighter pilot mentality that could be summed up by one of their well-known toasts that they would give in honor of a fallen colleague. "Here's to the next man to die." It was a pilot's farewell and the mindset they all adopted. Always the other guy—never them—and they didn't need unwanted household or family distractions. They just chose to believe that everything was always fine at home.

───────────

It would take Frank and the rest of the assigned team eighteen months to finish the investigation, and although he was never able to identify the actual cause, all the evidence led to an electrical short under Gus Grissom's seat combined with the pure oxygen inside and highly flammable materials, such as five thousand square inches of Velcro. There should have only been about five hundred square inches. But perhaps the ultimate failure was the failure of imagination to envision something as obvious as the actual causes that led to the fire.

Even if the exact origin of the fire couldn't be identified, someone would have to take the blame. North American removed the head of the Space Division, Harrison Storms, and NASA reassigned the director of the Office of Manned Space Flight, Joe Shea, to Washington after he suffered a nervous breakdown.

On April 7, 1967, the House Subcommittee on Space opened hearings into the Apollo 1 fire. NASA and the Apollo program were at a crucial turning point. Canceling the lunar program meant losing to the Russians and failing JFK, which was unthinkable to all the people who had worked tirelessly for years to reach their goal.

Susan helped Frank pack for what he hoped would be a short trip to Washington to testify on Capitol Hill. After the fire, Susan did her best to avoid media reports that did nothing for the spirits of anyone connected to Apollo, but she was now watching her husband on the evening news. Frank sat squarely in front of the committee and answered with both directness and candor the tough questions being thrown at him. Like most accidents, it was a daisy chain of factors from workmanship and quality control to the safety equipment on the launchpad. Frank's assessment was brief and to the point. "We in the space program had overlooked the obvious hazard of putting 100% pure oxygen into a spacecraft full of combustibles that was pressurized to more than 20 psi." The ultimate failure was not being able to envision that something so apparent could now possibly shut down a program designed, built, and operated by some of the smartest people on the planet.

Frank felt that some of NASA's harshest critics, such as Walter Mondale and Donald Rumsfeld, were more interested in earning political capital by calling for the abandonment of America's lunar program than in understanding the actual facts of what led to the fire. When several members of Congress implied the program should be terminated, Frank stopped trying to be diplomatic and just replied, "Stop the witch hunt, so NASA can get on with Apollo."

His testimony quelled most of the critics and any professional jealousy and criticism within the ranks of the astronaut corps. For men trained to be objective and highly pragmatic, it was clear NASA had chosen the right man for the job. "He handled himself with professional assurance and provided credibility to an investigation that many feared would be a whitewash. Frank is a practical and extremely able guy. As you read the names along the halls of astronaut offices, you see so much rank—all those colonels and navy captains. But Borman is one of those who would have reached that elevated status regardless of what career he chose," astronaut Walt Cunningham said.

When Frank's unflinching scrutiny of the fire ended, many at NASA believed his integrity and straightforward testimony before

Congress helped save the Apollo program and preserved JFK's pledge to the nation.

————————

In the months leading up to the Apollo 1 fire, everyone at the agency was confounded by something. America was in a race to the Moon, but where had their nemesis gone? Since Yuri Gagarin was first launched into orbit in 1961, the Russians had racked up a string of manned spaceflight firsts—then, mysteriously, in 1965, their launchpads went silent.

At first people around NASA were cracking jokes about the absent Russians, but that quickly turned to concern and worry. What were they up to? Was the USSR gearing up with new hardware to leap past the United States again and get to the Moon first?

Another two years went by, and the Russians still hadn't flown a cosmonaut into space. Finally, on April 23, 1967, US listening posts in Turkey picked up veteran cosmonaut Vladimir Komarov cursing at his superiors for sending him into space aboard a shoddy spacecraft. Komarov had rocketed to orbit alone aboard Soyuz 1, the capsule that had been designed for future lunar missions. The plan was to launch Soyuz 2 the following day to link up with Komarov to perform Russia's first rendezvous and docking of two manned spacecraft. It would be a great triumph for the country on the fiftieth anniversary of the 1917 Russian Revolution.

Russian space hero Yuri Gagarin inspected Soyuz 1 before the flight and had found more than two hundred structural problems that led him to pen a ten-page memo. In an effort to stop the mission, Gagarin gave the memo to a close friend in the KGB and asked him to make sure it found its way up the chain of command. When Komarov learned that the KGB contact and everyone who saw the memo was immediately demoted, he told his friend and colleague Yuri, "I'm not going to make it back from this flight."

Once in orbit, everything on Soyuz 1 went wrong. After several failed attempts to deorbit, analyst Perry Fellwock of the National Security Agency, stationed at the US airbase in Istanbul, listened to a terrified Komarov tell ground controllers in Russia that he was going to die. The Soviet premier Alexei Kosygin called to tell the cosmonaut he was a hero, and Komarov's wife was brought in to tearfully wish her husband good-bye and ask him what he wanted to tell their children.

On his nineteenth orbit, Komarov began reentry. By some miracle, Soyuz 1 made it through the fiery heat but was unable to deploy its main parachute. When Komarov released his backup chute, it became tangled with the first unopened one. Fellwock listened to the last horrifying moments of Komarov's life as he screamed just before Soyuz 1 crashed to the Earth.

The Russians publicly announced the death of the cosmonaut but released no details. In a gesture of goodwill, NASA offered to send Frank and astronaut Gordon Cooper to attend the funeral. Frank and "Gordo" were ready to make the trip, but the Russians sent word to Washington that the funeral was a "private matter."

Susan didn't need to be reminded about the dangers of the obsession to get to the Moon when Frank informed her that he wouldn't be going. She was well aware of the emotional anguish Valentina Komarov and the other Russian cosmonaut wives were dealing with.

What NASA didn't advertise, and the public was largely ignorant of, was the fact that astronauts White, Grissom, and Chaffee were only the latest casualties in the battle to beat the Russians. In the year leading up to the Apollo 1 fire, four other astronauts had lost their lives in training accidents. NASA's first astronaut widow was Faith Freeman. Her husband Ted's T-38 crashed after a bird struck the aircraft while it was on final approach for landing in Houston. Then, three months before the fire, Beth Williams lost her husband C.C. when his T-38 crashed on a flight to visit his parents in Alabama. Elliot See and Charlie Bassett were also killed when their T-38 crashed during a trip to the McDonnell Douglas facility in St. Louis. Ada Givens's husband, Edward, a Project Mercury finalist and Group 5 astronaut, was killed in a car accident a year after joining the agency.

Whether she was in a grocery store, watching television, or listening to the radio in her car, Susan was constantly reminded of the dangers of the lunar program, and had serious doubts that the sacrifice was worth the human cost. The weight on the families was enormous. The impact on the wives' physical and emotional health showed up in the form of everything from excessive drinking and pill popping to anorexia and agoraphobia. Despite NASA's mantra of risk mitigation, redundancy, and emergency contingencies, even before the first Apollo astronaut launched into space, they now had eight widows and seventeen fatherless children.

Pat White never received the professional help she needed to get back on her feet. Susan and the other wives tried to be there for each other, but it was a unique and extremely challenging time, not just for them but for all Americans. Everyone involved in the space program was desperately trying to deal with whatever was thrown at them next. Pat carried on for her kids but continued to struggle for fifteen years before the pain of Ed's death consumed her. In 1983, she took her own life.

Frank Borman's character and ability had impressed people like Deke Slayton and NASA flight director Chris Kraft from the first time they met him. Following his work on the Apollo 1 fire, there was no hesitation by the agency to assign him as the astronaut to oversee the new design of the command module. He took the job without hesitation and without talking to Susan. Frank didn't want another astronaut flying until the problems that came up in the investigation were fixed.

"I'll take the job. I know better than anyone what needs to be done," he told NASA's administrator, James Webb, and he did. What Frank didn't know and couldn't foresee were the months of frustration and battles ahead with North American Aviation, the company responsible for designing and building the space capsule.

It would be another long period of loneliness for Susan. She was used to Frank being gone for long periods—all the wives were—but it was different this time. Between the constant media presence and the underlying dread that something else might happen to another astronaut, they were all walking around with fake smiles and a cocktail or two. The wives wouldn't even admit to each other what they were all thinking: *Who was going to be next?*

12

50/50

AFTER SPENDING THE FIRST HALF OF 1967 at the Cape investigating the fire, Frank was at home just barely long enough to pack a suitcase before moving into another hotel room, this time in Downey, California. He had his work cut out for him when he arrived at North American to begin the redesign for the new Block II command module.

There was a meeting called almost as soon as Frank arrived. Bill Bergen, from Rockwell International, was brought in to assess things and got right to the point. "We know that there was a serious failure," he started out by saying. "This failure not only cost us three brave lives but also put the space program's future in jeopardy. It's clear that not everyone was doing their job. Take a good look around this table, because one of the people beside you will be gone tomorrow."

Frank was given free rein to do whatever he needed to ensure that quality control was the highest priority. When Frank found out that most of the engineers who were working on the highly complex spacecraft were going across the road to a bar for lunch every day and having a few beers, he had a chat with their union leaders and made sure that stopped. No alcohol until your shift was over. The union backed him up immediately and issued the directive. After that, the only real flak that Frank had to deal with was from his fellow astronauts. They would fly there, unannounced, to try and get Frank to agree to something else they thought the capsule should have.

Every astronaut wanted input into the command module redesign, but no one more than Mercury veteran Wally Schirra. Wally was unrelenting, and Frank had way too much work that needed to be done to get distracted by Wally's bullshit. Frank finally had to call NASA and tell his bosses to keep Schirra and everyone else away from the North American plant so he could do his job.

At the end of 1967, Frank was working seven days a week and had no idea what was going on at home. He called one evening, and Susan sounded especially upset.

"What's wrong, hon?" Frank asked as he rubbed his forehead. He was exhausted and hoped that it wasn't anything big. He just didn't have the energy for it.

"I went to see the doctor," Susan said quietly. "I've been having some problems, and I need to get a hysterectomy as soon as possible." She started to cry.

"When is your surgery?" Frank asked. He had no idea what to say, or what it was like for a woman to go through something like this.

"It's in a week," Susan said, hoping her husband would offer to return to El Lago to go with her.

"I will try to be there, but I don't know if I can." Frank knew that he could go if he needed to but was completely wrapped up with the redesign.

"I understand, Frank. You do what you need to do." Susan hung up the phone, quickly wiped her eyes, and went to check on the boys. They were her lifeline, and she knew that they would be there for her even if her husband wasn't.

In early 1968, Frank was still in California working on the command module when Deke Slayton assigned the prime and backup crews for the first three missions of the revamped Apollo schedule.

It was no surprise that Wally Schirra was given command of the first manned mission. It was a test flight of the command module in Earth orbit, which had been designated Apollo 7. Wally was highly critical of the power NASA had given Frank during the redesign and made enough noise and had the seniority to ensure that he got the first flight.

Jim McDivitt got the next slot as commander of Apollo 8 and the prestigious job of making the very first test flight of the lunar module in Earth orbit.

During a rare weekend at home, Susan knew something was up the minute Frank walked through the door. Although he'd just been assigned to command Apollo 9, he was disappointed it would basically be a repeat of McDivitt's planned Earth orbital flight. Susan tried to be sympathetic and assured her husband that he'd more than proven his value to America's lunar program. Frank was hoping for more of a challenging flight but understood what was expected of him.

Only seven years since President Kennedy committed to getting to the Moon, it was an incredible accomplishment to have achieved in such a short time. It basically came down to one thing: commitment. Frank knew he was part of that and would do it all again to see the mission through, but the billions of dollars spent on the program were the least of the costs.

When the new Block II command module emerged from the ashes of the Apollo 1 fire, it cost more than half a billion dollars in changes. The major reengineering fixes included a hatch that took only three seconds to open, compared to the nearly two minutes on the Block I spacecraft. The pure-oxygen environment that had been used on Apollo 1—and every manned spacecraft since Al Shepard's Mercury flight—was replaced with a safer nitrogen-oxygen mix. The cabin interior included new paint and fireproof fabrics.

Although costly, the 1,341 changes had been done swiftly and efficiently. Nearly everyone agreed that if Frank had not insisted on keeping the other astronauts out of the process, the goal of reaching the Moon before the end of the decade would have been impossible. With his work at North American accomplished, Frank focused on his new assignment—being the commander of Apollo 9.

To round out Frank's crew, Deke assigned Mike Collins as command module pilot and slotted in rookie Bill Anders as lunar module pilot. Anders was a Naval Academy graduate who'd chosen an air force career. The word among the astronauts was that Anders was another Borman—intense, inflexible, and no-nonsense.

Not long after the Apollo crew assignments were announced, Mike Collins started complaining about numbness in his hands. Surgeons discovered a bone spur in his neck, and although it wasn't a career ender, Deke Slayton was forced to move him to a later flight and replace him with Jim Lovell, who'd already flown with Frank.

Frank was back at North American in California training in the new command module simulator with Jim and Bill when an engineer popped his head through the hatch. "Colonel, there is a phone call for you."

Annoyed, Frank barked back. "Can't you see we're busy here? Take a message!"

"It's Mr. Slayton, sir. He says he needs to talk to you now." Frank told Lovell and Anders to continue their work as he marched off to a nearby office to take the call.

"Borman, I need you to get your butt back to Houston right away. I have to talk to you."

Frank shook his head as he rubbed his eyes and said irritably, "Talk to me now. I'm busy, Deke. The module has still got some problems."

"Dammit, Borman, I can't talk over the phone! This is classified. Grab an airplane now!" Deke hung up the phone before Frank could say anything else.

It was the middle of August 1968 as Frank landed his T-38 in Houston and taxied toward a waiting ground crew. Still in his flight suit and sweating from the Texas heat, he made his way to the Manned Spacecraft Center and up to Deke's office. Deke's secretary waved him in, and more annoyed than curious, Frank walked into the office to find Deke staring out the window chomping on a cigar. The chief astronaut turned to him with a look Frank had never seen before. "What is it?" Frank asked curtly.

Foregoing any pleasantries, Deke ordered Frank to close the door.

———————

The Borman boys were spending their summer working on their cars and training for the upcoming football season at League

City High School. With Frank away from home most days, Susan was the cook, coach, and confidant. She instinctively knew that all the boys needed was her unconditional love and encouragement to follow their passions and they'd discover who they were on their own terms. If they were responsible and accountable for their behavior and respectful to others, she stayed out of their way.

Frank was a tougher disciplinarian when needed, but those moments were few and far between. Frederick and Edwin never had to be lectured or reminded of the Borman code. Service was something they'd absorbed from both their parents.

Like their father, the Borman boys loved sports, especially football. Susan's teenage athletes trained hard, which meant she would spend the better part of each day grocery shopping and cooking. After stopping in to check on Pat, Susan drove to the butcher's to buy several pounds of pork chops. Although Frederick was seventeen and Edwin just fifteen, her teenage boys towered over Frank and seemed to convert every ounce of protein they consumed into muscle. She'd just finished peeling a pot full of potatoes and had turned on the electric frying pan when she heard someone enter the house.

Susan assumed something was terribly wrong when Frank walked through the front door because he was supposed to be training at Downey. "What are you doing home?" she asked, dreading the answer.

Frank could see the worry in her eyes and came over to hug her right away. "Everything's OK, Susan. Deke called me to come in for a talk we couldn't have over the phone. The CIA just told NASA that the Russians are planning a manned lunar orbital mission before the end of the year. They want me to command Apollo 8 now and take my crew on a lunar orbital mission in December."

Susan could hardly believe her ears. Images of the fire, Pat White, and eighteen years of funerals swept through her mind. She knew NASA was trying to make up for lost time after the Apollo 1 fire and the command module redesign. "It's August and the launch has been moved up to December? The capsule hasn't even been tested yet. You usually train for over a year, and you have barely four months?"

Frank tried to rationalize how NASA director George Low had come up with a simple yet risky idea that would put the program back on track. "We knew that the Russians were hell bent to do the same thing," Susan admitted later in an interview, "and NASA was determined to get there first, but I really didn't think they'd be able to come back. I just didn't see how they could. Everything was for the first time . . . everything."

Frank went on to explain that if Wally Schirra's Apollo 7 mission to test the new command module in Earth orbit, scheduled for October, wasn't perfect, then Apollo 8's lunar mission would be scrubbed, but that did little to settle Susan's concerns.

Frank had dinner with Susan and the boys, and early the next morning, before the boys were out of bed, he kissed her good-bye and was on his way back to North American.

Susan couldn't stop the runaway thoughts that this was a mission that couldn't possibly succeed. Rushing this kind of massive undertaking was simply . . . reckless, and her fears were completely legitimate. Five days later, Susan quietly celebrated her thirty-eighth birthday with her sons.

In the early morning hours of Wednesday, October 9, the massive doors of the Vehicle Assembly Building rolled open to reveal the largest, most powerful rocket ever built. Words seemed inadequate to describe the Saturn V. The height of a thirty-six-story office building, the shiny white rocket was a marvel of engineering. Once the crawler-transporter delivered Apollo 8 to Pad 39A, engineers and technicians would spend the next ten weeks going through the rocket's five-thousand-page checkout procedure.

Just before noon two days later, Apollo 7, with astronauts Wally Schirra, Walt Cunningham, and Donn Eisele headed for low Earth orbit atop the smaller Saturn 1B. It was not only the first manned flight of the Apollo program but NASA's first manned mission in twenty-two months. If Apollo 8 had a chance to beat the Russians to the Moon, it would be up to Wally and his crew to ensure the new Block II command module was fit for service.

While Apollo 7 was in orbit, the CIA returned to NASA with troubling news. The intelligence agency reported reconnaissance photographs that revealed the Russians had rolled out a rocket similar in size to the Saturn V with the capability of sending cosmonauts to the Moon. Even more troubling was the fact that the Russian launch window would open in late November, with December 6 being the last possible day they could send a manned mission to the Moon ahead of Apollo 8.

With the exception of a few minor problems, the new Apollo command module's hardware and software performed as advertised during the Apollo 7 test flight. The service propulsion system (SPS), the all-important single engine, was fired eight times and performed within 1 percent of the engine's expected thrust parameters. During Apollo 8, the SPS would have to work perfectly to get the spacecraft into lunar orbit and then be fired once again to free the spacecraft of the Moon's gravity to return Borman, Lovell, and Anders to Earth.

The Cold War race to the Moon was coming down to the wire. In mid-November, Russia's new Zond 6 flew to the Moon and returned to land in the USSR. The spacecraft had carried scientific probes and detectors and taken photos during its lunar flyby. Also on board the flight were the first terrestrial organisms to travel to the Moon. Flies, bacteria, and turtles would stand in during what NASA considered to be a Russian rehearsal for a manned circumlunar flight. What the CIA and NASA didn't know was that cosmonauts Alexei Leonov and Oleg Makarov were already deep into training and ready to go for a planned mission to orbit the Moon. Although the Russians reported that their unmanned Zond 6 had been successful, the spacecraft lost pressure during reentry and landed badly. Either one of those failures would have killed anyone aboard.

The failed landing of the unmanned Zond 6, along with the death of cosmonaut Komarov, had suddenly made the Russians cautious and risk averse. Alexei Leonov was the first human to walk in space and had been assigned as commander of Russia's first lunar mission. In a heated argument with his superiors, Leonov asserted he and Makarov were willing to risk a lunar flight if it meant delivering a fatal blow to the Americans. "People in our country assumed we'd be the first to land on the moon because we had always been first, but it was the indecisiveness of our chief designer at the time, Vasily Mishin, that caused us to fall behind in this program."

Unaware of what was really happening inside the Russian lunar program, NASA breathed a sigh of relief on December 6 when their launch window came and went. For the first time in nearly a decade, Apollo 8 was now America's best chance to win the battle of the space race against the Russians.

The 1960s was an incredibly tumultuous decade in America. NASA was its own universe, so no one who lived in the bubble of the space program understood or grasped all the social unrest and changes that were going on, from JFK being gunned down in 1963 to the horrors of the war in Vietnam, to the violence that accompanied the civil rights movement.

The year 1968 was especially bleak. Robert Kennedy and Martin Luther King Jr. being assassinated within a nine-week span were just two of the horrific tragedies that happened to make it a year in which the country desperately needed some hope. The American people were losing faith in their government and in the institutions that they had never really questioned before. Music started getting political and angry, and antiwar demonstrations were becoming more widespread and violent. It all seemed to come to a head in August as thousands gathered in Chicago to protest the Democratic National Convention in Grant Park. Police moved in with tear gas and began to club anyone who refused to move. It was a powder keg waiting to go off.

With the clock ticking, Borman, Lovell, and Anders trained day and night for every possible contingency they might encounter on mankind's first journey to the Moon. Their backup crew for Apollo 8, Neil Armstrong, Buzz Aldrin, and Fred Haise would play an integral role ensuring Apollo 8 had all the support they needed to complete their accelerated training schedule.

When George Low proposed his "Hail Mary" plan to send Apollo 8 to the Moon, NASA administrator James Webb was apoplectic. "It's insane! This will put the whole program at risk!" he fumed. "If these three men are stranded out there and die in lunar orbit, no one . . . lovers, poets . . . no one, will ever look at the moon the same way again." America had endured enough pain in 1968. Apollo 8 had to succeed.

The Apollo 8 crew and their wives were invited to the White House for dinner about two weeks before the launch. It would be the last time that Frank would see Susan before the mission. She told him she didn't want to come to the launch at the Cape and would stay home with the boys in Houston. He never asked her why. He didn't really want to know.

While in Washington, Frank got to meet aviation icon Charles Lindbergh. Frank experienced a serious case of hero worship, and even though he himself was about to make history, meeting the pilot of the *Spirit of St. Louis* was the highlight of the evening for him.

Susan flew back to Seabrook the next morning and gave Frank what she believed would be the last kiss that she would ever give him. She made sure that he believed that she was fine and told him how proud she was and then walked away before he could see the tears falling down her face.

On the evening of December 19, Frank's parents arrived from Arizona to be with Susan for the launch, and she hosted a cocktail party in honor of the mission with family and a few of the NASA wives and friends.

In the six years they'd lived in Houston, the Bormans had become quite close with NASA's flight director Chris Kraft and his wife, Betty Anne. Chris never thought of Susan as a frail person. He had always seen her as a strong woman and partner to Frank who could handle anything thrown her way. She gave everyone around her the impression that she was unflappable.

When Susan got her chance, she cornered Chris as he sipped on his cocktail. "Chris, I need you to level with me," Susan said as she looked him right in the eye. "What are the chances of Frank actually coming home safely?"

Chris would normally tell a white lie if he was talking to any of the other wives, but because it was Susan, he didn't. "You really mean that, don't you?" Chris looked at her, paused for a moment and then answered, "My best guess at this point is 50/50."

"OK . . . thank you for your honesty," Susan responded.

Chris then admitted to her that it was the riskiest mission for NASA yet, perhaps even more than the first lunar landing would be, and it confirmed to Susan what she was fearing. She believed in her heart as she walked away that she would be planning her husband's funeral very soon.

Frank had no idea about his wife's state of mind. With little more than a year left to meet JFK's deadline, he was keenly aware Apollo 8 could be the turning point in getting the program back on schedule, and knew it meant delivering a crippling blow to the Russians. If he could get himself, Jim, and Bill to the Moon and back home in one piece, as far as he was concerned, the Soviets could consider themselves officially beaten. Once he returned Apollo 8 safely, he believed the stage would be set for a lunar landing.

On the eve of his flight, Frank stepped out of his small room inside the Manned Spacecraft Operations Building to stare up at the Moon 239,000 miles away. He tried to imagine what that silver dot so far away would be like up close. While the crew shared a common living area, each of them had a modest private room with a single bed, nightstand, and telephone. The only art on the walls was the kind of painting you might expect to find hanging in a cheap motel room.

After a quiet dinner, Frank bid Jim and Bill good night and headed to his room to try and get some sleep. Neither he nor Lovell had slept the night before their Gemini mission, and he wondered in what universe the NASA doctors might expect them to sleep on the night before flying to the Moon for the first time. There was nothing to say, no pep talk or lecture on the significance of what they were about to do—he was confident Lovell and Anders were ready. As for the other four hundred thousand people that worked on Apollo, Frank took solace in his belief that all of them had done everything in their power to ensure the tragic death of his close friend Ed White and the crew of Apollo 1 crew hadn't been in vain. Just to be sure he'd covered all his bases, Frank knelt beside his bed and recited the Lord's Prayer.

At a time prearranged by NASA, Frank picked up the phone beside his bed to call home one last time. Susan was determined to sound cheerful and upbeat. She knew that Frank needed her strength right now more than ever, and she had never let him down on that score. "Everything is going to be all right, Su Su," Frank assured her.

"I know it will, darling," Susan lied.

"I'll be perfectly safe."

Susan was silent for a few seconds. "I love you, Frank Borman."

"I love you, too. I'll be home before you know it," he said with confidence. Whatever fears they both had about the mission remained unspoken.

She went over to the bar cart and poured herself another drink, then sat down at the kitchen table and started to work on Frank's eulogy. All she could see in her mind was that her soul mate was about to be taken from her.

Susan knew that NASA would try and control everything and spin it in their favor if anything happened to Frank, just like they attempted to do with Ed White's funeral. *I'll be damned if anyone tries to tell me how to honor my husband*, she thought, hoping this was the one thing that she could control.

While she was furiously writing things on a pad of paper, Edwin walked into the kitchen. "What are you doing, Mom?" he asked as he walked over to her.

For the first time ever, Susan didn't try to shield her boys from what she was feeling. Susan looked up and, in a calm but resigned voice, said, "I am writing out your father's memorial service. Just in case there is a chance that he won't be coming back, I want to be prepared."

Edwin gently took the pen out of her hand. He leaned over and looked at her. "Just remember, Mom," he said softly, "no one gets to choose how Dad goes. It isn't up to us. You taught us that."

Susan just stared at him and felt ashamed that her teenage son had to remind her of the very thing she had told them since they were old enough to understand the dangers of their father's chosen profession. The boys were dealing with the possibility of losing their father with a courage that she couldn't seem to access.

It wasn't her fault. No one at that time really understood the ways that repressed trauma manifests itself or how it gets triggered. The fear of losing someone else so important to her had been lying dormant since she was thirteen years old, and as proud as she was of her husband, there was a seed of rage growing inside of her that he *chose* to put himself in harm's way time and again. Susan wasn't conscious of it, though, and was just trying to do everything that she could to be what Frank and the rest of the world needed her to be.

Susan said goodnight to her in-laws Rusty and Marjorie Borman and then sent Frederick and Edwin to their rooms to try to get some sleep. A few of the astronaut wives, along with some close friends, would be arriving first thing in the morning to be with Susan and the boys during the launch, which was scheduled to lift off from the Cape at 7:51 AM.

Emotionally, there was little hope in her mind she was going to sleep that night or anytime soon. It was just after midnight, and if all went according to plan, Apollo 8 would be on its way to the Moon in less than eight hours. Susan went to her bedroom to remove her makeup and brush her hair. The thirty-eight-year-old glanced in the mirror and wondered who the tired old lady was staring back at her. She slipped out of her dress and pulled her nightgown over her head, knowing she would have to "put her face back on" for the world again in a few hours.

When it came to doing his job, Frank Borman didn't waste time analyzing his emotions. But tonight—tonight was different. After their phone call, Frank knew that Susan was putting on a brave face to prevent him from worrying about her. It was something he tried not to think about, but at a press conference earlier that month while Jim, Bill, and he were being pelted with questions about the safety of the upcoming mission, he responded when one of the reporters asked about the risks of the flight: "Of course there are risks. But if we believe that what we are doing is worthwhile, then we accept those risks. When it stops being worthwhile, I'll quit."

What no one knew, including Susan, was that Frank had already quit. He signed up to beat the Russians, and he was about to accomplish that. Going back up to collect some rocks, or to add to people's knowledge about what was up there didn't interest him. He would fulfill this mission and then he would be done. Anyone watching would be shocked to know that the man standing before them, looking like the perfect image of what an astronaut was, could walk away so easily. Frank wasn't in it for the fame and was beginning to see the immense toll it was taking on his family. He wouldn't put them through that again.

Going over to the small writing desk in his room, he pulled out a pad of paper from the drawer and began writing. He kept the letter short and to the point. It wasn't poetry by any measure, but he hoped that the words might help reassure his wife that nothing would ever keep them apart. Frank slipped the single sheet of paper into a stamped NASA envelope and left it to be mailed to Susan after the launch.

Teddy the family dog had given up following Susan as she paced around the house. Part of her felt like if she stopped watching the clock and just kept moving, time might speed it up.

She felt for the boys. They must be able to feel her fear, which she was certain filled the house with a sense of dread. Finally, just before 4:00 AM, Susan lay down on the top of the bed. Teddy was right there and jumped up for a snuggle. After she last spoke with Frank a few hours earlier, she'd turned on the "squawk box," the tiny green speaker NASA installed in each astronaut's home a few days before a launch, allowing the family to listen in on communications between the astronauts and Mission Control. As she closed her eyes, she hoped the din of chatter between controllers and engineers would lull her to sleep.

At 5:04 AM Susan heard a calm, reassuring voice. At first, she thought she was dreaming, but her brain finally recognized the familiar voice. "It looks very, very good," Frank said. He had just entered the spacecraft and was reporting to the test conductor on the status of the command module. Over the course of the next six days, that small speaker would be Susan's only link to Frank.

December 21 may be the shortest day of the year, but the winter solstice of 1968 was the longest day of Susan Borman's life.

13

MISSION VS. FAMILY

THE CREW OF APOLLO 8 rode the high-speed elevator up the launch tower, 320 feet to the waiting command module atop a rocket filled with five million pounds of fuel. Walking across Swing Arm 9, Frank could see hundreds of tiny headlights in the distance as people swarmed to the Kennedy Space Center to witness the first human beings launch to another world.

Just seven years after President Kennedy committed the nation to the Moon, Frank grabbed the "towel rack" above the hatch and pulled himself inside the spacecraft. He slid into his "couch" on the left side of the command module and plugged into Apollo 8's oxygen and communication systems. He'd flown the simulator day and night for weeks but now sat inside the flight-certified Apollo spacecraft he had helped redesign. The instrument panel in front of him had 566 switches, 71 lights, and 40 event indicators. Blind-folded, he could find each one.

Frank lay awake most of the night staring at the ceiling. He knew that he had chosen a very dangerous profession but was feeling it even more keenly now. He didn't allow himself to feel fear; it was something every fighter pilot was taught to control. But when he thought of Susan and the boys, he agonized over what he was putting them through.

That's where the conflict of interest lay. "The mission always comes first" had been pounded into his brain so many times it was imprinted there. The conflict would always exist—mission versus family. Frank knew that he would choose the mission every time. There really was no choice for him. He *had* to go.

Susan had supported him since the day she said "I do," but he knew in his gut that she'd gotten the short end of the stick. He hoped in that moment that she could feel how much he loved her and the boys. The very second he got as close to heaven as anyone ever had, he would ask God to let her know.

Deke Slayton had woken the crew at 2:36 AM, but the chief astronaut knew they had moonshot insomnia. The routine physical exam conducted by three NASA doctors was followed by the standard astronaut breakfast—steak and eggs—with Slayton and Neil Armstrong's backup crew.

In the suit room there had been very little small talk. Frank placed the same photo of Susan he'd taken with him on his Gemini flight into the small, fireproof bag NASA supplied each astronaut. The technicians helping them don their new fireproof suits were scope-locked on their singular task, which was just one of countless moving parts. Silently, Frank ran through the list of key mission events that would occur during the first eleven minutes of the flight, which would place Apollo 8 in orbit 114 miles above Earth. As the technician secured Frank's fishbowl helmet to its locking collar, he chuckled to himself, remembering how Susan couldn't stop laughing when he told her that it cost NASA an extra $45,000 to have his helmet modified because his head was so big. "I guess the nickname Squarehead that my football teammates back in Tucson gave me was right on the money," he said when she finally stopped giggling.

Just after 5:00 AM, Jim Lovell crossed the hatch threshold and wedged himself into the center couch between Borman and Anders. Frank was very proud of all the work his crew had done preparing for this moment, and he knew having them on board vastly increased Apollo 8's chances of success. "Anders was one hell of a worker, a superb technician, and all in all a great guy. I'm not sure he ever got used to my rough sense of humor or Lovell's freewheeling spirit," Frank later joked. As the lunar module pilot, Anders was flying on a mission without an actual lunar module, so NASA assigned him the critical job of photographing potential landing sites for Apollo 11, scheduled for the following summer.

Lovell had become an expert in navigation. As a navy man, it would be up to Lovell to keep his eye on the sextant and his hand on the rudder to ensure Apollo 8 stayed on course. If all went as planned, the figure-eight flight path would take the spacecraft around the Moon for ten orbits before returning to Earth for a splashdown in the South Pacific.

Frank couldn't imagine a better man or astronaut at his side for this first voyage to the Moon. Frank and Jim were close, but unlike other crews, they didn't socialize. "Susan and Marilyn did more socializing with each other than we did. Jim and I saw enough of each other during the week not to feel compelled to make it a seven-day relationship."

With no existing procedures on many key events of the mission, Apollo 8 required high-speed planning. Sixteen weeks earlier, Frank and flight director Chris Kraft had led a meeting that laid out a flight plan and defined objectives in less than four hours. "Once he got a whiff of that moon, he gave it the same merciless attention a pointer gives a covey of quail," said Mike Collins.

To mitigate risk, Frank wanted to do as few orbits as possible and get home safely, but he also saw the logic in staying for ten full orbits to gather data and photographs for future landing sites. In an effort to remove anything that wasn't necessary to the success of the mission, Frank was initially against the idea of having a television camera on board, but NASA overruled the opinionated commander. "I was wrong about some things at times. I was terribly wrong on the television. That was stupid on my part. Americans deserved to see what they'd paid for and so did the rest of the world," Frank admitted later. His main goal had always been to do everything possible to increase the favorable odds of completing the mission safely. "I was unreasonable at times, yet I felt justified being conservative in trying to maximize my crew's safety," he confessed.

Frank needed to keep everyone focused, including the press. The agency considered Apollo 8 a dress rehearsal for the "big mission" and discussed keeping Frank and his crew together to fly Apollo 11 for the first lunar landing. Deke Slayton wanted Frank to be the first man to walk on the Moon, but Frank interrupted him before he could even finish the question.

"No thanks, Deke. I've been away from home way too much since the Apollo 1 fire. Except for a few stolen moments I've not seen Susan and the boys in two years. If I can get Apollo 8 home safely, it will be my last flight."

Susan knew that Frank had done his best to protect her from any worries associated with the extremely risky lunar flight. She also knew he had enough to worry about without the added stress of knowing that she was certain he wouldn't make it home to her. Susan had always believed they were a team, and despite her

constant fear, wanted to know everything he was up against flying to the Moon. What she didn't overhear during Frank's phone
conversations, or from the other wives, she got from the media,
who took every opportunity to remind Americans of the drama
and extreme danger of the first lunar mission.

Early on, Susan chose to believe that Frank's skill and competence would keep him safe. Even if the machine failed him, she
absolutely trusted he could find a way out of any situation—which
he had proven time and again as a fighter pilot. That all changed
when Ed White was killed. She knew that everyone working at
NASA was doing their best, but it was the brand-new, barely tested
hardware and software she couldn't trust. Rightfully so. When
Frank's original mission had suddenly changed to a lunar flight
and was moved up to four months instead of eighteen, Susan felt
there were way too many technical unknowns and variables to
return Frank home safely to her.

The precision of navigation required to send the gumdrop-shaped
spacecraft on a 480,000-mile round-trip mission was staggering.
The math was the responsibility of Dr. Charles Stark Draper
and his MIT team. The average age of the engineers calculat-
ing the precision trajectory and navigation was twenty-four
years old, which some of the press loved to remind everyone
about.

The "tall foreheads" in Boston had been working on the
problem since the moment Apollo was announced. The computer commands needed to get Apollo 8 off the launchpad and
back home to its splashdown area in the Pacific Ocean 160
hours later had to fit on a computer with only 4K of memory—less storage space than that of a handheld calculator. The
mission was akin to throwing a dime from MIT in Boston and
having it land in a parking-meter slot two hundred miles away

in New York City. All with less computer storage than is needed
to send an e-mail.

The NASA "squawk box," the tiny green speaker with plastic
chrome trim and a NASA logo, served as Susan's lifeline during
the mission. Most of what she heard on this party line was incom-
prehensible jargon and acronyms that even the flight controllers
found tedious. But she, Marilyn Lovell, and Valerie Anders hung
on every word. All they cared about was hearing their husbands
say anything—even if it sounded like gibberish. It meant that they
were still alive. NASA told Susan that if anything went wrong,
they'd turn it off so she wouldn't be able to hear.

Susan hadn't slept and had barely got her clothes on when the
doorbell rang at 5:30 AM. As the door swung open, she was greeted
by the film crew she knew was coming to the house to film her
and the boys during the launch. Susan was simply too tired and
distracted to care any more about the intrusion and cared even
less about getting all dolled up.

The producer of the film, Francis Thompson, and director Theo
Kamecke were considered among the best nonfiction filmmakers
in America at the time. Thompson had won an Oscar for his 1965
documentary short *To Be Alive!*, which Kamecke had directed.
With support from NASA and backed by MGM Studios, the filmmakers planned to capture key Apollo events for a feature-length
film to be released after the first landing, later titled *Moonwalk
One*. Unlike most documentaries, which employed smaller 16mm
film cameras, the production rolled in a large 35mm camera like
those used for Hollywood feature films, which also required more
lighting and setup time.

Susan had pushed back hard on the idea of allowing a film crew into her home on launch day, when she had found out about it two months prior. Part of the reason for not going to the Cape was to avoid the public "death watch" as well as a possible repeat of the "fearful wife photo" taken of her at the launch of Frank's Gemini mission.

Frank was distracted as usual and dismissed her concerns as he was rushing out the door again to get back to solving all the problems that NASA had handed over to him and his team before the launch. "Susan, this is good for the program, so we're doing it."

She just stared with disappointment as the door closed and walked into the kitchen without saying another word, even though it was tearing her apart.

The Borman boys and their grandparents hadn't slept much either, and the ruckus of the morning events got them out of bed. As they walked into the living room, the bright camera lights were already blazing. Pat Collins, along with a few other astronaut wives—Faye Stafford, Pat McDivitt, Joan Aldrin, and Barb Young—were starting to arrive to lend their support. But there was one family member Susan intentionally hadn't invited—her mother.

Two days earlier, Ruth Bugbee had shown up without informing her daughter and held her own press conference on Susan's front lawn. Since Ruth's son-in-law was commanding the first mission to the Moon, she was eager for any attention she could get. She'd never had any use for Frank before, but now that the whole nation was paying attention to him, she wanted to bask in whatever fame that she could. Susan watched in horror from their front window as her mother held court. She didn't even bother to try to see Susan or ask how she was doing.

After leaving the Bormans' yard, she drove to Florida to make sure she was front and center at the Cape for the launch. She didn't have an official invitation, but once she told everyone she was commander Frank Borman's "proud mother-in-law," she was given access to the VIP area. It was very clear to Susan and the boys that her mother cared far more about the press knowing who she was than she did about her own daughter's and grandsons' feelings.

To everyone's surprise, Ed's widow and Susan's closest friend, Pat White, made an appearance that morning. Most often when an astronaut wife became a widow, like Beth Williams or Martha Chaffee, she left Houston to start a new life. It had been about two years since Ed had died, but Pat was still struggling to get on her feet. Her identity and sense of security were still firmly entrenched in El Lago and being an astronaut's wife. She couldn't imagine taking the kids out of school there and making a home somewhere else.

Susan had been with Pat every step of the way since Ed was killed and had been an invaluable support during the worst time of her life. Understanding the fear Susan was going through, it took every ounce of strength Pat could muster not to run home, but she was determined to return Susan's kindness and loyalty, no matter what happened.

———

It had been only a year since the Saturn V Moon rocket was ready for its first of two unmanned flight tests—Apollo 4. Launched on November 9, 1967, it represented NASA's hope to get the program back on schedule by launching the full Saturn stack in an "all-up" test of the rocket's three stages all at once, which was much more dangerous. This first launch had been originally planned for late 1966 but was delayed by problems with the S-II second stage and defects found in the Block I command module—both built by North American Aviation. If Apollo had any hope of keeping the program funded and beating the Russians, every flight would need to be near perfect. To the delight of the Saturn's designer, Wernher von Braun, his colossal rocket performed flawlessly.

The same week the Borman boys were lining up to see the science-fiction epic *2001: A Space Odyssey*, spectators were gathering around the Kennedy Space Center to witness the second test flight of a real-life Moon ship. On the morning of April 4, 1968, a confident von Braun and his team launched the Saturn V on its second test—the unmanned Apollo 6. Just two minutes into its flight, Mission Control began recording violent vibrations racing up and down the length of the rocket. Just before the S-IC first stage was jettisoned, airborne cameras recorded pieces falling off the spacecraft. No sooner had the five J-2 engines of the S-II second stage been lit than the onboard instrumentation unit detected problems with engines two and three and shut them down.

The rocket limped into orbit, but the S-IVB third stage also encountered problems with its single J-2 engine. The "pogo effect" also caused structural damage to the adapter housing the lunar module. Had there been a crew on board, the ten Gs of force induced by the ferocious vibrations would have killed the astronauts. NASA concealed what a failure this was.

Later, as Susan watched the evening news, NASA administrator George Mueller struggled to explain the problem to Congress and alleviate their fears. Every member of the von Braun team was working around the clock to remedy the problem. Dampers and shock absorbers were added to the Saturn V, but there was no time before the launch of Apollo 8 to actually test the modifications.

The unknowns of the first manned lunar flight, combined with the known problems encountered on Apollo 6, led Bill Anders to a mathematical conclusion that the survival odds of the Apollo 8 crew were not in their favor at all: about a 30 percent chance of success. But like Frank, he lived by the Airman's Creed:

I am an American Airman.
I am a Warrior.
I have answered my Nation's call.

I am an American Airman.
My mission is to Fly, Fight, and Win.
I am faithful to a Proud Heritage,
A Tradition of Honor,
And a Legacy of Valor.

I am an American Airman.
Guardian of Freedom and Justice,
My Nation's Sword and Shield,
Its Sentry and Avenger.
I defend my Country with my Life.

I am an American Airman.
Wingman, Leader, Warrior.
I will never leave an Airman behind,
I will never falter,
And I will not fail.

Thirty percent odds were not enough to deter him if his pre-
diction was right. It was a creed he had lived by his whole life and
had been drilled into him since he was on the cusp of becoming
a man. In his mind, as well as Frank's and Jim's, this is what they
had trained their whole lives to do. So, Bill left behind a recorded
message for his wife, Valerie, and their five children if she should
find herself a widow that Christmas.

To the press, NASA emphatically declared Apollo 6 a success,
but in the mind of Frank and the other astronauts, the test flight
was a huge failure. The crippled mission went largely unnoticed

LEFT: Tucson High Badgers quarterback Frank Borman of the undefeated 1945 Arizona state champions. *Courtesy of the Tucson High yearbook student editor & staff*

RIGHT: Tucson beauty queen Susan Bugbee, age nineteen. *Courtesy of the Borman family*

Shortly after Frank and Susan were married, July 1950. *Courtesy of the Borman family*

US Air Force captain Frank Borman in the cockpit of his F-84F at Luke Air Force Base, 1951. *Courtesy of the Borman family*

ABOVE: Frank's parents, Edwin "Rusty" and Marjorie Borman. *Historic Images*

RIGHT: Susan with her mother, Ruth Bugbee, taken during Frank's Gemini 7 mission. *Historic Images*

Susan and Frank shooting hoops during some rare family time with son Edwin. *Historic Images*

Frederick assembles a model airplane under the watchful eye of Frank and Edwin. *Ralph Morse/Getty*

Alan Shepard, America's first man in space and chief of the Astronaut Office, confers with Gemini 7 commander Frank Borman before his record-setting fourteen-day mission in Earth orbit with Jim Lovell, December 4, 1965. *Courtesy of NASA*

Susan watching the launch of Apollo 8 with Edwin, Frederick, and Marjorie
Borman, December 21, 1968. *Courtesy of PBS American Experience,* Chasing the Moon

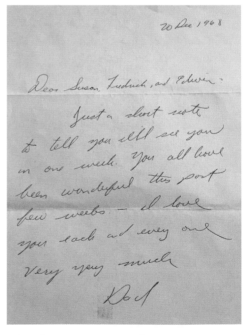

20 Dec 1968

Dear Susan, Fredrick, and Edwin:

Just a short note
to tell you I'll see you
in one week. You all have
been wonderful this past
few weeks. — I love
you each and every one
very very much

Dad

LEFT: The first humans to leave Earth and travel to the Moon on Apollo 8
(left to right): command module pilot Jim Lovell, lunar module pilot Bill Anders,
and commander Frank Borman. *Courtesy of NASA*

RIGHT: The note Frank wrote to Susan and the boys the night before Apollo 8
departed for the Moon. *Courtesy of the Borman family*

The first color photo of Earth taken by a human from the Moon during the third orbit of Apollo 8, by Bill Anders, December 24, 1968. *Courtesy of NASA*

Valerie Anders and Susan Borman receive word that Apollo 8 is headed home after emerging from the far side of the Moon for the last time, December 25, 1968.
Lynn Pelham/Getty

Frank was Eastern Airlines spokesman in many of the company ads during his tenure as CEO from 1975 to 1986. *Courtesy of the Borman family*

"All airlines fly at the same speed but bad service can make a flight seem longer."
FRANK BORMAN, PRESIDENT, EASTERN AIRLINES

Frank and Susan getting ready for one of many public events they attended as "Team Borman." *Courtesy of the Borman family*

Frank and Susan arrive at the White House prior to the Kennedy Center Honors, 1992. *Mark Reinstein/Getty*

Frank and Susan on the tarmac just before strapping into their two-seat P-51 Mustang. *Courtesy of the Borman family*

LEFT: Susan poses in front of *Su Su II* wearing her beloved turquoise jewelry. *Courtesy of the Borman family*

ABOVE: One of the last cards Susan was able to write to Frank before her Alzheimer's advanced. *Courtesy of the Borman family*

Frank with his vintage 1954 USAF T-34 trainer still flying on the fiftieth anniversary of Apollo 8, December 2018. *Courtesy of Larry Mayer*

Frank and Susan enjoy the warmth of Big Sky Country on their seventieth wedding anniversary, Billings, Montana, July 20, 2020. *Courtesy of Brenda Vidrine*

by the media and the rest of the country when another event eclipsed everything else. Almost at the very same moment the Apollo 6 command module was being hauled up onto the aircraft carrier USS *Okinawa*, Martin Luther King Jr. was assassinated in Memphis, Tennessee.

By December 21, 1968, there was no turning back. Four short months after NASA made the decision to fly astronauts aboard the mighty Saturn V, time was up. Frank Borman had a scheduled date with destiny.

―――――――――――

Everyone in the Borman living room was glued to the television set, waiting for the countdown to begin. As the camera panned the group of people that had gathered, it looked like a scene from a '60s cocktail party. All the attendees were dressed up and had a drink in their hand. The drink happened to be coffee, however, because it was around 6:00 AM with liftoff scheduled for 6:51 AM Houston time—7:51 AM at the Cape in Florida.

Frank's parents were animatedly chatting with the minister from Frank and Susan's church. It looked like a group of people that was excited and happy, until the camera got to Susan and zoomed in. She appeared haggard, like someone who hadn't slept in days (because she hadn't), and was very pale. The woman who never failed to look as though she was walking off the cover of a fashion catalogue was totally disheveled. She didn't seem to even notice that the film camera was there and did nothing to hide her distress.

Susan was crouched on the floor in front of the TV, and every time she brought her hands up to her face, they were shaking. Everyone around her seemed oblivious to her state, except for her oldest son. Fred was right behind her with his hand on her shoulder. He kept a fake smile on his face, because at seventeen he was already trained to deal with the media and everything that came with being the son of Colonel Frank Borman. He had been the man of the house more often than his father was able to be at that time, and he knew what was expected.

As the final countdown began, the filmmaker could almost feel Susan's anguish through the lens. Susan wasn't an actress, nor did she have any aspirations to be one. She was simply a wife and a mother who was still very much in love with her husband. She didn't care about NASA, the Moon, or any of the fame that came with the job description. She didn't care about the mission. She cared about one thing in that moment—Frank. And she was absolutely convinced that she would never see him again.

NASA public announcer Jack King called out the last moments of the countdown. At T minus one minute, the public voice of Mission Control announced the rocket's propellant tanks were fully pressurized and external power had been transferred to Apollo 8's internal flight batteries. The camera crew captured Susan's anguish as the blood drained from her face.

King's voice echoed the tension and immensity of the historic moment. "Final reports coming from Frank Borman, thirty-five seconds and counting."

At T minus nine seconds, King's iconic voice announced, "Ignition sequence start, the engines are armed." The Saturn V's onboard computer commanded the engine's turbo pumps to release four railroad cars of fuel every second. The five F-1 engines of the first stage unleashed a maelstrom of 160 million horsepower as they exploded to life. Nearly four hundred feet above the firestorm, a roar that sounded like the heavens were being torn apart filled the Florida air. Frank's eyes darted across the instrument panel. He knew the 6.2 million–pound Saturn had inched off Pad 39A as the mission clock started. The Apollo 8 command module shook like a bug perched on the end of a car antenna.

Susan clenched her hands so tightly they turned white as she pressed them into her cheeks. When she opened her eyes a few seconds later she saw the engines blasting 7.5 million pounds of thrust as they adjusted to steer Apollo 8 clear of the launch tower. For a moment, it appeared large pieces of the white Saturn were the being blown off the rocket, but the white fragments were 1,200 pounds of frost being shed from the supercooled propellant tanks before being vaporized in the intense fire.

High above the Apollo stack, the spacecraft shook so violently Bill Anders was certain the fins at the bottom of the first stage were shearing through the launch tower. To his surprise, Mission Control radioed that Apollo 8 had cleared the tower. "I felt like a rat being thrashed in the jaws of a terrier," said Anders.

Just a few feet from Susan's face, the camera only amplified her emotions. Behind her, Frank's mother, Marjorie, seemed to levitate with joy. As the camera panned the room, everyone but Susan was smiling and cheering. Rusty Borman didn't blink as he watched the massive rocket carrying his only child blast skyward. Everyone was witnessing history.

Three miles from the launchpad in the VIP viewing area at the Cape, people stood in awe as the apocalyptic fire shot from the flame trench before a shockwave slammed into everyone like a freight train. A thousand miles to the north, seismometers in New York registered the Earth trembling as Apollo 8 headed into the clear morning sky.

The Saturn V slowly tipped its nose over as it headed east over the Atlantic. The spacecraft was vibrating so violently Frank was unable to read the instrument panel. He could do little more than confirm the mission milestones as Collins called them out from Mission Control. While Susan felt her heart would burst from her chest as she stared at the TV screen, the flight surgeon monitoring the crew's vital signs never saw Frank's heart rate rise above 110 bpm.

Since the onboard computer controlled the Saturn V on its pre-determined ascent, the astronauts were merely passengers. Until they reached Earth orbit, the only control Frank had was if there was a major problem and he needed to launch the escape tower mounted above the command module to rocket them clear of the Saturn V. He gripped the T-shaped abort handle just like he'd done countless times in the simulator, but the shaking was so violent that he removed his hand. He told Anders later that he was concerned about aborting accidently and decided "he'd rather die than make a mistake."

One minute after liftoff, a pillar of flame more than a thousand feet long trailed behind the Saturn V as it raced into orbit. Susan was tuned into Mike Collins's voice on the squawk box in between Jules Bergman's commentary on ABC News. "Apollo 8, you're looking good." Her eyes lit up briefly as she heard Frank respond calmly, "Roger."

Passing through the sound barrier, Apollo 8 shook even more. Ninety seconds later, and traveling more than six thousand miles per hour, the S-IC first stage dropped away from the Apollo 8 and the five J-2 engines of the second stage roared to life. Staging threw Bill Anders forward with such force he instinctively raised a hand to shield his face from hitting the instrument panel. A millisecond later, the second stage roared to life and he was thrown back into his seat so violently the metal locking ring of the glove on his right hand gouged his clear fishbowl helmet. *Rookie mistake*, he thought to himself, until he learned Borman and Lovell had done the same thing.

As the spacecraft got smaller on her television screen, Susan's shoulders began to relax little by little. So far, her prayers had been heard. Still three minutes from Earth orbit, the crew started experiencing the same vibration problem that had nearly destroyed Apollo 6. "We're picking up a slight 'pogo' at this point," Frank let Mission Control know.

Flight director Chris Kraft stood up and removed his signature cigar from his mouth. The room got very quiet as all the flight controllers looked around the room with alarm and didn't dare to even breathe. Thirty seconds later Frank radioed, "Pogo damping out." There was a collective sigh around the room.

Eleven and a half minutes after liftoff, Frank confirmed they were safely in Earth orbit at a speed of five miles per second.

Even though she was completely exhausted, Susan knew that she had to go and give a statement to the press who were camped outside on her lawn. She stood up and went into the bedroom to change into something that would make Frank and the program proud. She put on the beautiful cream-colored dress and matching coat with the fur collar that they had bought in New York—it was her favorite outfit—and then made sure her hair and makeup were perfect. She got the boys and their dog, Teddy, and prepared to go outside and give the media what they wanted: the illusion of a happy and proud wife.

Susan had always been proud of Frank, and it had nothing to do with what he did. It was who he was. Pride wasn't something she needed to fake; pretending not to be afraid for him was the challenge. She put on the same smile that had gotten the Ford modeling agency's attention when she was younger and went out to tell all of the press how delighted she was.

She was poised and lovely. No one there had any idea how strong this woman really was.

It began to drizzle as reporters shouted questions, quizzing her about her thoughts and feelings. "Mrs. Borman, what did your husband have to say when you last saw him?" asked the first reporter.

"You mean when we said good-bye? Now, that's very personal, you know that," said Susan. "I'd love nothing better than to make a beautiful and profound statement for you that would be earth-shaking for everyone, but I'm just speechless."

She smiled and thanked everyone and then went back into the house to sit by the only thing that connected her to Frank. There were so many things that could still go wrong, and she just needed to hear his voice. "Come home to me, darling," she whispered like a prayer. "Come home to me, Frank."

———

Fred and Edwin Borman had never had much interest in the celebrity that came with being the son of the commander of the first mission to the Moon. They had been raised on military bases their whole life. It was the only life they knew. So they were able to ignore most of what was going on outside of their front door. They were more interested in fishing and football.

At times they needed to escape the craziness. So after they were finished with the media, they snuck out using their secret exit in the backyard and jumped into Fred's '63 Corvette to go hunting. The press somehow got wise to their escape and gave chase. Fred hit the gas and drove like an Indy race car driver to lose them. They knew that their father had just broken every speed record on the planet, but he would still strangle them if he knew how fast they were driving.

———

Cleared for flight status in September but too late to rejoin the crew for the circumlunar flight, Mike Collins had been assigned by Deke Slayton as the mission's CapCom, who talked to the crew. "All right Apollo 8, you are go for TLI."

Mission Control fell silent. No sooner had the words left his mouth that Collins had the sinking feeling he'd made a serious mistake. To the uninitiated, TLI was just another NASA acronym.

To Apollo 8, "translunar injection" meant the human species was about to break free of Earth's gravity and head out into deep space for the very first time in history. Well-read, intelligent, and articulate, Collins felt he should have said something more profound about the historical milestone.

No one cared—certainly not Frank, who replied, "Roger, we understand we are go for TLI."

The maneuver called for Apollo 8 to reignite the single J-2 engine, which was the same third stage of the rocket that had exploded during a recent test. Aimed at a point in space to intercept the Moon sixty hours later, Lovell pressed the PROCEED button and called "Ignition" as the J-2 engine came to life silently in the vacuum of space.

The astronauts felt the spacecraft accelerate as they approached their escape velocity of twenty-three thousand miles per hour. Apollo 8 established a new speed record as it raced past Pete Conrad's Gemini 11 apogee record of 815 miles. Given the events of the previous two years, in near disbelief, flight director Chris Kraft called up to the crew sounding more like a father encouraging his children, "You're on your way. You're really on your way!"

Five minutes later, the third-stage engine shut down as scheduled, no longer needed to get to the Moon. Frank triggered the explosive bolts that connected it to the command module and released the now-spent third stage to the depths of space. Jim and Bill looked out the window and watched the Earth getting smaller. Now twenty-one thousand miles from home, the crew of Apollo 8 looked back at something no other human had ever seen—the majesty of the Earth in its totality.

"Boy, it's really hard to describe what the Earth looks like," Jim reported. "I can see most of South America all the way up to Central America, the Yucatán, and the peninsula of Florida." It was an emotional experience, and the crew said nothing to each other.

Frank smiled to himself and thought, *This must be what God sees.*

So far everything was going as well as anyone could hope, until Frank started feeling queasy. All three astronauts had been inoculated for anything and everything, but now at the fourteen-hour mark, Frank had vomited twice and had diarrhea. Unfortunately, in the small and enclosed zero-G command module, it had nowhere to go and so it just floated around the cockpit. Frank didn't want ground control to know at first, so they kept it quiet. He wouldn't let a minor case of the flu get in the way of the mission and what they were there to do.

But eventually, they had to let Mission Control know that the commander of Apollo 8 was feeling less than ideal. Frank and the crew assured them that it wasn't serious, but NASA was still quite concerned. The future of the program was contingent on this flight.

With one ear on the squawk box, Susan distracted herself as she cleaned up the remnants of the early-morning launch party. It was after nine in the evening in Houston, and although her guests had gone home, the press was still blocking traffic and annoying the neighbors. Susan had just finished putting the last of the food away when her phone rang. Trying not to think the worst, she froze for a moment before snatching it up before it rang a second time.

It was Mission Control. NASA first assured Susan the mission was proceeding as expected, but Frank seemed to be sick. "Did he get the flu often?" they wanted to know. No one had to tell her of the stakes involved. "Do you think it will affect his ability to do his job?"

Relieved, and more amused than anything else, Susan's quiet laugh interrupted NASA's messenger before he could question her further. "Frank will never be the problem," she assured them. "He will always do his job no matter what, and he will always get it right."

Lovell and Anders actually felt some queasiness as well, but it passed quickly. Whether it was flying a plane or a spacecraft,

Frank had never had motion sickness in his life. He told Houston he thought it may have been caused by the sleeping pill he'd taken, or maybe it was the twenty-four-hour flu, but the world was watching, and there was no way in hell the commander was going to turn around and go home because he felt sick.

After catching a short nap, Frank assured Mission Control he was feeling much better. As astronauts flew more missions in the years to follow, scientists would conclude that Frank was most likely the first victim of *space adaptation syndrome*, which simply put is a short-term condition in space travel that causes disorientation and nausea.

Two days had passed since the launch, and Susan was still withdrawn. In her mind, she was continuously giving herself a pep talk. *Don't think too much, don't feel too much.*

She remembered her "bible"—Nancy Shea's *The Army Wife*.

1. Make a congenial home
2. Rear a family of which he will be proud
3. Strengthen your husband's morale at all times

Shea continued: "Your whole scheme of life revolves around your husband, your children, and a happy home."

After nearly two decades of following that manual, the pressure was finally getting to her. Between the drinking and bouts of depression that no one really understood at that time, she was starting to unravel. To her, mental illness was something that only "crazy" people experienced.

NASA had its hands full trying to stay on schedule, and Susan Borman was just part of the unintended collateral damage. For all the glory that the space program had brought to America, there was a darker, hidden side—though it was a story no one was interested in hearing.

During a mission, every day was an open house at the chosen astronauts' homes. People came in and out at all hours. Whoever was going to space, their wives were expected to entertain, and there were people around most of the time, sunup to sundown. Everyone was always very thoughtful; they would leave when they could see that you wanted to be left alone but in the afternoon would show up with a bottle to have a drink. It was just standard operating procedure. Susan and the other wives were grateful for the distraction.

Around this time on December 23, Apollo 8 crossed the threshold between Earth's grip and the Moon's gravitational influence, about two hundred thousand miles from home. For the first time in recorded history, the astronauts aboard Apollo 8 were in a part of the universe that separated them from the rest of world, a world they had just left far behind them.

During most of that day, Susan hadn't strayed far from the din of the squawk box. Now being pulled toward the Moon, Apollo 8 would be swinging around the far side and out of communication for the first time. Susan couldn't stop thinking about Apollo 8's single SPS engine. It had to work perfectly to slow Apollo 8 so it could safely enter lunar orbit. Then, twenty hours later, it would have to be refired for precisely five minutes to break the spacecraft free of the Moon's gravity and return Frank home.

Susan was hunched over in her seat by the squawk box. She had barely eaten anything for days, and the boys were starting to really worry. "Mom, please, you have to eat something," Fred said. Susan just smiled weakly and told him she wasn't hungry.

Fred marched into the kitchen and grabbed a container of potato salad that a thoughtful neighbor had brought over. He got a spoon out of the drawer and walked over to her. "Mom, look at me," he said. "Open for the airplane." He had a spoonful of the salad and was mimicking what she would do to him and his brother when they wouldn't eat their vegetables as toddlers.

Susan started laughing. It was the first time Fred had heard that beautiful sound in ages. While she was laughing, he put the spoon in her mouth. She looked up at him and started chewing. What would she ever do without her boys?

Edwin heard the clank of the mailbox lid, grateful that Fred had got their mom to finally eat something, and went to the front door to retrieve the last Christmas cards before the holidays. One envelope had no return address, but it was in a NASA envelope addressed to Mrs. Frank Borman. With a concerned look on his face, Edwin slowly came into the kitchen and handed the letter to his mother, who was still chuckling after her lighthearted moment with Frederick.

The envelope was postmarked Kennedy Space Center. She stopped laughing and took a deep breath, unsure what she might find, and carefully opened the envelope. The boys watched her as she gently removed the letter and unfolded it. Almost instantaneously her eyes got brighter, and she smiled a real smile for the first time in a very long while. It was the note Frank wrote her and the boys the night before he left for the Moon.

Susan cleared her throat and read the few sentences out loud.

Dear Susan, Frederick & Edwin,   December 20, 1968

Just a short note to tell you I'll see you in one week. You all have been so patient with me over this period of time. I love you each, and everyone, very, very much.

—Dad

14

LOSS OF SIGNAL

DECEMBER 24, 1968. It was 3:45 AM in Houston, and another day had passed without sleep for Susan. Pat Collins and Valerie Anders had both tucked their children in before arriving at Susan's for the anxious moment when communication with Apollo 8 would be lost as the spacecraft vanished behind the far side of the Moon.

To begin Apollo 8's deceleration into lunar orbit, twenty-four thousand miles from the Moon and traveling at five thousand miles per hour, Frank began the countdown to lunar orbit insertion. LOI required the big SPS engine be fired for a precise duration to allow Apollo 8 to be captured by the Moon's gravity. There was only one SPS engine, and it had to work flawlessly, not only to get Apollo 8 safely into lunar orbit but to return the crew to Earth. The precision required was staggering.

To complicate the technical ballet, the critical burn would occur when Apollo 8 was on the far side of the Moon and out of radio communication with Houston. Mission Control referred to the loss of signal with the spacecraft by the acronym LOS. Just the slightest malfunction or miscalculation, and Apollo 8 would crash into the Moon or be hurled into the abyss of deep space.

If the engine burned perfectly for four minutes and six seconds, and if the math was flawless, Apollo 8 would reappear on the Moon's near side, facing Earth, forty-seven minutes later. The maneuver had a sliver-thin margin of error, and it was LOS that Susan now feared the most. Frank and the crew would be all on their own. She couldn't help but think this would be the perilous maneuver that would steal her husband from her. If there was a catastrophe, she'd likely never know what had gone wrong on the far side.

Every mile the spacecraft got closer to the Moon, the greater the risks became. Mission Control began its final calls. "Apollo 8, Houston. You have five minutes until we go dark—all systems are go . . ."

"Thank you, Houston," Frank answered.

"Roger, Frank," the CapCom said. "I have a message from Susan, and she wants you to know that the custard is in the oven at three-fifty. Over."

It was a secret message that only Frank would understand. Long ago, when he was just starting out as a pilot, he told her, "You worry about making the custard, and I'll worry about the flying and getting home safely."

It was Susan's way of letting him know that everything was OK at home, when he might need to hear it the most. She was desperate to believe that it wouldn't be the last message he'd ever hear from her.

Five hundred miles to go before LOS, mission controllers ran through their final checks with Apollo 8. "All systems GO. Safe journey, guys."

Bill Anders responded for Frank, who was closely monitoring the computer that would execute the burn. "Thanks a lot, troops. See you on the other side." The squawk box in the Borman kitchen went silent. On Christmas Eve morning, Apollo 8 disappeared behind the far side of the Moon.

Frank now readied the crew for the big milestone. The computer flashed Go/No-Go, asking them if they were sure they wanted to initiate the LOI engine burn. With a steady hand, Jim Lovell pressed PROCEED. The computer took control of Apollo 8 and counted down the last few seconds. Five, four, three, two . . .

On "one," Frank's heart jumped to 130 bpm as twenty thousand pounds of thrust from the SPS exploded silently into the vacuum of space. Nine minutes after LOS, the crew sat in silence as Apollo 8 glided backward through the darkness.

"Wow . . . I can't see squat out there," Frank remarked. With the Moon between the spacecraft and Earth, Apollo 8 was submerged in unimaginable blackness. Frank lowered the cabin lights, and an ocean of sparkling stars filled his window. At T minus one minute, he scanned the checklist and each indicator light one last time. Bill Anders looked out his starboard window and the hairs on the back of his neck stood up. The sea of stars suddenly vanished behind what he described as a "gaping black void" before he realized he was staring at the Moon, the half that was then in shadow. It was the darkest night of their lives.

It would also be the longest forty-seven minutes of Susan's life. If all went as planned, Apollo 8 would come back in the view of Earth and she'd hear Mission Control call AOS, or acquisition of signal. Her head bowed as if she was praying, for the first forty minutes, Susan barely moved.

Mission planners had calculated the exact second the mission clock would let them know when Apollo 8 entered the sunlit area on the far side. Frank felt his stomach clench. Crossing the terminator between darkness and sunlight, the now bright, cratered surface filled Apollo 8's windows.

Lovell was the first to see it. "I've got the Moon!"

Anders barely got three words out: "Oh my God." At the very millisecond predicted, the "hostile face of the Moon" appeared below them. Frank pressed his face close to his rendezvous window. *This is what Earth may have looked like before life, back at the beginning*, he thought.

Many people refer to the unseen side of the Moon as the "dark side"; however, both sides receive equal amounts of sunlight. In a phenomenon known as "tidal locking," the time it takes the Moon to complete one rotation is perfectly synchronized with the duration it takes to complete one orbit around the Earth, and so the far side stays eternally hidden from terrestrial eyes. But that does not mean the far side is always dark. It is dark when Earth sees a full Moon but illuminated when Earth sees a new Moon.

There are remarkable topographical differences between the near and far sides of the moon. The landscape of the near side is mostly flat, while the far side has more craters and rough terrain, with few of the "mare," or basaltic seas, created by volcanic lava flows that are so visible from Earth. Over the past four billion years, asteroids have bombarded the enigmatic far side, leaving it battered with impact craters.

Huddled in the corner of her kitchen, Susan waited for the comforting chatter of the squawk box to return. It was nearly 4:30 AM, but no one seemed the least bit tired in the Borman household. Frederick and Edwin were in the next room watching the television coverage with their grandparents and a few friends, but Susan preferred to be alone. She took a deep breath and checked her watch. Time was up. Houston should have acquisition of signal any moment.

"Apollo 8, Houston . . . over." Susan was momentarily startled when the squawk box suddenly came back on.

"Apollo 8, Houston . . . over. Apollo 8, Houston . . . over."

Susan nervously fingered her pearl necklace as CapCom Jerry Carr's patient voice made six radio calls over a two-minute period.

Finally, Susan heard a familiar voice: "Go ahead, Houston, Apollo 8," responded a very relieved Jim Lovell. Susan looked up and was able to take a deep breath.

Frank disengaged the computer. Twenty-five years after Rusty Borman gave his son fifty cents to take his first plane ride, Frank was now piloting a flying machine that he could have never imagined would exist—in lunar orbit. In that moment, he suppressed the emotions rolling over him and told Lovell, "It's no time for congratulations. Dig out the flight plan!"

Sixty-nine miles above the lunar surface, Apollo 8 had settled into the first of ten planned orbits. Now, as Frank had time to look out the window, the Moon reminded him of his childhood home. "The far side was like a night without a Moon on a high Arizona desert. The skies are enormously illuminated by stars, more stars than you can imagine."

When Houston asked Frank to describe the lunar surface, he took a moment and then responded, "I can only speak for myself, but my impression is that it looks dark and lonely. A big expanse of nothing. It wouldn't be an inviting place to live."

Frank later reflected on everything and everyone that had made this possible. "It really was a miracle," he'd say. For the first time in history a machine made by Americans was now orbiting the Moon with three humans aboard. He couldn't help but feel a mixture of both pride and gratitude.

Life magazine had published the first photos of the far side of the Moon in 1959. Taken by Russia's Luna 3 probe, the grainy photos provided little detail. In the decade following, the United

States and Russia sent another eight probes, but none compared to the images Bill Anders was capturing through the lens of his Hasselblad camera. NASA had timed Apollo 8's arrival to provide Anders optimum lighting conditions to photograph the Sea of Tranquility, on the Moon's front side, the prime location for Apollo 11's future landing attempt.

Seventy-five hours into its mission, Apollo 8 was about to emerge from the far side of the Moon for the fourth time. Frank pitched the nose over to position the command module's five dinner plate–sized windows toward the lunar surface. "All right, we're going to roll." Using the lunar horizon as reference, the commander rolled the spacecraft 180 degrees to provide Anders the most advantageous position to photograph the desolate landscape.

Anders provided a running commentary as he clicked off a series of shots of a crater as it rolled out of view. "There is one dark hole. I couldn't get a quick enough look at it to see if it might be anything volcanic."

Frank was checking the scheduled flight plan when Anders exclaimed, "Oh, my God!" Frank looked up and saw something never seen before by any human eye: Earthrise.

It was an awe-inspiring moment, and Frank's heart pounded with the sheer beauty of it. "The lunar horizon was so stark and ugly, it amplified the beauty of the Earth."

"Wow . . . is that ever pretty," said Anders as he snapped off several black-and-white frames.

"Hey, don't take that; it's not scheduled," Frank said as he chuckled, referring to NASA's predetermined flight plan. Anders floated to another window for a better view and urged Lovell in the lower equipment bay to find him a roll of color film as quickly as possible.

It was the only object in the universe that had any color to it. How could this little blue ball exist in this vast universe of nothing? Frank thought.

Lovell passed Anders the color film, which he slapped into the back of his camera. Anders rushed to bracket a series of shots to ensure he'd capture at least one with the proper exposure.

"This is the most beautiful, heart-catching sight of my life," Frank reflected. "Everything we held dear, our families, our country, and all of humanity was back on that blue planet." With his arm extended toward the small window, Frank could cover the entire globe with his thumbnail.

When Apollo 8 appeared on the near side during its fifth orbit, the crew began its first television transmission. Susan still hadn't slept, but she promised herself she would get some sleep the moment Frank was free of the Moon's gravity and headed home. Margaret and Jim Elkins held vigil with her as the grainy images of the Moon filled her television screen. Susan closed her eyes and focused on Frank's voice, imagining she was next to him. Susan didn't care about the Moon. The only thing on her mind was the moment she would be reunited with her husband.

———————

In the harried days leading up to the launch, Frank had received a call from NASA's chief of public affairs, Julian Scheer. He reminded Frank that if all went according to plan, Apollo 8 would be broadcasting live from lunar orbit on Christmas Eve. "You're going to have the largest audience that's ever listened to or seen a television picture of a human being."

"Well that's great, Julian. What are we doing?" Frank answered, not even trying to disguise his annoyance. Scheer just deferred the decision to Frank.

"Say something appropriate to the occasion."

Frank knew that whatever they said from 240,000 miles away needed to be meaningful and hoped that Susan might have a solution. She gave it a lot of consideration, but despite her best efforts and those of the Lovells and Anderses, everyone was at a complete loss. Frank needed a solution, but there was barely enough time in the flight schedule "to take a leak."

Frank ended up contacting his friend Si Bourgin from the US Information Agency, who then discussed the dilemma with former White House press secretary Joe Laitin. The pair of professional wordsmiths decided to come at the problem from two angles—the epic nature of Apollo and the turbulent events going on in America that year.

It was well after four in the morning when Christine Laitin rolled over and found her husband missing. She threw on her robe and half-heartedly called out to him, "Joe?" Sleepy-eyed, she followed the sound of typewriter keys being hammered in frustration. A snowstorm of crumpled typewriter paper covered the kitchen nook's vinyl floor. Out of paper and out of time, Joe explained his dilemma to his half-awake wife.

"Start at the beginning," Christine said without hesitation. Exhausted and bewildered, Joe just gawked at her like she was speaking a foreign language. She briefly explained her idea, twirled around, and like a winged messenger glided back to bed.

Everyone involved agreed that Christine's idea was brilliant and befitting of both Christmas and the historic occasion. Days before the launch, Frank ordered that the message be printed on fireproof cards.

Jim and Bill rose from a brief five-hour rest period as Apollo 8 began its ninth orbit. Frank had been on watch and was already preparing the cabin for their Christmas Eve television broadcast. Bill pointed the TV camera out the port window, filling the frame with the bright lunar landscape.

For the first few minutes of the broadcast, these men tried to access their inner poets, taking turns giving their personal impressions of the terrain sixty-nine miles below.

"The Moon is very different to each of us," Frank began. "I know my own impression is that it's a vast, lonely, foreboding type of existence—a great expanse of nothing."

"Frank, my thoughts are similar," added Lovell. "It makes you realize and appreciate just what you have back on Earth."

Just a few minutes were left in the broadcast before Apollo 8 was scheduled to disappear behind the far side of the Moon for the last time and begin its journey home. With time running out, Frank handed Jim and Bill their lines to read.

Anders began with the first four verses of the first book of the Bible—Genesis: "In the beginning, God created the heavens and the Earth."

For the next two minutes, a third of the world's population was transfixed. People on all the seven continents listened to the voices of three only children from three everyday, working-class American families, speaking to them from the Moon. Borders and boundaries vanished. In an unequaled and singular moment, the world was silent and momentarily unified.

Susan's eyes welled as Jim Lovell continued with verses five through nine. And then, as if he were speaking directly to Susan, Frank concluded the broadcast with "And God said, let the waters under the heaven be gathered together unto one place, and let the dry land appear: and it was so. And God called the dry land Earth; and the gathering together of the waters called he Seas: and

God saw that it was good. . . . And from the crew of Apollo 8, we close with a good night, good luck, a Merry Christmas, and God bless all of you—all of you on the good Earth."

Susan wiped away the tears rolling down her cheek as the television screen went dark.

CBS News anchor Walter Cronkite fought back his emotions and struggled for the right words. He took a moment to clear his throat and then looked straight into the camera. "Apollo 8, humankind's first flight into the orbit of the Moon, an event sure to be written larger in the books of history than any our generation has seen. A year of trouble and turbulence, anger, and assassination is now coming to an end in incandescent triumph. Apollo 8 achieved every one of its major mission aims and something else. It lifted the spirits of earthbound mortals and carried them too, if only for a while, out of their own horizons."

Borman, Lovell, and Anders didn't speak for a while after. "It was a very, very sobering thought, to see that little blue marble in the middle of all that darkness and you realize how lonely we really are on this wonderful Earth," Frank later reflected. "I think it gave a lot of people hope and transcended national boundaries. I want to believe that at least for that instant in history—people looked upon themselves as citizens of the Earth."

In stark contrast to the conflict and tragedies of 1968, it was a dream the country needed to come true. For a brief moment, three billion humans, alone on a small blue planet in the vast emptiness of space, were one.

Christmas Day was less than an hour away in Houston. Apollo 8 had one last hill to climb before it could begin its long fall back to

Earth. Susan invited Valerie Anders to the house that evening for the trans Earth injection (TEI) maneuver and acquisition of signal.

Now on its tenth and final orbit, Apollo 8 would swing behind the far side one last time and fire the SPS engine for two and half minutes. If the TEI burn went as planned, Apollo 8 would appear on the near side, break free of the Moon's gravity, and accelerate home.

Frank didn't have any presents to open Christmas morning, but Susan made sure he had a special message from her. CapCom Jerry Carr from Mission Control described it to him: "Colonel Borman, your wife wanted me to tell you that your home is decorated with four big evergreen wreaths sprinkled with powdery snow and red bows. A tree in the den awaits your safe return, and she and your sons plan to stay home for the midnight blast out of Moon orbit." Normally they would attend midnight services at St. Christopher's Episcopal Church, but they decided to go to the Christmas Day service at 7:00 AM instead.

"Since there are no young children in your home, family Christmas gift-giving will simply wait until you get back from the fantastic miracle of your flight to the Moon and back."

Frank smiled to himself. He couldn't wait to see them.

On December 24, at 11:40 PM Houston time, Apollo 8 vanished behind the far side of the Moon for the last time. Orbital mechanics required Apollo 8 to fire its SPS engine out of sight of Mission Control. If the engine performed to spec, they'd be back on Earth in sixty hours.

NASA had trained the crew for nearly every eventuality while in space but never briefed them on how they might handle one unfortunate event: that they couldn't make it home. The agency had a blueprint for a complex and expensive rescue mission—but it was quietly shelved. If the SPS engine failed and the crew were marooned in space, they'd have four days of oxygen left.

"Well, did you guys ever think that one Christmas Eve you'd be orbiting the Moon?" Lovell inquired.

Anders shook his head and then quietly said what all three of them were thinking: "Let's hope we're not doing it on New Year's."

With countdown to ignition approaching, Frank tried cracking a joke to lighten things up, which was a bit out of character for him. "I'll tell you one thing—these long flights are good for me. An old fatty like me, I bet I've lost a lot of weight."

Anders was solemn as he commented on the view, "Pretty sunrise."

One last check on the numbers. The display keyboard flashed 99, asking Lovell if he was sure he wanted to fire the SPS engine. With a look Lovell had seen a thousand times before because of their shared history, Frank gave the command without speaking. PROCEED.

Before she left home late that evening to go be with Susan and hold their vigil together by the tiny box that they had been hovering around for what seemed like forever, Val Anders retrieved the good-bye tape recording Bill had made for her in the event he was unable to return home. Feeling confident she'd never have to play it, she hid it away.

Just before midnight, Susan and Val sat silently together in the corner of the Borman kitchen awaiting acquisition of signal. *Life* magazine assigned a photographer to the Bormans to capture Susan's reaction, regardless of how events unfolded. There had been such a crush of reporters and photographers over the past few weeks, they'd become invisible to Susan.

She rubbed her arms to warm herself. She'd thrown a sweater over her shoulders, but she couldn't seem to shake off her chill.

I shouldn't be surprised, she thought, and shook her head. *I have barely slept in nearly five days.* She checked her watch. 12:14 AM, Christmas Day. Time was up. The trans Earth injection burn should be over. If acquisition of signal came at the predicted moment, she'd finally know her husband's fate and her family's future.

Susan's clenched hands looked like a prayer demanding God bring Frank home. Her mind flashed to Pat White, who'd never had the chance to tell her husband good-bye, and to Valentina Komarov, who told her husband she loved him for the last time moments before the crash of his spacecraft. Susan fought the impulse to consider the terror of either situation.

Frank never spoke to Susan or the crew about worst-case scenarios. Despite the insurmountable odds of this historic flight, Frank Borman had never been one to entertain failing in anything he set out to do, and he chose to trust the technology.

At the predicted time of acquisition of signal, CapCom Ken Mattingly made his first radio call. "Apollo 8, Houston. Over." Patiently waiting for the decisive moment, the *Life* photographer framed Susan and Valerie and gently rested his index finger on the shutter release.

"Apollo 8, Houston. Over."

Two minutes later, the lighthearted voice of Jim Lovell released the pressure, "Houston, Apollo 8. Over. Please be informed there is a Santa Claus."

Life captured and later published the moment Susan looked skyward to give thanks as she pumped her fists in the air with joy. Frank was on his way home.

A few hours later, Susan was squeezing into a pew with her boys and Frank's parents for Christmas morning service at St. Christopher's Episcopal Church. The Reverend James Buckner had become close with the Borman family and was appreciative of Susan's heart and compassion for others. Frank took an active part as a lay reader whenever he was home and was disappointed he wouldn't be able to participate in the holiday service. So Frank improvised and asked fellow parishioner and Mission Control engineer Rod Rose to help him out with something.

When Apollo 8 reappeared from the far side of the Moon, after Anders took the soon-to-be-iconic Earthrise photo, Rod Rose recorded Frank reciting a prayer he had written to be played at church on Christmas morning. Before he began, Frank declared, "This for people everywhere," but he hoped Susan would understand it was mostly for her. "Give us, Oh God, the vision to see the love in the world, in spite of human failure. Give us the knowledge that we may continue to pray with understanding hearts and show us what each of us can do to set forth the coming of the day of universal peace. Amen."

Reverend Buckner concluded the service asking God to "watch over and protect, we pray, the astronauts of our country."

Susan left church that morning with her arms wrapped around the reel-to-reel tape. For the first time since Frank told her he was going to the Moon six months earlier, she started to have faith she might actually see him again.

———————

With each mile Apollo 8 got closer to home, the more buoyant everyone in Mission Control became.

"'T'was the night before Christmas, and way out in space, the Apollo 8 crew had just won the Moon race. The headsets were hung by the consoles with care, in hopes that Chris Kraft soon would be there. Frank Borman was nestled all snug in his bed . . ." joked CapCom Harrison "Jack" Schmitt.

Even Deke Slayton, usually stern and serious, commandeered the radio and said, "Good morning, Apollo 8, Deke here. I would just like to wish you all a very Merry Christmas on behalf of everyone in the control center and I'm sure everyone around the world. None of us ever expected to have a better Christmas present than this one. Hope you get a good night's sleep from here on, and enjoy your Christmas dinner tomorrow, and we look forward to seeing you in Hawaii on the twenty-eighth."

Frank looked at Lovell and Anders in disbelief and smiled; he'd never heard Deke sound so jovial and almost carefree. "OK, leader. We'll see you there."

It wasn't Susan's cooking, but Frank enjoyed the best meal that he and the crew had had since liftoff. Christmas dinner aboard Apollo 8 consisted of real turkey meat packed in thick gravy wrapped in foil and adorned with festive ribbons of fireproof plastic. "Santa Slayton" had even included four travel-sized bottles of Coronet VSQ Brandy.

It was a nice gesture, but there was no way in hell Frank was going to take any chances, even though Apollo 8 was very close to the goal line. "I knew if something went wrong, the media would blame the booze and poor crew judgment, so I ordered Lovell and Anders to put the bottles back in the food locker. We could drink and celebrate once we were safely back on Earth."

On December 26, Susan agreed to NASA's request to talk to the press one last time before the mission ended. She was getting ready to be in front of the cameras again, trying desperately not to worry about the boys. She hadn't seen her sons in hours. She gave Teddy a good brush so he didn't look like a homeless dog and gave herself a quick once-over in the mirror.

Just as the press were arriving, Edwin stole into the house sporting a cast on his right hand. "What happened to you?" Susan rushed over to him looking both upset and relieved.

"It's no big deal, Mom. I got in a fight with Fred last night in the bathroom and I punched him in the head and broke my thumb." Rather than give their mother something more to worry about, the boys waited until that morning and Fred drove his brother to NASA, where a doctor X-rayed it and set the broken digit in a cast.

"What were you fighting about?" Susan asked, looking concerned. She knew that she had been totally distracted for a while, and had not been the mother the boys were used to being able to rely on.

Edwin looked at her sheepishly, "I actually don't remember, but as soon as we heard my thumb snap, we tried to laugh it off and made up."

Frank spent the last day methodically going through the reentry procedures, checking time, velocity, and position. Unlike an aircraft that could "go around" and make another landing attempt, if something went awry during approach, Apollo 8 had only one chance to make a successful landing. Hurling toward Earth at the twenty-five thousand miles per hour speed required, Apollo 8 had to enter a corridor only two degrees wide. If their angle was too high, they'd skip across the atmosphere and be hurled into deep space again. If they came in at too steep of an angle, even their heat shield wouldn't protect them from being incinerated.

In the event the computer failed during reentry, Frank was trained and ready to take over and fly the spacecraft manually. As Apollo 8 hit the top of the Earth's atmosphere, Frank looked up and saw the Moon rising above the horizon. He knew that he would never look at it the same way again. Free of the service module, the crew of Apollo 8 proceeded to obliterate every speed record in history as the command module slammed into Earth's atmosphere.

After a week in zero Gs, Frank could feel the capsule rapidly slowing and sensed they were in for one hell of a ride. "Hang on!" he warned his crew. Flying tailfirst, Apollo 8 was moving too fast for the air to get out of the way of the blunt end of the spacecraft. Even though the computer automatically rolled the spacecraft to dissipate some of the heat, Borman, Lovell, and Anders were nothing more than passengers. Inside the blowtorch of fire, the enormous thermal load on the heat shield reached five thousand degrees Fahrenheit. Unable to make radio calls through the fiery plasma gas that enveloped the spacecraft, Apollo 8 would be out of communication one last time, for a period of three minutes.

"This is a real fireball!" Frank shouted. Lovell called out "Six Gs" as the deceleration pushed the crew deeper into their seats. For the next six minutes just taking a breath felt like an elephant was sitting on their chests as the sustained G-forces increased their body weight to more than nine hundred pounds. The computer fired the control thrusters, rolling the spacecraft 180 degrees again to coast higher into the atmosphere to unload some of the Gs. Out of his window Frank could see the stream of fire get brighter as Apollo 8 pitched over to continue its deceleration toward Earth.

Because they were landing at night, there would be no live images of the splashdown, so Susan stood in the kitchen where she could both see the television coverage and still hear the squawk box in her bedroom.

During Apollo 8's ten passes behind the far side of the Moon, along with the final three minutes of reentry, loss of signal with Frank and the crew had lasted nearly eight hours. The week-long mission was difficult enough, but those eight hours added a dimension to the separation Susan hadn't anticipated. In her mind, during each period of LOS, she felt as if she died a little. In those moments, Susan felt Frank was just a dream, a figment of her imagination who never really existed, and she really was all alone. Then as the dream began to descend into total darkness, acquisition of signal would come back and Frank would be real again.

"Houston, Apollo 8. Over," Frank called out.

"Go ahead, Apollo 8, we read you broken and loud," replied Mission Control.

"We've got a real fireball propelling us, and it's looking good. We're in real good shape, Houston."

Apollo 8 would be the first manned mission to splash down in total darkness. Mission planners had suggested adding another lunar orbit to the mission so that Apollo 8 could land during daylight to help both the crew and the recovery ship have a visual if anything went wrong.

"I don't want to spend any more time in lunar orbit than absolutely necessary," Frank argued. "What the hell does it matter? If something doesn't work, we're all dead anyway, and it won't make any difference if nobody can see us."

Apollo 8 landed in the ocean about one thousand miles from Hawaii. The impact was jarring, and when it hit the water, the spacecraft turned nose down. The three astronauts—some would say the most famous men in the world at that time—were hanging upside down for a short time like bedraggled monkeys. When the capsule finally righted itself, it was a terrible boat that bobbed around so much Frank got seasick from the motion. It took an hour and a half for the frogmen to come and get them because it was too dangerous for the navy-trained swimmers to be in the ocean in the dark.

At dawn the froggers were dropped in the water from the helicopter hovering above, and when they finally opened the hatch, Frank took a deep breath of fresh sea air and felt more appreciation for the beautiful planet he lived on than ever before.

The mission was successful, and it was over. The three exhausted and scruffy men were loaded into the helicopter and then taken to the aircraft carrier named the USS *Yorktown*. All Frank wanted now was to shave, shower, and see Susan and his boys.

———————

It was just after breakfast in Houston, and Apollo 8 was officially safe, 147 hours after lifting off from Florida.

As soon as she confirmed that Frank and the crew were back on Earth and officially on their way home, Susan turned off the squawk box, unplugged it from the wall, wrapped the speaker cable around its plastic green shell, and placed it in the corner of her clothes closet. She hoped that she would never have to look at it again.

Frederick and Edwin followed their mother back onto the lawn so she could make her last statement to the press. Susan seemed to float out of the front door, lighter and unburdened. As the press huddled around her, she took Frederick and Edwin by the hands to keep them close.

"I'm still speechless. Just tremendous relief, and it's just truly the happiest day."

The tragedies and heartache that enveloped the nation in 1968 were replaced by a hope and dream fulfilled.

With frayed nerves and a week of sleepless nights behind her, Susan began the first step back to what she hoped would finally be some kind of a normal life. With Teddy tucked up against her, a physically and emotionally exhausted Susan Borman crawled into bed and finally fell fast asleep.

Once again, fate had been a hunter in the life of Frank Borman. For a moment, he allowed himself a moment of reflection. A deep sense of gratitude, humility, and reverence for his part in the epic journey of Apollo 8 filled him with emotion. "I honestly believe God was shining on us from the very beginning."

Frank was now one of the best-known people in America and had become a global celebrity. Three humans had traveled to another world only to discover the majesty of Earth. Bill Anders's photo would grace the cover of newspapers and magazines all over the world. *Earthrise* would be one of the most recognizable images of the twentieth century and would be heralded as "the most influential environmental photograph ever taken."

By every standard, the mission commanded by Frank Borman was an unmitigated success. Launched at the height of the Vietnam War, Apollo 8 had projected American values without engaging in warfare and provided humanity with a new perspective on its collective self.

The only thing that Frank had requested be waiting for him on the helicopter that picked them up from their ocean landing spot was a razor. Using one in space wasn't an option, and he couldn't wait to get rid of his beard.

As they landed on the flight deck of the *Yorktown* and listened to the men on board cheer and salute them, Frank closed his eyes for a moment and realized that he would never experience this kind of high again in his life. He was deeply moved by their excitement. They were all far away from their own families at Christmastime, but they didn't seem to mind. They weren't just cheering for three astronauts but for their country. It had been a year of division and tragedies, but no one was thinking about that on the morning of December 27, 1968.

The next day, the three astronauts flew off of the carrier and received a huge welcome when they landed in Hawaii. Slung in the seat of an air force C-141 transport plane, which flew the crew home from Hawaii, Frank reflected on the blur that had been the last two years. Since January 1967 he'd lived inside the NASA bubble, oblivious to the outside world and the lives of his family. Over the previous twenty-three months, he investigated the Apollo 1 fire, testified before Congress, helped redesign the command module, and commanded the mission many at NASA considered to be the most dangerous of the entire Apollo program.

Later that afternoon, NASA announced the names of the crew assigned to Apollo 11, the mission that would make the first landing attempt. It would fly the same trajectory as Apollo 8, but the last sixty-nine miles to the lunar surface would be in the hands of Frank's backup, Neil Alden Armstrong.

It was 2:30 AM when the crew finally touched down in Houston. More than two thousand NASA employees had gathered on the ramp awaiting the triumphant arrival of the first human beings to travel to the Moon. Mission controllers, engineers, technicians, administrators, and janitors had all come to celebrate their collective and historic victory.

Even before the door of the aircraft swung open, Frank could hear the roar of the crowd as the engines wound down. As they stepped out onto the landing of the stairs, Frank, Jim, and Bill were hit by a tsunami of adulation.

Frank waved back in appreciation as he squinted through the bright lights looking for the only thing he cared about seeing—his family. It didn't take him long to find his beautiful blonde wife dressed in her cream-colored winter overcoat, grinning from ear to ear.

He bypassed everyone in his path, and with a huge smile on his face made his way over to her and placed the red and purple lei that he'd brought with him from Hawaii around her neck. He pulled her in close and held her and felt her kissing him all over his face, then hugged his sons.

Someone from NASA cleared his throat behind him, trying to get his attention, and Frank reluctantly had to leave them for a moment. He stepped up to a microphone on a makeshift podium beside Jim and Bill, with Susan's red lipstick smudged all over his cheeks.

"Thank you, everyone, for coming out so early in the morning to welcome us," Frank said with gratitude. Jim Lovell made a few comments as well and then they stood for photos and shook a lot of hands. It was way past time for the exhausted astronauts to go home, but the huge crowd didn't want to let them go.

When all the families finally got in their cars to drive home, they could see the masses of people in their rearview mirrors waving good-bye.

None of the men said very much about their experience on the drive back to their homes. They just kept telling their families how happy they were to see them and that they couldn't wait to eat real food and sleep in their own beds.

They'd had years of practice putting a mission behind them as soon as it was over and not philosophizing about it. It was why NASA needed men like this. They had climbed into an unproven and untested machine and made everything work, without making too much of it. Reluctant heroes but heroes nonetheless.

Frank read just a couple of the telegrams that people from all over the country had sent to Houston when he had landed early that morning. The one that stood out and that he would never forget was from a female American citizen, not a celebrity or politician: To the Crew of Apollo 8. Thank You. You Saved 1968.

CBS News anchor Dan Rather was a thirty-seven-year-old correspondent when Apollo 8 made its historic flight. He had spent most of that year reporting on one shocking and distressing thing after another. He got emotional in an interview many years later about what this triumph meant for the whole country—if not the world:

> It was one of the most traumatic and consequential years in history, but out there, up there, is the great dream of putting a man on the moon. It seemed almost unbeliev-able, and the nation collectively held its breath worrying about are they going to make it? Such a miraculous thing is against the odds but maybe, maybe we can make it.
>
> When the pictures started coming back of the Earth from that distance, the sense of American achievement, the sense of how great the cosmos, how small we are, how fragile the Earth is, all of those things began to bounce around like electricity in your brain and touch a very spe-cial part in the heart.
>
> For those of us that lived through that time, we were reminded that darkness does not last.

Frank Borman wasn't a man who ever looked into the meta-phorical rearview mirror, but he couldn't help but feel a little sentimental about the previous six years, since he'd been chosen as an astronaut. "It's only when you get into deep space that you experience the total immersion of the heavens. The Earth was the only thing with color in the entire universe, and everything else was an inky black void. It was suspended there with a beautiful blue hue to it—the blue marble. Everything I held dear was on that Earth. And when I got off the airplane in Houston, there they were . . . my girl, and my boys."

When Susan ran up to kiss him passionately and welcome him home, and then Frederick and Edwin embraced him tighter than they ever had before, Frank would never forget the look of love and pride in their eyes and realized in that moment that he hadn't felt such an overwhelming sense of relief and euphoria since Susan had agreed to marry him eighteen years earlier.

15

MORAL COMPASS

As Frank walked into his house in El Lago, he found
a Christmas tree lit up with all the presents still unopened.
Susan wanted to celebrate Christmas when he returned, so they
all got to sit down and do what other families had done three days
before. Susan opened her gift from Frank first. It was a beautiful
dress that he had bought for her weeks before he made history. It
was a thoughtful gift but not one that said, "This might be the last
gift that you ever receive from me."

Frank hadn't allowed that to enter his mind; therefore he had
absolutely no idea that his wife had been so convinced that he
wasn't coming home that she had already begun the grieving
process. She was obviously relieved that her worst fears had not
been realized, but the emotional stress had taken a huge toll.

Frank also didn't notice that she had lost weight or that there
were dark circles under her eyes. He was still coming down from
the biggest high that he would experience in his lifetime, and so
he was understandably oblivious to anything else.

The weeks after Apollo 8 were consumed with parades, medals, and fancy dinners with politicians and dignitaries. America
was heavily invested in all the pomp and circumstance, with
ticker-tape parades across the country. It began at the White

House on January 9, 1969, with all three men getting Distinguished Service Medals from President Lyndon Johnson and continued from there. Frank was asked to speak to a joint session of Congress, along with Jim and Bill, and as he walked up to the podium where legendary figures like Winston Churchill and Dwight Eisenhower had stood (whom Frank had always had the greatest admiration for), he couldn't help but smile to himself. He looked up at the visitors' gallery where Susan and the boys were beaming at him and shook his head in wonder. How did he end up here?

As he started to speak, he realized he wasn't nervous at all because he believed that he had something important to say. "Exploration is really the essence of the human spirit," Frank said with conviction. "To pause, to falter, or to turn our back on the quest for knowledge is to perish." He ended the speech with a quote from the poet Archibald MacLeish, who summed up what Frank saw way up there much more eloquently than he ever could: "To see the Earth as it truly is, small and blue and beautiful in that eternal silence where it floats, is to see ourselves as riders on the Earth together, brothers and sisters on the bright loveliness in the eternal cold . . ."

Despite all the celebrations and accolades, the three men never forgot about their fellow officers and brothers serving and dying in Vietnam. Men no one would ever know about but their friends and families—the crew of Apollo 8 endeavored to keep them in their thoughts every day.

———————

Even though Apollo 8 was to be Frank's last flight, he stayed with NASA for another year and a half. He was just about to turn forty and needed that time to get the twenty-year full retirement benefits from the air force. He informed NASA that when the eighteen months were up, he would like to get some kind of administrative job.

Frank also started getting tired of the "apple pie" image that the reporters and media painted of the astronauts, one that seemed to imply that they were all cut from the same cloth, like clones of each other. "I don't think you could find a more diverse group of people," he told a reporter during an interview. "The only thing we really all have in common is our commitment to the space program."

On January 20, 1969, Richard Nixon was inaugurated, and Frank and Susan not only got an invitation but were seated right behind the new president as he was being sworn in. The new administration initially told NASA that it wouldn't be as supportive of the space program as Johnson's was, but it seemed now that Nixon saw it as a great way to distract the American people from the war in Vietnam.

He took a personal interest in Frank and wanted him as the program's representative, which Frank accepted. The Nixons invited Susan and Frank to dinner at the White House after the inauguration, and Susan and Pat Nixon left the men almost immediately after dinner to talk about redecorating the presidential residence. Susan and Pat started a friendship that day that continued for years.

Frank and President Nixon ended up becoming quite close as well. They liked and respected each other, and when Nixon would discuss things with Frank, he genuinely listened to what Frank had to say. He would take his advice, even if it was contrary to what his advisers were saying. He trusted Frank, even more so because he wasn't a politician.

Nixon called Frank into the Oval Office one day and asked him to go on a goodwill tour of Europe. "Mostly goodwill," he said, "but I also want you to check on how our NATO allies are doing with their space programs."

Frank accepted immediately with one request: "I want to take my family with me, sir."

"Of course," Nixon said.

On a chilly morning in February 1969, after many state briefings about protocol, the Borman family left Andrews Air Force Base for London. It would be a three-week trip that would also take them to France, Germany, Italy, the Netherlands, Belgium, Spain, and Portugal. They were flying in style because Nixon had given them *Air Force Two* to use.

Susan was especially concerned about her wardrobe. She would be meeting the queen of England, among many other important dignitaries, and while her secondhand clothes may have been OK for TV appearances, she felt quite self-conscious about it now. Her husband just wore a classic black suit everywhere, which was always appropriate, but she needed to have multiple outfits for all the dinners and ceremonies. She was also a bit nervous about the etiquette, doing and saying everything in the right way. It was another challenge that she just figured out, and as she sat on a couch at Buckingham Palace chatting with the queen of England, Frank looked over at the pair. The queen looked charmed and relaxed, and he thought proudly, *That's my girl.*

Frank and Susan's schedule in Europe was very controlled, but Fred and Edwin had a lot more freedom to come and go. They were old enough to take off by themselves and jumped at every opportunity to do so. It was a great adventure for two young men. During the day they went sightseeing and in the evenings met with royalty.

Frank was greeted as a hero in every place that they stopped. He did interviews and met with anyone who might benefit the

United States politically. People couldn't get enough of his account of mankind's first trip to the Moon.

When one of the reporters asked him why so much money was being spent on space exploration when there was misery everywhere to overcome, Frank responded, "My hope is that space exploration will bind the people of the world together, so we will all begin to look at ourselves as earthlings, rather than Germans or Dutch or Americans."

In Rome, the Bormans were told that Pope Paul VI had granted them an audience. Susan had been debating on what to wear as soon as they found out and decided on the nicest thing that she had packed, a lovely gray suit. But just hours before they had to leave for Vatican City they were informed that there was a dress code and they would all be required to wear black. No one but Frank had the right clothes, so they had to go last-minute shopping in Rome for Susan and the boys. It wasn't an economical shopping trip at all, as they were short on time, but when they arrived at the Vatican, Frank and Susan were very moved. Although they were committed Episcopalians, they were treated with the utmost honor and respect.

Their visit was supposed to be only fifteen minutes, but the Bormans ended up staying for over an hour. They received medals and gifts, and as they were about to leave, the pope looked at Frank and said, "When your Apollo 8 crew read from the book of Genesis on Christmas Eve—in that particular moment of time, the world was at peace."

Fred and Edwin had their eyes opened when they arrived in Germany and saw firsthand the differences between communism and a free society. From the windows of the hotel they were staying in, they could see the shocking contrast between the vibrant lights of West Berlin and the utter blackness of the East part of the city. The boys were missing school to go on this trip, but they were learning far more valuable lessons than can be taught in a classroom.

While in Spain at yet another dinner in honor of the Bormans, hosted at the American embassy, Susan saved the day—or the evening, to be accurate. She always seemed composed and had a way of making everyone feel at ease around her. Frank, on the other hand, was a no-small-talk guy who appreciated getting to the point in all things, so he relied on his wife's charisma and grace in big social situations.

The US ambassador's wife appeared to be quite drunk in the receiving line as people were making their way into dinner, and she started getting extremely loud and obnoxious. Her husband looked horrified and was trying to get her to quiet down as calmly as he could without much success.

When Susan got to her in the line she took her hand and whispered in her ear, "Mrs. Wagner, I would love a tour of the rest of the embassy. I've heard about your skill at decorating and would especially like to see your bedroom."

Mrs. Wagner blinked and looked confused for a moment and then nodded slowly and let Susan lead her away. When they got to the bedroom, Susan gently coaxed her into her bed with a promise to check on her soon and came back downstairs to join Frank for dinner.

Not long after they arrived home from their whirlwind tour of Europe, Frank got a call from an investment banker who informed him that he and Susan were now millionaires. Apparently, Ross Perot, the software magnate, had somehow put a million dollars in Frank's bank account as an incentive to come and work for him.

Frank met Mr. Perot in 1969 when he started working on the prisoner of war situation in Vietnam—something Ross was a big advocate for. After a meeting with Frank about the plight of the POWs, Ross Perot was so impressed with the famous colonel/ astronaut that he tried to hire him on the spot.

"I'm flattered sir, and interested," Frank said, "but I have to talk things over with my wife."

"If you come to work for me, Frank, I will make sure that you'll be financially independent so that you can focus all of your attention on this," Ross said.

The Bormans never had a lot of money in the bank, as Frank was still making a military salary, even though you could argue that Colonel Frank Borman was one of the most famous men in the world at the time. He was very tempted but knew that he had to get Susan's thoughts about it.

"Frank," Susan said in a serious tone after he told her, "you know we can't take that money. There would be strings attached to it, and he would own you. No amount of cash is worth that. You know that I am right."

She continued to look her husband straight in the eye until she felt him acquiesce. Frank let out the breath that he had been holding and just nodded because he knew even before he told her that Susan's integrity would never accept something like this. She *was* right, dammit. He slowly got up to call the banker and declined the money. The financier thought he was crazy—he knew how much military men made.

Yet again, the Bormans' moral compass was revealed, and the banker ended up with a grudging respect for this couple, who walked away from an easy fortune. In the end, it is always character, not affluence, that will be the measure of a human life.

Ross Perot ended up becoming a lifelong friend of Frank's even though he had been turned down, and Frank continued to work on the POW crisis in Vietnam on behalf of the White House until he left in 1970. He worked tirelessly to improve their conditions and get them home.

It seemed like a thankless job, but a few years later when a number of POWs were finally released when the war ended in 1975, Frank got a few telephone calls thanking him for his efforts on their behalf. One of the calls he received was from former POW John McCain—the same John McCain who would become a US senator from Frank and Susan's home state of Arizona and end up running for president twice.

Frank was still working as field director of the Space Station Task Force as liaison between NASA and the White House. As Apollo 11 got closer, he was asked to speak at college and university campuses around the country to talk about the importance of the space program. He had no idea when he accepted the request that he would be encountering outright hostility at most of the engagements.

It was a disaster. He was booed off stages and had things thrown at him. He had to arrive and leave in a helicopter at one of the scheduled talks to avoid the massive protests over the military. It wasn't just the students. Teachers and professors were egging them on and decided that Frank should bear the brunt of their censure over Vietnam. They didn't see him as an American hero but as someone who represented the military establishment and all of its sins.

Frank tried to shield Susan from as much of this as he could, but she was with him on the tour. She didn't attend every university engagement but wanted to go with Frank to Cornell. Professor Carl Sagan, the cosmologist and astrophysicist, was to be their host. Frank was escorted into the lecture hall by armed policemen, and fortunately the talk went quite peacefully. The students were polite and had good, thought-provoking questions to ask the ex-astronaut. It wasn't until later that things got hostile, when the Bormans were invited to Carl's house for dinner.

Professor Sagan invited some of his favorite students to come over as well and then proceeded to encourage them to rip into Frank about Vietnam for the whole evening. It was an ambush disguised as a dinner party.

Frank knew everything there was to know about fighter jets and how to get to the Moon but not enough details of the controversial war that had been going on for well over a decade. That wasn't his job or his mission, but no one at the gathering cared about that. When Frank and Susan left, it was with a barely civil good-bye.

Susan was devastated by the attack on her husband and lost all respect for their host. She was a firm believer in having convictions, but she felt there was a time and place to voice them—a "friendly" dinner party was not it.

Frank vowed to find out every detail at his disposal about Vietnam so that he could at least be armed with some good intel before he got confronted again.

———————

Frank was more than happy to get back to his duties at the White House as the launch of Apollo 11 got closer. While in Washington, Frank was invited to attend the annual dinner of the Alfalfa Club in Washington. The Alfalfa Club is an exclusive social club composed of top business executives and influential politicians, including several presidents of the United States. They would have an annual black-tie dinner at the Capital Hilton in Washington, DC, which the press was never allowed to cover. The Soviet ambassador happened to be there and asked Frank if he would consider coming to visit the Soviet Union with his family. Frank was completely shocked, as was the president, and Nixon urged him to accept.

Nixon was very interested in a joint space mission between Russia, the country that Frank had always seen as the enemy, and the United States. The president wanted Frank to feel them out on the possibility and advised Frank to make it the priority of the visit.

While Frank was getting ready for the trip to Russia with a big dose of both trepidation and skepticism, NASA was writing a script for the president to deliver publicly when the astronauts landed on the Moon for the first time. The agency was hoping that by playing to the president's ego, it would get more support for the program. So it encouraged the Nixon administration to take the credit for Apollo 11's hopeful success.

It was pure politics, and Frank was livid. It was also a great distraction from the upcoming goodwill trip. He left Nixon a terse message: "You can't do this."

The president called him as soon as he got the memo. "Why don't you like what NASA wants me to say, Frank?" Nixon barked.

"With all due respect, sir, you had nothing to do with getting to the Moon or what it will take to land on it. You can't take the credit." Frank didn't even try to be diplomatic. "You're the fortunate recipient of this mission if it succeeds—and will get tarred and feathered if it fails. But if you say that you were the father of this endeavor, it's just plain wrong."

"OK, Frank, just what should I say, then?" Nixon asked, clearly annoyed but wanting Frank's opinion anyway.

"Something simple. Something nonpartisan. Just a few words of congratulations and then get off of the air," Frank answered bluntly.

Nixon was infuriated but knew he was right and eventually thanked Frank.

Frank was standing just off camera, behind Nixon, when he called Neil Armstrong and Buzz Aldrin from the Oval Office the day they landed on the Moon, July 20, 1969. He recited what Frank had suggested and had his staff write up for him:

> This is certainly the most historic telephone call that I have ever made from the Oval Office. Because of what you have done, the heavens have become part of man's world. As you talk to us from the Sea of Tranquility, it inspires the rest of us to redouble our efforts to bring peace and tranquility to Earth.

16

"SPACE COOPERATION AND GOODWILL"

SUSAN WAS SITTING IN HER SEAT on the airplane with her hand tucked into Frank's arm. She could feel the tension coming from him even though he hadn't said very much on the long flight to Russia. They both had mixed feelings about this trip, for obvious reasons. The last seven years of their lives had been consumed with beating a nation they had never met in actual combat, to make a statement about the strength of America and to avoid another war. Susan was hoping for the best but preparing herself for possible conflict and hostility and knew that Frank was feeling the same way.

As the Borman family got their first glimpse of Moscow from the window of the airplane on July 2, 1969, Edwin turned to his father. "Dad, this place reminds me of a black-and-white movie— there is no color anywhere."

His description was accurate. Everything seemed monochrome, from the clothes people wore to the cars that they drove. They would realize very quickly into the trip not to judge the country based on its capital.

The Bormans were met by three cosmonauts when their plane finally landed, as well as the vice president of the Union of Soviet

Societies for Friendship and Cultural Relations with Foreign Countries—the organization responsible for their official invitation.

The purpose of the trip was at the forefront of Frank's mind as he made his first speech in the airport at the reception held in their honor: "I expect this visit to promote friendly cooperation between the United States and the Soviet Union to further the investigation into space." He would repeat this many times in the numerous speeches and toasts he was asked to give—and there were many, many toasts over the course of the next two weeks—always with Russian vodka.

One of the cosmonauts assigned to travel through Russia with them made a magnanimous gesture after introducing himself: "Colonel Borman, if there is anything that you would like to do, any place you would like to visit, please let us know. Our country is yours." Most Russian people were captivated by status and prestige, and Frank's notoriety made him more of a celebrity than an enemy.

Frank jumped on this immediately. "That's great! There are two things I would really like to see. First, your supersonic transport jet, the TU-144, and then we would like to see your launch site."

The other cosmonauts standing nearby looked at each other in mute dismay as though Frank had asked for all their state secrets. They cleared their throats a few times and finally one of them said, "We are sorry, Colonel, but we cannot fulfill those requests."

Frank got his first taste of the Soviets' proclivity for secrecy and distrust of outsiders. He got the impression, though, that the cosmonauts themselves were just following orders and would have shared more if they could. They were secretly quite curious about everything the colonel knew but believed they could never ask.

The Bormans left Moscow almost immediately with their Russian entourage. Their next stop was Leningrad (now St. Petersburg). It was a beautiful place and celebrated treasure, a perfect example of the Russians' deep respect for history, even if they happened to rewrite it on occasion.

The one thing that the Borman family didn't expect was to have such an affinity with the Russian people. They found many things in common with them. They had a wonderful sense of humor and wanted the same things for their own families as any American would. Frank was starting to see them as people instead of a threatening enemy.

The Bormans were taken to a reception given by Leningrad's mayor on their first night there. Susan approached Frank quietly and asked him if she could say something to the crowd.

He was initially surprised and then told her a bit sarcastically that they had "less than twenty-four hours left in the city" and to keep it short.

Susan responded by giving him "the look." She took the floor and gazed out at everyone gathered there and then gave them all a dazzling smile. She communicated through her interpreter, Anna.

"I have wanted to meet the Soviet people for a long time so that I could look into the eyes of the ones that are responsible for the fact that I am an astronaut's wife," she began, alluding to the competitive nature of the two space programs. "The Russian cosmonauts' wives—now my sisters—understand exactly what I mean. . . . So I would like to propose a toast to the wives of the cosmonauts, who know only too well the heavy burden of both fear and glory."

The place erupted in applause. Susan Borman stole the show.

Susan and their interpreter bonded almost immediately. Anna was a tall, statuesque young woman with flaming red hair. Fred and Edwin affectionately nicknamed her "Big Red." Anna was a historian by profession and thoroughly enjoyed talking to someone as intelligent and charming as Susan Borman.

In no time at all, Susan and Anna were chatting like old sorority sisters, but Susan eventually started to get concerned that the close friendship that was growing between them would get Anna into trouble. Susan genuinely cared about people, and so they responded in kind. It didn't seem to matter where in the world Susan Borman traveled; she always found friends—because she was one.

The schedule was very tight, but Susan needed to deal with her hair and asked Anna if she could recommend a salon to get her hair done. Anna set it up, and when Susan finally got back to their small, drab hotel room—a five-star Russian hotel made a Holiday Inn look luxurious—she was chuckling to herself.

"How did it go?" Frank asked when she walked through the door.

Susan shook her head. "I have never seen anything like it. It's all self-service," she said. "You stand in line for a shampoo, wait your turn, and then wash your hair yourself. Then you go to another line to wait for a spot at the mirror and roll and set your hair yourself. Then it's on to another line for the dryers, which you operate yourself, as well."

"Seriously?" Frank said, laughing. "Toto, we're not in Kansas anymore."

Even though things in Russia seemed antiquated and backward to the Bormans, the people that they encountered were always welcoming and hospitable. Frank was shocked to find that most Russians, even the military and especially the cosmonauts, had a respect and affection for America. With all the Russian anti-American propaganda that he knew they had been inundated with, it was, quite simply, remarkable.

While at a state reception, a Soviet Air Force general made his way over to Frank and waited patiently until he had Frank's full attention. "Colonel Borman," he said in very broken English.

"I know that our two countries are not friends. But I will never forget how you helped us defeat Hitler. I flew one of the planes that your country gave us to fight the Nazis. I want you to have these."

He proceeded to unpin his pilot's wings from his uniform and handed them to Frank. Frank was very moved and totally speechless. In that moment he recognized the brotherhood of airmen, regardless of the country where they were born, and was humbled by the sincere and heartfelt gift.

Frank decided to propose a game while on a long flight to their next stop on the tour. He called it "Capitalist Versus Communist." His hosts were very hesitant at first, not wanting anything to escalate into a heated argument on what was supposed to be a goodwill visit.

"Listen, we won't be debating or arguing," Frank said, trying to reassure them. "I just can't think of a better way to get to know one another. I won't make a capitalist out of you and you can't make a communist out of me, but it could be a starting point for friendship. I believe the only way that we're going to end up true friends is if we try and understand each other. If I can understand what you believe in a bit more, and you can try and understand what I believe in, we are sure to find some common ground."

The cosmonauts started off apprehensive but began to enjoy the game almost immediately, as did their wives. It turned out to be fun and the best icebreaker that anyone could have imagined.

Their next stop was Star City, where the cosmonauts all lived. Frank, Susan, and the boys were treated like the most honored of guests.

One of the cosmonaut's wives pulled Susan aside after observing Fred and Edwin for a while. "Your boys are so good," she said to Susan through Anna. "Our children have become spoiled and vain because their fathers are well known in the country. How did you keep them so humble?" She looked sincere but troubled.

Susan thanked her for the compliment, not really knowing how to answer, but beamed with secret pride over these two young men of hers who consistently conducted themselves with modesty and respect for others.

The Russians threw a big party for the Bormans while in Star City, and every cosmonaut who could make it was there. Frank got to meet Alexei Leonov—the first man to walk in space and someone Frank had always thought of as a nemesis. Alexei was also known to be a very talented artist, and later in the evening he walked over and handed something to Susan. He had sketched an image onto a napkin. It was the dove of peace with an olive branch hovering over the Moon, with the words APOLLO 8 printed on the dove. Susan was deeply moved and graciously accepted it.

The wives wanted to show Susan all the things that they were most proud of in their small cosmonaut community, which was advanced by Russian standards. They certainly lived better than the average Soviet citizen.

The first place they took her to was their daycare center. They were excited for her to see how modern and organized it was. When they got there, Susan looked around and saw a cold, starched, and sterile environment. It looked more like a laboratory.

"I don't like this at all," Susan said bluntly as she shook her head. "This is not the kind of atmosphere that children should be raised in. I hope we never see anything like this in America."

Instead of being offended, they were just shocked. But both Frank and Susan believed their Russian hosts actually admired their candor.

Frank made sure to keep bringing up the possibility of a joint US-Soviet space flight. It was met with resistance at first, but as the trip continued, their hosts seemed more and more open to the idea. He was there to plant the seed and would find out later that it had definitely been sown.

Anna sat by Susan on their next flight, to Simferopol, with her ever-present notebook. She was constantly writing down things that Susan would mention to someone or say directly to her. She called them "Susan's Sayings." Susan talked to her about religion, politics, and anything else that came up. Susan was so used to her husband being the center of attention that it was extraordinary for her to be the one whom someone sought out and listened to.

Susan leaned over as Anna wrote down something else that she had just said. "Anna, I don't think that you should record and keep the things that I say to you anymore. I don't want you to get into trouble."

"But I love the way you put things, Susan," Anna replied. "We discuss topics that I don't get to talk with anyone else about."

"I love our chats as well, Anna, but I'm worried for you," Susan said in a low, urgent voice. "I can say and believe these things and I won't be held accountable, but you will—and I don't want anything to happen to you."

Anna feigned nonchalance, but when they got off of the flight at their next destination, she realized that she had left her notebook on the plane. All the blood drained from her face, and she rushed back to the aircraft to retrieve it. Fortunately, she found it before anyone else. When she walked back toward Susan, she was shaking. Susan had never seen anyone so scared, and got a real sense of the fear that these people lived under and what a police state really meant.

———

After going full speed for over a week, the Bormans landed in Novosibirsk, and when Susan got off of the plane, she started feeling sick to her stomach. It was quite cold there, and they were staying at a lovely little dacha (cabin) near a river. By the next morning, she couldn't function at all, much less get out of bed. She was worried about ruining whatever was planned for that day and had absolutely no idea where to get any kind of medical care.

Susan seemed to be burning up, and Frank was getting concerned. "I am going to get a doctor for you, Su Su. Don't be upset about this, OK? I'll take care of it."

Frank got hold of their hosts and told them what he needed. In a shorter time than he expected, considering they seemed to be in the middle of nowhere, two women showed up at the door. They had white lab coats on, but besides that looked nothing like doctors. But they made house calls.

Neither of them spoke any English and their bedside manners were nonexistent. They were brusque as they took Susan's blood pressure and temperature, exchanged words Frank couldn't understand, and then proceeded to put her shoes on. They gave Frank a look that said "stay out of our way," then lifted her out of the bed. Supporting her between them, they made Susan walk out of the cabin toward the river, carrying along a blanket.

That was the last Frank saw of his wife for a couple of hours. He was somewhat troubled and had no idea what the hell was going on, but he decided to have some faith that their hosts sent them medical professionals who wouldn't make Susan any worse.

The two large Russian women marched Susan to the edge of a stream. It was quite chilly outside, and the current was moving fast. Through a few abrupt hand gestures, they let her know that she needed to take her clothes off. Susan was so sick at this point that she didn't really balk at the idea, and they proceeded to help her with the task. When she was ready, they both picked her up and plopped her into the icy stream.

Their manner was so brisk and efficient that Susan felt safe, even though it was the most bizarre medical treatment she could ever conceive of. They kept patting her on the back and made her stay in the icy water for as long as she could. Just when Susan thought that she had lost all feeling in her legs and most of her body, they helped her out of the water and wrapped her in the big warm blanket and sat with her under a tree. Susan fell asleep immediately, and when she woke up about thirty minutes later, she felt amazing.

They got her back to the cabin, where she slept a few more hours but no longer felt sick. The next day she was back to herself, completely refreshed, and for the rest of the trip she felt better than she had in a long time. These two women had given her the best prescription possible—no tests, no drugs—just an ice bath in a mountain stream and sleep.

———

On their last night in Moscow before returning home, Frank, Susan, and the boys were picked up in a limo and taken to a hangar several hours away. Frank was finally able to see one of the Russian planes that he had been hoping to check out—a TU-144. It was the world's first supersonic passenger aircraft.

Frank was beyond excited because he didn't think he would be allowed to see it. But he got a detailed tour of the airplane, and then they all sat down to a dinner that was brought into the hangar.

It was a perfect end to a trip that had reaped more benefits than he ever imagined. He was an airman among fellow pilots, united by common experiences and the love of flight. From the air, there are no such things as borders between countries; they are just lines on a map. Frank had expected even more animosity from the Russians than he'd received while touring US college campuses but instead found himself among comrades.

When they finally got back on US soil, Frank reported to the president personally on the trip. He answered the many questions that Nixon had, and Frank urged him to return the invitation and let the cosmonauts see anything that they wanted at NASA, in the spirit of openness.

Frank continued to press for a joint space venture. On July 17, 1975, after Nixon resigned from office and Gerald Ford became president, an Apollo spacecraft docked in orbit with a Soviet Soyuz spacecraft.

Apollo commander Tom Stafford, Frank's test pilot instructor from Edwards, made his way through the tunnel linking the two ships and shook hands with Soyuz commander Alexei Leonov. Frank was also pleased that this last Apollo flight included his old friend Deke Slayton. Besides being the director of flight crew operations, he was also an original Mercury 7 astronaut, though he never got to fly. Deke finally got into space after being grounded for sixteen years for that slight heart murmur.

It was a shining moment of alliance in the dismal years of the Cold War. It showed the world what could be on this blue sphere that is home for us all and why Colonel Frank Borman was so proud of a mission that he never flew.

17

MOONMAN

I N 1970, FRANK WAS NEARING THE END of his twenty-year military career with both NASA and the air force. He was trying to figure out what was next. He didn't really know what he wanted to do but knew that a change of pace was needed for Susan.

Fred had graduated and was now a cadet at West Point, and seventeen-year-old Edwin was about to enter his last year of high school. Frank was starting to field job offers in the private sector when Eastern Airlines showed up to make their pitch to him. They were a company in trouble and needed some strong leadership to pull them out of the debt and mismanagement that they were in. It just so happened that his good friend Jim Elkins was on the board at Eastern and strongly urged them to approach Frank with an offer.

Eastern's Floyd Hall became Frank's most persistent professional suitor. He instinctively understood that Frank wouldn't be won over with a big salary but needed a challenge. Eastern Airlines could definitely deliver on that. They were the fourth-largest airline in the country but were hemorrhaging money and had been dealing with internal problems for a while. Eastern offered Frank half the salary that other airlines were offering him but dangled the carrot of being president of the company within a few years.

It was a mission to save a sick but established airline and eventually be in charge. On July 1, 1970, Frank joined Eastern Airlines officially. It meant moving to Miami, where their headquarters were located, but there would be many unforeseen challenges he would be facing with his new job.

When Frank told Susan that he had accepted Eastern's offer, she smiled and gave him the support that she always had, but she had no intention of leaving her youngest son in Houston until he graduated high school.

After Fred left to go to West Point, the house felt empty. Susan was used to Frank being gone, but the boys were her reason for doing everything. The depression that she increasingly struggled with was getting harder to conceal. No one really knew anything about mental illness then, and it was never discussed, especially in the military. Susan started to become more isolated, not wanting to ever be seen as the scared, emotional astronaut's wife that the media had already portrayed her as.

Alcohol was the only thing that helped. It helped with the extreme anxiety, and it alleviated the darkness that would come over her like a black hole ready to suck her inside. The years of constant stress and pressure were catching up with her in a way that was becoming almost impossible to manage. She was on her own with this and the shame that came with it. She wouldn't dream of burdening Frank with this thing she didn't understand herself, and disguised it as best as she could hoping that it would pass. Unfortunately, every time it did pass, it came back.

Frank started his job at Eastern with the optimism and confidence of someone who was used to winning. He quickly encountered an environment of hostility that he wasn't remotely prepared for and realized that he had taken on a bigger challenge than he had anticipated. That was saying something, considering that he was the man who pissed off and stood up to so many people at both NASA and North American while investigating the Apollo 1 fire and simultaneously training to get to the Moon.

Frank Borman was no stranger to massive obstacles, but this one was in a category of its own. It was the first time in his life he had encountered intelligent people with big egos who didn't have a code. In the military he was used to butting heads with individuals who thought their way was best, men who seemed larger than life. But in the end, they always put that aside for the mission, because they believed in something bigger that their own personal opinion. The people who ran and worked at Eastern Airlines had no such code.

Frank was at a loss as to what to do about it. The only person whom he confided his disillusionment to was Susan. He had no idea what she was dealing with herself and so he asked her to do the worst thing possible for her at that time: "Susan, please come here and leave Edwin with my parents. I have already talked to them, and they will move into our house in Houston and look after him. He'll be fine, but I need you right now."

Susan did what Frank just took for granted that she would do. She came to Miami as soon as she organized everything for her youngest son, and with a broken heart that was grieving the loss of her boys and her identity as a mother, she boarded a plane for Miami.

Frank was so happy to see her at the airport, he didn't notice that she had lost weight again or that her eyes were swollen from crying. He didn't pick up on the extreme sadness that was emanating from every part of her. All he could see was that his best friend was there to support and comfort him.

But he was never home. It was history repeating itself. Frank promised her that things would be different now that he had a civilian job, but the issue wasn't the vocation—it was his nature.

———————

Things were getting worse at Eastern. Frank was trying to deal with everything using a bit more finesse and diplomacy than he was used to. His typical approach to problems wasn't working, because this was a completely different playing field.

The only thing he had to compare it to was his time at the White House. There was a lot of political bullshit that was part of the airline culture, and he now had a new "call sign," one that Eastern employees whispered behind his back: "Moonman."

"What is old Moonman going to do next?" became the phrase that made its way back to Frank on a frequent basis. They didn't trust the celebrity astronaut who, in their opinion, was given too much authority too soon. No one comprehended the near-impossible challenges that he had been asked to solve, to get to the core of Eastern's financial plight and do something about it.

Frank Borman was committed and tenacious, but he continued to encounter nothing but resistance. He was starting to lose all faith when something happened to restore it, something horrible that no one would ever wish for but made everyone in the company band together: the crash of Flight 401.

When Eastern Flight 401 crashed into the Florida Everglades on the night of December 29, 1972, Frank was now senior vice president of Eastern Airlines. He got the life-altering call at midnight and proceeded to enter into what could only be described as a nightmare. The rescue efforts to get to the remote crash site weren't happening quickly enough, so Frank jumped into a helicopter and was one of the first to arrive. It was pitch black, but he immediately jumped into the deep wetland. Everywhere he turned there were people crying for help. He could smell leaking jet fuel and knew that alligators would be around looking for an easy meal. Frank made his way through the fetid water by following distressed voices calling out, and all around him the dead and dying were bobbing up and down in the murky swamp.

Frank had a moment and realized that this was what combat would have been like. He trained his whole life for this kind of scenario but had to leave the military to experience it. It was as horrific a scene as had been relayed to him by the men he helped bring back from Vietnam.

Frank quickly shook it off and started by unpinning victims trapped under pieces of wreckage until he heard a woman screaming that she couldn't find her baby. He made his way toward her and finally got the hysterical woman to tell him what the baby had been wearing. He searched everywhere, determined to find this tiny human who had basically just come into the world. He didn't stop until he finally found the tiny, lifeless body among some wreckage. Frank made his way back to her and let her know as quickly and as compassionately as he could, knowing it was too awful to process in that moment. He continued on to save as many people as he could find. The smell of jet fuel mixed with swamp water was overwhelming, and all Frank could say to himself over and over was, "Please don't let it catch fire." How the plane wasn't burning already was both a mystery and a miracle.

More rescue crews were starting to show up but had very little space to land. Frank rushed over and started using flashlights to guide the choppers to safely set down. He refused to leave the scene until the last rescue craft departed and then demanded to go to the hospital to check on the welfare of the surviving passengers. Running on adrenaline, he didn't think about the hours he had been in the water or that he hadn't eaten or slept.

Frank looked across the chopper at two Eastern flight attendants who had survived the crash. They had worked tirelessly to help the surviving passengers and did what needed to be done. He could not have been prouder of them. They were sitting with the woman who had just lost her baby. She wouldn't leave the crash site until they forced her to. She was still in shock and couldn't accept what had happened. They took turns trying to comfort her.

In the aftermath of the crash, Frank made sure that treating the survivors and their families with humanity and kindness was the priority. It wasn't a public relations scheme to try and avoid lawsuits but a genuine concern for the victims. Eastern Airlines representatives made themselves available at every hospital to make phone calls, shop for clothing, and do anything else that needed to be done.

Throughout the tragedy, Frank realized that his employees had gone above and beyond, and for that they earned his respect and gratitude. His faith in the company had been restored, and he vowed in that moment to do whatever he could to save it.

When he was finally able to call Susan, he got a bit emotional. "You know, hon, this airline has some really amazing people," he said as though he had made some kind of miraculous discovery. Out of a tragic disaster came a deep love for this company that wasn't an inanimate corporation anymore. It was a living entity made up of magnanimous, strong-willed human beings. Eastern Airlines was worth fighting for.

Frank hung up the phone with Susan feeling like he had just turned an important corner. He had no idea how close he was to another catastrophe.

18

"NEVER BOTHER YOUR HUSBAND WITH TRIVIAL MATTERS"

SUSAN BORMAN WAS IN THE APARTMENT in Miami that Frank had quickly found when he started at Eastern. She was on the couch just staring at something beyond the wall. She had a drink in her hand, and her eyes were red, even though she hadn't cried in days. There were no tears left.

She kept telling herself to get off of the couch and get ready. Fred was coming for a visit! She hadn't seen her precious oldest boy in months, and even though she had come to Miami because Frank told her that he needed her, she never saw him. He was dealing with the aftermath of the crash, and she felt more alone than she ever had before.

No boys to take care of. No military wives to get together with. It was just her and the voices in her head, and they wouldn't stop. Not for a second. They would start to remind her about how much she still missed her father and how abandoned she felt when he left her. It was something that she had refused to think about for years . . . and how angry she was with him for leaving her with a mother that could barely stand her.

She then jumped right into living with the threat of losing her husband on a daily basis because he had a burning obsession to be the best, regardless of what it cost his family. There was a constant churning inside, along with a darkness that had always been nipping at her heels and had now finally caught up to her. It was a combination of deep trauma and a mental illness that refused to disappear.

The only respite from all of it was when she had a drink, so she started the day out with one and didn't stop. Anything to keep from being sent to a place that she couldn't come back from.

Susan knew that she was losing control but had nothing left to fight with. There was no one to be strong for anymore. Fred was due to arrive soon, but she continued to stare into the void. She would get off the couch and brush her hair in just a few minutes, just not right now. She looked over at the bottle on the side table, grabbed it, and had another splash. *How many was that today?* she tried to remember as she took another sip of vodka. *I'll just close my eyes for a minute.* She laid her head back and waited for the blessed oblivion to come.

Depression is one of the most sinister diseases for an individual to face. You can't see it. There is no physical manifestation to alert anyone to its presence unless you take the time to look deep into someone's eyes who is suffering from it. The spark that should be there is simply gone.

Humans are hardwired to survive, but the kind of deep pain that doesn't seem to have a light at the end of the tunnel is almost impossible to bear. It just gets darker and darker until you believe that you will never see illumination again. So, you pray that you won't have to. You pray that when you close your eyes, you won't have to open them ever again. It's better than holding on to the hope that it will eventually get better, when it never has. There are brief respites. Times where joy is just within reach . . . and then slips away like a mirage.

You can distract yourself with worthwhile causes, loved ones, or passions—but when you dare to look over your shoulder, the darkness is right there, always ready to draw you back.

If you have already been to hell, there is not much else to fear. Especially death. Anyone who has experienced this is fighting a war that is almost impossible to win. Whether you do or not, you are a warrior.

———————

"Mom, Mom, I'm here!" Fred sounded tired but excited as he came through the door. He had knocked but no one answered, so he let himself in to the condominium he had visited only once before. An Eastern car service had dropped him off, one of the perks of being the son of the vice president of the company, and he had been treated very well on the flight from New York.

He couldn't wait to tell his mom about everything that was going on at school, some of it challenging but most of it really great.

That's weird, Fred thought as he made his way into the kitchen. *I can't smell dinner.* He had missed his mom's cooking so much, and she always made his favorite when he came home—fried chicken.

"Mom, where are you?" Fred was starting to feel uneasy. This wasn't like her. It was too quiet and dark in the apartment. Was she lying down? "Mom?"

Fred stepped into the living room and then he saw her. She was on the couch, and she didn't seem to be breathing. There was a glass tipped over on the carpet and a bottle of vodka on the coffee table.

Fred came over and shook her leg. "Mom!" She didn't move. "Mom! Please wake up!" He started to panic. "Mom," he pleaded, "please wake up. Please talk to me."

Susan finally moaned, and Fred almost fell to his knees in relief. She was trying to open her eyes but didn't seem to be able to. She made some noises like she was trying to say something, but Fred couldn't understand any of it.

"Mom, I am going to call the ambulance." Susan was still mumbling but incoherent. Fred's hands were shaking as he picked up the phone and called emergency services.

"Hello, what's your emergency?"

"It's my mom, she can't speak, and she doesn't seem to be breathing well," Fred said frantically. "Please send someone right away—please," he pleaded. He gave them the address and kept looking at Susan, who had just rolled to her side and started vomiting.

"She is throwing up. What do I do?" Fred had never felt so helpless. This was the woman who had always taken care of him, who always knew what to do every time he or Edwin got sick or did something stupid and hurt themselves.

"We are on our way, sir," said the dispatcher. "Roll her onto her side and make sure that her airway is clear."

"I will . . . please hurry!"

Fred hung up the phone and went over to his mom to make sure that she was breathing. As soon as he felt her breath on his hand, he ran into the bathroom to get a towel to clean up the vomit, then grabbed whatever bowl or container that he could find in case it happened again.

He sat down on the floor beside her and pulled back her hair from her face. "Mom, please talk to me," he whispered. "Please be OK."

Fred realized right then that he didn't even think to call his father. Not only did he have no idea where he was, but he was so used to Frank never being available for any emergency around the house that it never crossed his mind. It had always been just the three of them—the three musketeers—and his mother had always known what to do. So, he stayed on the floor beside her holding her hand, and prayed that the ambulance would get there soon.

Eastern Airlines had its own chief medical officer, Dr. Julio Serano, and as soon as Susan was admitted into the hospital, he was called to come and examine her. When he arrived, he found a catatonic woman in the bed and a distraught young man beside her.

He came over and placed his hand on Fred's arm. "Can you tell me what happened?" he asked. Fred was trying to keep his emotions in check and told the doctor what he found when he came into the apartment.

The doctor nodded and immediately took a look at the tox screen to find out what she had ingested. "Fred, does your father know?" he asked. "Do you know how to get a hold of him?"

"No, sir, I don't," Fred said with a trace of bitterness.

"I will call the head office and track him down. In the meantime, why don't you go home and get some sleep? I promise we will take good care of her and that she will be OK."

"I don't want to leave her," Fred insisted, looking at the doctor like he was crazy.

"Son, your mother is going to have a very difficult time trying to talk to me about this when she finally can, and I promise you that it will be more difficult for her if you are here."

Fred knew that the doctor was right, and as much as he hated to admit it, he wasn't sure that he really wanted to know. "OK, sir," he said, "I will go home, but I will be back tomorrow."

Dr. Serano nodded. "She's in good hands."

Fred walked out of the hospital in a daze, hailed a cab, and went back to the dark apartment.

Dr. Serano asked a nurse to keep trying to get hold of Frank. Finally, she was able to track him down at the Eastern headquarters in Cleveland, where he was still dealing with the aftermath of the Flight 401 crash.

Frank was in the hangar when he noticed an Eastern agent running toward him. "Mr. Borman, system control has been trying to reach you. Your wife is ill and was admitted to the hospital."

Frank rushed to the closest phone he could find before the agent even finished. He called home, knowing that Fred was supposed to be there.

"Hello," said Fred. He sounded exhausted.

"Fred, it's Dad, what is going on with your mom?" Frank tried to keep his voice calm but sounded more like a drill sergeant.

He could hear Fred take a deep breath. "Well, Dad, I'm not exactly sure what is wrong. She was on the couch and hardly breathing when I came into the apartment, and she couldn't speak. She started throwing up, and so I called the ambulance and got her to the hospital."

"Thank God you were there," said Frank.

Fred paused. "Yes, Dad, thank God, because you never are, are you?"

Frank closed his eyes and dropped his head. Fred's arrow pierced right through his heart. "I will get on the first flight that I can and be there as soon as possible."

"OK, Dad," Fred finally said. "I'll see you when you get here."

Frank hung up the phone and stopped for a moment as the guilt came over him in waves. He had to keep it together, but deep inside he had never been so afraid. He knew. He knew that something wasn't right with Susan, but the mission of saving this damn airline took up all his time and mental energy. He had put her in second place yet again, and if anything happened to her, he wasn't sure he would ever forgive himself. He picked up the phone again and dialed.

"I need to get back to Miami as soon as possible," Frank said.

The flight back to Miami seemed interminable. Frank had no idea what actually sent Susan to the hospital but had known for a while that she was struggling. This time his approach to a problem wasn't going to cut it. She wasn't a machine that needed to be fixed, and as much as Frank hated to admit it, he was out of his depth.

Dr. Serano met Frank in the lobby of the Coral Gables hospital when he arrived. He looked at Frank with compassion for a moment and then said bluntly, "Your wife is very sick and has had a nervous breakdown. She needs help. There is a place that I think she should go. It's called the Institute of Living in Hartford, Connecticut, which is a treatment center that I highly recommend."

Frank just nodded and said wearily, "Whatever you think will help her, Doctor. I need her to be OK . . . whatever it takes."

Susan had been heavily sedated and wasn't allowed any visitors. Frank sat numbly in the waiting room and tried not to obsess over what had brought her to this place. *How had he not seen that she was in that much trouble? Did he just not want to see?*

The next morning, he finally got to go into her room and just held her hand until he felt her stir. She was disoriented and had a hard time talking but kept trying as tears ran down her face.

"Frank, this has been going on for a long time," she finally said in a broken whisper. "I'll do whatever it takes to get better."

When Susan married Frank Borman, she ended up marrying one of the most competitive pilots in the US Air Force. Duty was the driving force behind everything that Frank did and would always trump everything else—including her and the boys. She adopted this philosophy because she believed there was no other choice . . . and she was in love.

Susan absorbed her copy of *The Army Wife*. She took every suggestion as a command and followed it to the letter: *Perfect comportment and behavior at all times. Participate in officers' wives' activities. Children must always be neat and well-behaved. Show deference to senior officers' wives, even if you don't respect them at all. Never bother your husband with trivial matters.*

To Susan it was holy scripture, and in 1950, as a young air force bride, it *was* as important as your religious faith to be completely dedicated to your husband. She didn't resent the regimented discipline or the denial of herself and her own needs—she was used to it, thanks to her mother.

She truly accepted she was a part of something important, something bigger than herself, and believed in it as strongly as Frank did. Whatever separation or setback came along, she took it all as part of the deal. To do otherwise might hurt Frank.

Little did she know that she would need this training to be thrust into the spotlight as the wife of an astronaut. At first it was kind of exciting. One minute she was just one of hundreds of wives at Edwards Air Force Base, and the next she was part of a small, exclusive group of women who would become known all over the country, *the astronauts' wives*.

Susan continued to play the role throughout her time at NASA. She never complained, kept all fears to herself, and made sure that she was raising two boys that anyone would be proud of. Frank's priorities were hers.

Susan worked hard to try to adopt her husband's "it always happens to the other guy" viewpoint. But it was happening to the other guy *all the time*. At every base where Frank was a fighter or test pilot, they attended multiple funerals for fellow airmen. It created fissures in the foundation of that belief. For a girl who'd lost her father and her sense of security at thirteen years old, she would not and could not accept the possibility of losing Frank. Frank had subconsciously taken her father's place and she wouldn't entertain any thought of his death, so she sent him off on every mission with a smile on her face.

Even though she was warm and engaging to everyone she met, Susan was actually an introvert who found most people quite draining. Extroverts need people to recharge, but introverts tend to get depleted by people—especially groups of them. She relied on the boys for her social interaction and was able to project an image of the perfect military wife because she never let many people get close.

The boys, however, took their family's nomadic lifestyle in stride. It was all they knew, and the friends they had growing up were in the same boat. What was abnormal to most families was perfectly normal to them.

Any stress or fear Susan felt, she repressed. She kept everything to herself, so even the boys had no idea that anything was ever wrong. Fred and Edwin seemed to inherently know to take their cues from their mom. *Don't ever show anything but pride.*

No one in the astronaut community really discussed anything with anyone. The wives themselves couldn't support each other emotionally because of the fierce competition that their husbands dealt with. When they got together, they would pour themselves a drink, light up a cigarette, and pretend that everything was fine. The only time they let their guard down was when one of them became a widow, and then they took turns making sure that the latest victim of the program was fully stocked with food and booze.

That was the way both NASA and their husbands wanted it. You *would* do your part even if it meant wearing a phony smile to hide whatever was really going on. Every one of them felt pressure to portray the most well-adjusted woman in the world. But there would be a huge price to pay, and no one was more cognizant of that than Mrs. Frank Borman.

Susan had internalized her feelings since she was a young girl with no idea that all that pain would need to be released at some point. There would have to be a reckoning.

Her foundation started to crumble in earnest after the Apollo 1 fire, when Ed White was killed. Fred and Edwin were getting older and more independent. They didn't need her constant presence, and so she spent every moment she could with Pat White and her kids, doing everything she could think of to comfort them, which also meant putting herself in a widow's shoes night after night.

It started to feel as though it had actually happened to her, and the feeling wouldn't leave. When the "other guy" was bigger, stronger, and just as smart as Frank, that theory no longer held up in her mind.

She wasn't the only one deeply affected. After the Apollo 1 fire, tensions between astronauts and their wives reached a tipping point, and NASA stepped in to deal with the emotional crisis. Their solution was to get the agency's flight surgeon Chuck Berry to intervene. He started handing out tranquilizers to keep the wives numb and quiet, and strongly recommended that every wife take them. It was the "just give someone a pill" remedy that continues to this day.

Susan chose to stay away from the pills, because she had already discovered something that helped, which was a big part of the military culture as well. It started out with a couple glasses of wine with Pat White while she watched her slowly unravel, night after night, and gradually became her way of coping with the stress and scrutiny of Apollo 8. It then became a refuge from the dread and anxiety, and was the only break she had from the dark voice that repeated, *Frank is not coming back from this mission.*

19

"IT'S TIME FOR
A RECKONING"

SUSAN SAT SILENTLY IN THE AIRPLANE BESIDE FRANK, who was beginning to realize just how blind he had been to what was going on with the one person he relied on more than anyone else. Susan had barely spoken a word since she found out that she was being sent to a psychiatric center over one thousand miles away from her new home that didn't feel like a home at all.

Frank sensed that she felt betrayed. He had never felt anger like this from her before but was feeling it now as he looked over at her again staring out the window. She refused to look at him. *Did she think he wanted to take her so far away? Didn't she know that he was beside himself with worry and guilt? Didn't she see how helpless he felt?*

No, she did not, and for once she couldn't care less.

For the first time since they were wed, it wasn't all about him and the support that he needed. The trajectory of their relationship was changing dramatically, and he knew in his gut that nothing would ever be the same.

When they finally arrived at the Institute of Living, Frank was relieved that it looked more like a beautiful New England college campus than a hospital. All around there were ivy-covered buildings that were in the style of classic English architecture, and the picturesque grounds gave an impression of serenity. It was a beautiful setting that Susan would eventually come to appreciate.

Just not today.

The Institute of Living was built in 1823 in Hartford, Connecticut, as a psychiatric facility. The institute's philosophy was:

> Recovery is a process centered on the whole person and his/her goals, rights and responsibilities. Each individual's potential for restoration is engaged through participation in the treatment process. The journey to wellness is a unique function of autonomy, self determination, and available resources. . . . Many of these practices evolved from the philosophical framework of "Moral Treatment." Moral Treatment was an approach to mental illness based on humane care and the recognition that the signs and symptoms of mental disorders reflected illness. The Institute of Living . . . embraced this approach to caring for the mentally ill. By involving these individuals in therapeutic settings, they were treated in a dignified and humane manner. The approach minimized the use of restraints and seclusion and maximized medical, psychological, social, occupational, and spiritual modalities.

Frank led a silent, visibly anxious Susan to the front doors, where they were met by the senior psychiatrist of the institute, Dr. Richard Brown. He looked to be in his early to mid-sixties, was about Frank's height, and had eyes that exuded warmth and compassion. He was actually about to retire but took Susan on as a favor to Frank, who had called and begged him to help with their situation.

Dr. Brown was gentle and had a calm, soft voice. Susan would eventually come to trust and open up to him in ways that she never imagined.

Frank was in agony over having to walk out of the building and leave his precious wife and partner behind, but he didn't know what else to do.

"Susan, please look at me," Frank pleaded as he tried to get her to turn around. "I will come back to see you as soon as they say that I can."

Susan refused to move at first, and then slowly turned to face him with tortured eyes. "I don't want to stay here, Frank. I promise you that I will beat this. You can't leave me here. Please don't leave me here."

Frank looked over at the doctor. In his whole life he had never felt so miserable or powerless.

"Susan, I want you to know that you will be OK here," Dr. Brown said. "I believe that Frank loves you very much and just wants to see you get better."

Susan wiped away the tears that escaped and nodded jerkily. "OK, I'll do whatever I have to." She stepped forward to give Frank a quick kiss on the cheek. "Tell the boys I love them and that I'll be home soon." She gave her husband one last look as she turned to follow one of the nurses to what would be her room for the foreseeable future.

"We'll take care of her," Dr. Brown said to the devastated man standing in front of him. "It will be a long road, but something tells me that she is stronger than anyone, including herself, realizes."

Frank was too emotional to answer, so he just gave a brief nod. He walked out of the institute in a complete fog and tried to not to think about how he was going to get through the next six weeks without the other half of himself.

"Nervous breakdown" isn't an actual medical term and isn't indicative of a particular type of mental illness, even though it usually points to one—for instance, anxiety or depression or both. There are also many reasons why people with depression are more likely to be heavy or dependent drinkers.

One of the biggest is that people struggling with depression use alcohol like a medicine, to "treat" the symptoms. Antidepressants work for roughly one-third of people with mental illness, and so the desperation to get relief drives them to self-medicate. For some, alcohol does relieve things. It takes away anxiety, and as long as you don't drink to massive excess, it makes you feel the closest to "normal" that you ever have—so it's a very easy thing to rely upon. The more pain and stress that life dishes out, the more you believe that you need it. Statistically, women do not assimilate alcohol as readily as men, and therefore are more prone to be at risk for alcohol-related death and disease.

Alcohol dependence is also three times greater among people with depression compared to people who don't suffer from the disease. In the 1950s, '60s, and '70s, everyone drank. It was the accepted norm of most adults. The dangers of alcohol consumption were not talked about or understood as they are today.

When Barbara Cernan gave her "What it's really like to be an astronaut's wife" speech that became national news, she told her husband Gene when he phoned to talk to her about her newfound fame: "It's amazing what you can do after two tranquilizers and three martinis." In other words, it was the culture of the time, and NASA supported it one hundred percent.

When Susan Borman had her mental breakdown in the early 1970s, no one talked about mental illness, coping skills, or ways to deal with stress and trauma. It was a taboo subject. Pills of any kind were out of the question if you were married to Frank Borman as well. He thought taking an aspirin was a problem—not that there were many antidepressants available at that time. If you suffered from this horrible disease, you were essentially on your own. Combine that with being put under the spotlight of a high-pressure and extremely stressful lifestyle lived out in front of a news camera, and you have a disaster in the making. It's not *if* it will happen—it's *when*.

Many factors contributed to Susan's problems. Her childhood. Learning at a very young age to suppress anything painful. Marrying one of the most ambitious and intense men God saw fit to create. And to top it all off, she had a genetic predisposition to both depression and extreme anxiety. The fact that she was so poised and never showed a hint of any of it while in the spotlight, or when Frank was at home and needed her, is nothing short of a miracle. She raised two amazing boys and gave them the childhood that she never had, one full of love and security. She was just as much of a hero as her husband but couldn't begin to believe that.

And now she was in a "loony bin." She had never felt so humiliated or angry with herself. *What will everyone think?* she wondered, feeling completely hopeless. *I have let my boys down. I have let Frank down.* She put her hand over her mouth to keep from sobbing out loud. *I am a complete failure as a wife and mother . . . as a human being. I have to get out of here as soon as possible.*

Dr. Brown found Susan sitting on the floor as he let himself into her room when she didn't answer the door. He quietly sat on the floor beside her for a few moments. Susan refused to look at him.

"Susan," he said quietly, "I know you don't believe me right now, but you are going to get through this, and I will be with you every step of the way."

Susan finally raised her head. "Please, Doctor," she said, "I just want to go home to my family." *But that was the problem, wasn't it?* she realized in that moment. *There was no one to go home to, no one who needed her.* She was alone most of the time with no purpose, and she had to acknowledge to herself that if she went home right now, she would end up in the hospital again. Something was wrong. Something inside of her was broken. She knew she was sick, and now *her* mission was to heal and return home as whole as possible.

Susan looked at Dr. Brown. "OK," she said in a stronger voice. "I'll do whatever I need to do."

Dr. Brown smiled and got up from the floor and helped her stand up. "Well, Susan, the first thing we need to do is go and have something to eat," he said. "I have a feeling that you haven't eaten much for a while."

"No," she said in a dejected voice. "I haven't, and that is just one of the many things that I need to do better at."

Dr. Brown turned to look at her. "Susan, I need you to hear this. You have done the best you can in extraordinary circumstances. My guess is that you have been sick for a very long time and did a good job of hiding it because your husband and your sons relied on you so much. You never let them down—not once, from what I have been told. Nor did you let the American public or NASA down. It's only now that your body is finally able to get your attention because there is no one at home that needs you. It's OK to look after yourself for a change, Susan." He paused. "It is why you are here. Now it is all about you, and that is OK. It's time for a reckoning. It is difficult for you to hear that because you have been trained to ignore yourself, but it is absolutely necessary in order for you to heal."

Susan had no idea how much she needed to hear those words until he said them. Although it made her uncomfortable to think about putting herself first, there was a secret part of her that had been begging for this her whole life. A place to be heard and seen. Not as a prop or someone's version of who they wanted her to be—just to be Susan Bugbee Borman.

A heartbreaking fact then presented itself—she actually had no idea who that was. But she hoped over the course of the next few weeks, she would get to meet her.

20

"I WILL PROTECT HER
FROM NOW ON"

FRANK HAD NEVER BEEN someone to dwell on past mistakes. You make one—you learn from it. You move on. But this was different. He now had to think about how he had contributed to his wife's illness. He knew that he had taken Susan's support for the last twenty years for granted. He'd always believed that she was as content with their marriage as he was. He was terrified that he might be wrong about that.

> *My dearest Susan,*
> *Here it is tomorrow already. The plane trip back from Connecticut was the longest of my life. No sooner had I arrived home, when I got a call from Fred. He finished in grand style and graduates from West Point on Friday. I'll take all kinds of pictures so that you can enjoy his pride.*
> *Susan, all is going fine here. Please don't worry. Just concentrate on getting well. I expect you to be a tennis star and a great piano player when you leave Hartford. I want to tell you how much that I love you even though you might not believe that right now. I do and always will.*
> *All my love, Frank*

Frank knew that he probably wouldn't get a response from her right away, but he had used letters once before to convince her to come back to him. He was hoping and praying that it would work again.

> *My dearest Susan,*
>
> *I know the days have been long. The long weekend was really long! But time does pass. It's been two weeks now since you went to Hartford. The boys and I are figuring out ways to make the days go by faster. You and I have so many reasons to be proud of our boys. Edwin has the respect of everyone that I talked to now that he is in the Ranger school. His [tactical] officer told me that he was a great young man and a natural leader. I wish you could have been there to see his reaction when he was told. Fred made sergeant and has his feet firmly on the ground as you and I know so well now. I think that I have brought you up to date on everything since I last wrote. I hope that you will write me back. I think a letter is even better than a phone call because they can be read over and over again. Susan—there are so many things that I want to say. So many times that I wish I could just hold you and say them to you. Temporarily I can't, but what I can tell you is that without you my life has no meaning at all. I can also tell you that far from looking upon you as a possession as you suggested you thought I did, I look upon you as a wonderful companion with whom I want to spend the rest of my life. I love you a great deal more than I can express but will try in the future to do a better job. Honey, please continue to do the things that the doctor requests.*
>
> *The boys and I need you home—it isn't a home at all without you.*
>
> *All my love, Frank*

As Frank sat down in their Miami apartment to write Susan another letter, he started looking around at all the things that she had done to make the place seem more like a home, something else that he had always taken for granted. He hung his head and whispered a prayer. "Please tell me what I need to do," he pleaded. "Please help her to get well and come to home to me. I don't know how to live without her."

> *My Dearest Susan,*
> *The days are long, and the nights are very lonely. It has been almost three weeks since the Friday night things came unglued. I've had ample time for a great deal of thought. I've reached a fundamental conclusion. A conclusion based not on emotion, but the realities of life. As I sit here at home at 4 am, I want no success at Eastern or anywhere else at the expense of our marriage. At times I am almost overcome with guilt when I realize how insensitive I was to your needs and feelings. I must confess that I was on occasion feeling pretty sorry for myself lately. Thoughts like stopping the car and just walking away from everything—even myself— crossed my mind more than once. But in retrospect I realize that I could and can find no meaning or purpose to life without the woman that I love. Our boys are also seeing things differently. Our family as an entity has suddenly been threatened, and its true value is much clearer. I hope you'll notice the change in me. You are constantly in my thoughts and prayers.*
> *I love you, Susan*
> *Frank*

It took six weeks just to get Susan to a place where her physical body started to seem healthier and stronger. She was eating nutritious food on a regular basis and taking vitamins that helped to provide all the nutrients she was lacking. She was playing tennis almost every day and getting back to her love of music—something she had always enjoyed as a young girl but never had time for—by playing the piano in the music room. She loved country music and was learning some of her favorite songs.

Being in a peaceful environment away from all the stresses of the world, she was finally in a sanctuary that made her feel protected and safe, something she hadn't felt for a very long time. Long walks on the beautiful grounds, surrounded by the huge trees that seemed to provide a canopy of tranquility, seeped into every part of her. The only thing that was robbing her of complete serenity was being away from Frank. It wasn't completely rational, as he had been away from her for so much of their marriage, but she couldn't shake the guilt of not being there for him. It had always been her job.

But a big part of her was very angry with him, something she had never been able to admit to herself before. Angry for all the times that he was away and distracted. Angry for not seeing how much pressure that she was under throughout his career and especially during their time at NASA. Furious for putting her through hell and expecting it to never affect her or the boys. She resented every time she had to put on a fake smile and pretend that everything was fine. Some days that anger threatened to choke her, and without the alcohol to numb it, she felt it burning through her like a fire.

Susan couldn't respond to Frank's letters—not yet. Not until she worked through all this rage. It seemed like an overflowing river that was gushing out everywhere. For someone who had been raised to never show or express negative emotions in any way, she felt completely lost and overwhelmed. But every day, through group therapy sessions and the self-care that she had avoided most of her life, she was slowly coming to terms with everything that she had repressed.

Susan was getting to a place where she started to see that her anger toward Frank was tied up with the anger she had toward her father for leaving her and for having to carry the weight of his death around her neck like a noose that got tighter with each passing year. But admitting that out loud felt like a betrayal to the first person who she felt ever truly loved her.

Finally, Susan was able to sit down and write Frank a letter back.

> *Dearest Frank,*
> *I need you to know that you and the boys have been in my mind and in my prayers every minute since I have been here. I so very much want for the both of us to reach for new and higher horizons in our relationship with each other. We are so blessed. Through thick and thin we have always had love. How I miss you. I try so hard to be aware of the things I struggle with and I am learning to stare them in the face because I want to be the best version of myself that I can be. I just don't seem to know who I am anymore now that the boys don't need me like they did when they were small. I still have work to do, but I believe that you will be there on the other side. You will never know the source of strength that our love is. I am trying not to think of all of the years I fought the simple truth. I will get through this, because I have so much to live for.*
> *All my love, Su Su*

When Frank got that letter in the mail, he felt profound relief. He kept it by their bed on the side table like a talisman that everything was eventually going to be OK.

The six-week period that Susan had initially committed to was up, which meant that Frank could finally visit and they would be able to talk on the phone.

Susan stood at the pay phone in the hallway by her room and took a deep breath. In over twenty years, she had never gone for so long without talking to Frank. She was nervous. His letters were full of regret for all the ways he had let her down, but what if he decided that he was better off without her after so much time apart now that the facade of her being the perfect wife had been demolished? Frank hated weakness. He had always despised it in others. Would he despise her now?

Susan picked up the phone. If she had learned anything over the last month and a half, allowing fear to control you would always take you somewhere your soul didn't want you to be.

"Hello, darling," Susan said when Frank answered. "I think I am ready to come home now," she said in a rush. "I feel so much better and miss you terribly."

Frank had to wait a moment to answer her. He cleared his throat to disguise his rising emotions. "Hello, Su Su," he said. "It is so good to hear your voice. You have no idea."

"I think I might," she replied.

"How are you? How are you feeling?" he asked. He would never take for granted just being able to hear her voice again.

"I'm a lot better, darling. I just want to come home."

"What does Dr. Brown think?" asked Frank. "Does he think that you are ready to leave?" Frank closed his eyes and prayed that it was true.

He could hear Susan hesitate on the other end and then she finally answered, "No, he doesn't think that I am ready yet. He's concerned that if I leave now, I will have to come back, but I don't agree. Frank, I want to come back home now. It's been six weeks, and I feel much better."

Frank felt like his heart was in a vise. "Susan, I want you to come home more than you can possibly know, but I need to know that you will be OK once you are here. I need you to come home healthy, no matter how long that it takes."

He could hear her start to cry on the other end, and he felt like part of him was dying. He had no idea what to say, and the guilt he felt for all that he had done to contribute to her pain came at him in full force.

"I am so sorry, honey," he said. "You can't know how sorry that I am. That I didn't see it . . . that I was so distracted with things that I thought were more important."

Susan was silent for what Frank felt was an eternity. "So, you're not disappointed in me?" she finally asked. "You don't think that I am weak because I used alcohol to deal with all of the stress and fear?"

Frank was initially shocked and then felt ashamed. This was the first conversation they were having after six weeks of being apart, and the first thing out of his wife's mouth was "Are you disappointed in me?"

In that moment Frank understood that he needed therapy as much as she did—maybe more. What had he done to this amazing woman? How could she believe that? He needed to figure it out.

"Susan, I care about one thing right now, and that is you. I clearly have not done a good job of letting you know how very proud and in awe I am of you. I have been too focused on things that I thought were important—but I never meant to make you feel like you took a backseat." He stopped and cleared his throat again so that he wouldn't start to cry. "I need to know that you have taken the time that you need to heal. I will be fine, but I need you to be more than fine. You have always put me first—it's your turn now."

"OK, Frank," Susan finally said. Frank knew that she was crying, but as usual she tried to hide it. "I will talk to Dr. Brown and find out how much longer he thinks I need to stay. I really trust him now and will do whatever he thinks I need to do to get home to you healthy."

"I love you so much, Su Su."

"I love you too, darling."

Frank hung up the phone and dropped his head into his hands. He felt like his insides were unraveling. He had to stay strong for her. She needed him to support her this time, and there was no way he would let her down. He picked up the phone again and dialed. It rang a few times, and then a friendly voice answered.

"Hello, you've reached the Institute of Living. How can I help you?"

"Hello, it's Frank Borman. I need to speak with Dr. Richard Brown as soon as possible. Is he available?"

"Just one moment, sir. I will see if I can locate him."

Frank sat on hold for a couple of minutes.

"Hello, Colonel Borman," said the doctor in the calm voice that Frank was becoming more familiar with. "What can I do for you?"

"I'm not sure what the protocol is, doctor, but can you tell me how Susan is really doing? I know we have talked periodically over the last six weeks, but she wants to come home and I want that too, but only if she's healthy enough."

Dr. Brown could hear the anguish in Frank's voice, so he chose his words carefully. "Colonel," he started.

"Please just call me Frank."

"OK . . . Frank," he began again, "Susan is a remarkable woman, but you already know that, and she is doing a lot better than she was six weeks ago. But I will be completely honest—you need to pray that she doesn't try to leave yet, because while her physical body is getting stronger every day, the mental part of her needs more time to heal. She has to continue to deal with all of the pain that she has never been allowed to express. She also needs the tools to handle stress and sorrow without alcohol—and I just don't believe she is there yet."

Frank knew in his gut that the doctor was right, but he missed her so damn much.

"How much longer, doctor?" Frank asked dreading the answer.

"I wish I could tell you for sure, Frank, but each person heals at their own pace, and I refuse to rush anyone through something like this."

Frank slowly let out the breath that he had been holding. "Of course—I understand, and thank you for being honest with me."

"I would like you to come for a visit soon, though. I would also like you to participate in some of her therapy sessions if you would be open to that."

Part of Frank would rather walk over hot coals than have anything to do with a psychiatrist. His experience with the ones at NASA wasn't exactly positive, but he also had acknowledged to himself that he needed to deal with all the ways that he had contributed to the problems that Susan was facing.

"I think you know that I'll do anything for her," Frank finally answered.

"Yes, I believe I do," said the doctor. "She's going to be OK, Frank. I wouldn't tell you that if I didn't believe it. It will be her decision every day to heal and will take an extreme amount of courage, but I really think that she has it. She wouldn't have survived the life you have led up to this point without it. She also has an immense amount of love for you and the boys, and I know that she will do whatever it takes to get home to you."

Frank thanked the doctor again and hung up the phone. He had no idea what the next few weeks and months would bring, but he did know that their life was going to change—because it had to. Susan needed more . . . of what he didn't know yet, but he would do anything within his power to make it happen.

> *My Dearest Susan,*
>
> *I just talked to you this morning and I also just talked to the photo shop. They say that Edwin's graduation pictures are ready so I will go right away to pick them up and send them to you. Hopefully you will get them before Sunday.*
>
> *Susan—let's just take this one day at a time. I will be there to see you next Friday and from then on perhaps we can spend the weekends at West Point which is so close to where you are or take some trips to New England. You have given me support and love in some very tough times. Now it's my turn and I refuse to let you down. I know that you are worried and confused and I'm sure that's a very natural reaction. Questions like "who am I?" are tough for anyone. I've tried to answer that myself lately. The best I can figure is that I am a damn fortunate man who loves his wife and sons who gets up and tries to give a reasonable effort on a daily basis. Some days I succeed, some days I don't. But even when I don't, your love and support sustain me. You know Susan, by any reasonable standard you have succeeded over and over in some very difficult times.*
>
> *An awful lot of people love you.*
>
> *At least three need you a great deal and those same three are very proud of you.*
>
> *All my Love, Frank*

Susan was just finishing her morning walk around the grounds of the institute. It had become a daily meditative part of her new routine, and she was so grateful for the peace that she had found in this place. As difficult as it had been when she first arrived to come to terms with being there, she could see now how desperately she needed to face everything that she had pushed into the corners and crevices within her mind and heart. It seemed that as soon as she dealt with one thing, there was another in the queue that needed to be acknowledged. She closed her eyes for a moment beneath her favorite tree and started going over the session in her mind that she'd had with Dr. Brown the day before.

"Good morning, Susan," Dr. Brown had said in that quiet voice that instantly helped Susan relax as she walked into his office and sat down. "How are you feeling today?"

"I feel good," Susan said. "I have been eating and sleeping so well. . . . I didn't realize how much of a difference that would make—but it has."

Dr. Brown just nodded and gave her an encouraging smile. "You have really committed to the physical part of this program, and I can tell just by looking at you that your health is coming back more every day. But now we need to start really working through some of the things that I believe are at the root your breakdown. It wasn't just the alcohol, Susan," he said. "We need to go back to where it started—something that was extremely painful for you . . . losing your father very suddenly and being blamed for it by your mother. And until you left home, she continued to control and demean you. She was supposed to protect you, but instead she tried to make you feel like it was your fault."

Susan looked down at her clasped hands that were getting clammy. She knew that once she started to look at all that pain, it might consume her. But she had promised Frank and her boys that she would do anything she had to—so she took a deep breath and then looked up at Dr. Brown and nodded. "OK, where do I start?"

Dr. Brown looked at her thoughtfully, "Why don't you tell me how angry you are with your father for leaving you when you needed him so much? You must have felt abandoned."

The question startled her at first. She was hoping that she would never have to admit that out loud, not even to herself. It had been a part of her for so long, especially when her mother became unbearable—which was most of the time. Dr. Brown could see that she was struggling to come to terms with the anger, but he patiently waited until she was able to speak.

"How can I be angry with him?" she finally said. "He didn't choose to leave. He had a medical condition, and he died from that."

"That doesn't mean that you didn't feel abandoned, Susan," he said. "And then your mother blamed you . . . which was so very wrong of her."

Susan felt a sickening feeling in the pit of her stomach that had been lodged there since she was thirteen years old. It was always there, always churning, tormenting her with the thought that if she had just been a bit faster, she might have saved her father.

"Susan, I need you to look at me. This is very important," he said. "You are not to blame. You were only thirteen years old. Your father was a physician, so he especially knew how important it was to keep an oxygen tank available at all times with his condition. That was *his* responsibility, not yours. Never yours." Dr. Brown sat forward so that Susan could see how serious he was. "Would you hold Fred or Edwin responsible for something like that when they were thirteen?" he said without breaking eye contact.

Susan shook her head. The thought was deplorable. "No! Absolutely not—not ever," she said.

"I know that, Susan, and that is why deep down you are so angry. Your soul knows that you did everything that you could to save your father but got blamed anyway and then had to live with this massive guilt that was never yours to carry.

"Susan," he said, "I want you to close your eyes and imagine that you as an adult now can go back and talk to yourself at thirteen. What would you say to comfort her and assure her that none of that was her fault? What would you say to one of your sons at that age to relieve them of a burden that no young person should ever have to deal with or feel any guilt over?"

Susan started to shake. She had spent so many years trying to forget the horror of all of it. To willingly go back to that awful day seemed intolerable.

"I know that what I'm asking is hard, but you will never move past it unless you face it. I promise that you are safe in this room. I am here with you, and I want you to allow whatever needs to come up—no matter how terrible it feels."

Susan wanted to scream at him—he was asking too much. She felt like she was on the brink of a full-blown panic attack. But thinking of one of her boys being blamed for something that they had no control over made her so furious that she did what he asked. She closed her eyes and saw herself that day. She watched herself race to the pharmacy and beg the pharmacist to come with her to get there as fast as possible. She saw herself run through the door and see her dad on the floor—dead. She saw that sweet girl start to sob uncontrollably and then watched as her mother coldly looked up at her and said, "You're too late—you killed your father."

Susan was able to access her maternal nature and felt a flood of love and compassion for the younger version of herself. She walked up to that brokenhearted girl and pulled her into her arms, and she started to whisper to her that none of this was her fault. She wasn't to blame and did everything that she could. She told her that her father would have been proud of how hard that she tried . . . and then the adult Susan looked up and with hard eyes stared at her mother.

"How dare you," she said. "How dare you do this to your own child?"

Susan held on to her younger self, took her hand, and walked out of the house. "You're OK now . . . I've got you."

Susan slowly opened her eyes and felt like a thousand pounds had just been lifted. This weight that had been smothering her for so many years was finally gone. She felt liberated but adrift at the same time. She took a deep breath and let it out slowly. Dr. Brown could see that something powerful had just taken place.

He placed his hand on her arm. "How do you feel, Susan?"

It took a moment for her to respond. "I feel so much relief but also a loss. That shouldn't be, should it? I should be extremely glad to let this go. It doesn't make sense."

Dr. Brown nodded. "It makes perfect sense, because this has been a part of you for three decades. It's a big part of your identity, and even though it was harming you, it was familiar. You will feel a bit unmoored for a while until your mind and heart accept that you don't need it anymore. It will come back and try to get your attention, and when it does, I want you to do the same thing that we just did here. Can you do that?"

"Yes, I can," said Susan as she sat up straight in her chair. "I will protect her from now on."

21

SECOND HONEYMOON

My dearest Susan,
Sundays are tough! I wanted to jump through the telephone lines and be with you so badly last night while we were talking. But remember, I will be there next Friday and we can have a great weekend around the beautiful countryside in New England. Everyone here sends their best to you. I am so glad that I finally get to visit you!

I love you dearly, Su Su. I will call you tonight and am counting the seconds until Friday.
Your O.A.O. Frank

Dearest Frank,
Your love, loyalty and friendship (in that order) have saved a lot for us—helped me more than you know. I recognize it and adore you for it and thank you for it. I have learned the hard way that it's better "out than in" when it comes to my feelings. I have believed for so long that it was my job to keep all of that to myself. I now know how detrimental that was. Thank you for trying to understand

everything that I am struggling with. I can't wait to see
you my darling . . .
Love Susan

Frank arrived at the institute on the Friday as promised and was both excited and nervous. He missed Susan more than he thought was possible, and although he could barely wait to see her after so many weeks without actually looking at her face, he also knew that there were things that he had to be accountable for and would have to deal with.

Unbeknownst to Susan, he had been speaking to Dr. Brown regularly on the phone, not only to check on her progress but to discuss with him some of the ways that he had contributed to her illness. Frank had also committed to having sessions with Dr. Brown on his own while he was there. He was carrying a lot of guilt and knew deep down that if he didn't deal with it that it would get in the way of the two of them moving forward. He would be lying if he didn't admit that he was dreading it. But if Susan could be a fighter and do whatever was necessary, so could he.

Frank walked down the long hallway and paused outside of her room. The last time he had been in this building was one of the most difficult moments he'd ever experienced.

She would never know just how hard it had been to walk away and leave her there.

He felt like he was seventeen years old again, standing outside of her house in Tucson waiting for her to come out for their first date.

He brought her favorite flowers and was wearing the sports jacket that she liked so much. "Man up, Borman," he murmured to himself. He raised his hand and knocked quietly on her door. It opened immediately, and it took only a second to notice how much healthier and vibrant his wife looked. She launched herself into his arms, and he almost dropped the bouquet of flowers.

"Darling," she said as she kissed his cheek and nuzzled his neck, "I have missed you so much." Frank felt like crying. He held on to her tightly with his free arm and just breathed in her scent. He didn't want to let go. Not now—not ever. "I have missed you too, sweetheart," he managed to get out. "You have no idea."

She pulled back and placed her hands on either side of his face. Her eyes were bright with unshed tears as well but her smile lit up her whole body, and Frank realized that he hadn't seen that smile since they first got married. She seemed unburdened by the weight of all that she had been carrying, and had never looked more beautiful to him than she did in that moment.

He cleared his throat and handed her the bouquet of gerbera daisies that were a bit crushed, but she didn't seem to care. "My favorite," she said as she held them up and inhaled their fragrance. "Thank you, darling."

She spun around in her small room and found something to put the flowers in, added some water, and then turned back to Frank. "Would you like to go for a walk before dinner?" she asked.

"As long as I'm with you, I don't care where we go," said Frank, still feeling like this was a dream—one that he had been imagining for more than six weeks.

———

It was the perfect weekend. It seemed like they were on their second honeymoon instead of being at a hospital. They held hands everywhere they went, just like when they first started dating, and talked more than they had in years. Their conversations were raw, honest, and beautiful.

Although somewhat uncomfortable at first, Frank's sessions with Dr. Brown were revealing. He was absolutely willing to admit all the ways that he had contributed to Susan's anxiety and insecurities. He talked about the guilt that he carried, knowing that the military career he had chosen had been much harder on Susan than she let on.

If he was truly honest, he didn't want to know. He didn't want anything to get in the way of "the mission," and because she deeply understood that, she suffered in silence. Frank knew that she had always put him and the boys first, and he was just now beginning to comprehend the steep price she had paid.

"Dr. Brown, my job right now at Eastern, it requires so much time and travel. I think I should quit so that I can be there for Susan," Frank said. "I fully acknowledge how goal-driven I am and I took this challenge on to save this company, but I feel like Susan needs me more. I don't want her to ever suffer like this again." Frank looked away to try and get himself under control.

"Frank, I don't want you to do that, and I will tell you why. Susan's recovery isn't dependent on you becoming something that you are not. You need a challenge. It is how you are wired. It is who you are, and she has always known that. She never stops talking about how proud she is of you and of all that you have accomplished in your life. Now that you are aware of what she is going through and how much your decisions affect her, I am believing that you will find a balance that works for both of you. She would never ask you to walk away from a commitment—and to be honest I believe it would make her feel like a burden if you did that. You just need to talk to her more, Frank, and make her feel like she's a part of whatever your missions will be in the future. She revealed to me that she feels you omit things in regard to your work, because you don't think that she is smart enough to understand."

"What?" Frank sounded shocked. "How could she ever think that? She is one of the smartest people that I know. She has kept me from making some really bad decisions in life . . . her ability to read people is amazing. I would have been lost without her—I still would be." Frank felt sickened by the thought that his wife doubted her value to not just her family but to everyone that knew her.

Dr. Brown just nodded. "You may think she should just know that, Frank, but she needs to hear the words. You are not exactly an easy man to live up to—or to live with," the doctor said.

Frank came out of the session with Dr. Brown realizing that he needed to communicate with Susan more openly in every way, to give her more information and details about what he was doing and what he was involved in. She was his partner in life, but he needed to make her a partner in his work as well. Enough to know that there are always risks, but he would never be reckless or allow his ego to lead. She needed to know how much he relied on her, not just to make a beautiful home or be a perfect hostess—but for the emotional intelligence that she brought to every situation. Frank had always known that he had an intelligent mind and the ambition to match every challenge thrown his way. But Susan was the heart—she was *his* heart and the most important part of the equation. Without her, nothing he had accomplished in his life meant a damn thing.

> *My Dearest Susan,*
> *It was another long flight home. But tonight I have a great deal more serenity than I did the last time that I left you in Hartford. I also have a far greater appreciation for what it is that counts in life. This weekend was one of the most wonderful of my life. These past seven weeks—although difficult—have given me a new perspective and a new*

understanding of just how much you mean to me and how fortunate I have been to spend all of these years with you.

Susan, I love you and I am exceedingly proud of you. The future is ours!

All my love, Frank

My dearest Frank,

Well here we are hoping like crazy that there is a safety net below . . . somewhere! We are okay though, because we haven't spent our nine lives yet. I'm way better off than you are on that score ☺ I'm ever so proud of you so please keep on hangin' and scrappin' like you always have.

Eastern is lucky to have you and I know how challenging this has all been for both us. We have lots of years ahead and I truly believe they will be the best years for us both!

I do love you, but even like you better every day . . .

Your OAO, Su Su

Susan applied herself with even more determination to everything Dr. Brown asked her to do. With her typical fortitude, she responded very quickly to both the treatment of her alcohol addiction and to therapy. She was tireless in facing everything that she had to in order to get back to her family. Every phone call and letter that she and Frank exchanged was both wonderful and excruciating. Wonderful, because they were speaking more honestly and authentically than they had—well, ever. Excruciating, because she found herself falling even more in love with her husband all over again, and being so far apart was agonizing.

She kept herself as busy as she could and had become quite close to a young woman named Amy who had just recently arrived at the institute to be treated for alcohol addiction. Susan took her under her wing and learned that she had no family support at all. They had disowned her. Amy came from a wealthy family in New York, and they'd sent her to the institute to get rid of her because they were ashamed. They told her to get straightened out and never come back.

Susan was heartbroken for her and also could relate to having a family that would turn their back on one of their own. She vowed that she would do whatever she could to make sure that this young girl knew she wasn't alone.

Frank Borman had never done a lot of soul-searching in his life, but during the long months that Susan was in Hartford he started to look at things—and himself—through a different lens. He realized that he was using work and had always used work as a way to escape the things that he didn't want to dwell on. When he finally stopped to do some self-analysis, he was consistently overcome with both guilt and grief.

He started remembering all the things he did that may have seemed small at the time but knew deep down had hurt his wife. All the times that he chose work over time spent with his family. Chose to put the mission before everything else. Making her allow a camera into their home during the Apollo 8 mission when she begged him not to. And more recently—the weekend that he had taken her on a business trip to Singapore just before she had her breakdown. When she contracted the flu on the trip, he accompanied Eastern's clients to China and left his extremely sick wife in a hotel room by herself in a strange country. It was just a few memories of so many things that had contributed to her finally shattering.

But through all of it, Susan gave her support and loyalty. He was finally understanding that he took it for granted and never stopped long enough to really look at anything from her perspective. He discussed this with Dr. Brown at the last session that they had.

"That's why I feel responsible," Frank said hoarsely. "I've always put my job and my goals first, and I just don't know what to do with all of this guilt." He looked down at his hands and tried to get himself together before continuing. "I'm still the same guy that I was in the air force and NASA. I even work weekends at Eastern trying to learn the business as quickly as possible. I have left Susan alone so much—even after I made her move to Miami and leave our youngest son, Edwin, behind."

Frank paused. "It's the conflict I have struggled with my whole married life. . . . I took a picture of Susan with me on both Gemini 7 and the Apollo 8 flights and refused to look at it because I didn't want to be distracted."

"How would that be a distraction, Frank?" Dr. Brown asked.

Frank didn't seem to hear the question. "Did I make her feel that way, like a distraction?" he implored. "Did I make her feel like she did as a girl growing up in a house with a mother that made her feel unwanted?"

Frank couldn't breathe. He was full of one agonizing thought after another. *How could he have done that?* He felt desperate to do something immediately to fix it. "I've put too much pressure on her—ignored her. I'll quit Eastern and do whatever it takes to make her well," he burst out.

"Frank, quitting your job is not going to help Susan. Working to accomplish a goal is who you are and how you are wired. We have already discussed this," Dr. Brown said. "You have just pushed her too hard for a long time, but she is going to be all right. From now on, the demands that you make of her need to be explained and the time away because of work has to be justified. You need to communicate why you are doing what you are doing—and she is starting to stand up for herself when she needs to. She is learning to give herself the same consideration that she has always given you."

Dr. Brown stopped for a moment to let Frank process. "Frank, she needs the support that she has always given you. Can you do that?"

Frank couldn't speak, so he just nodded.

"Frank, I am going to ask you one more thing today. More than once in our sessions you have brought up this conflict between the importance of a mission and your commitment to your family. Have you been asking yourself in the last few weeks if the missions were worth it?"

Frank looked at him gravely and nodded. "Countless times."

"What was the answer?"

Frank didn't hesitate. "They were. They were all worth it." His eyes were tortured as he said it.

Dr. Brown nodded. "Do you think Susan thought that they were worth it as well?"

Frank looked down and didn't answer for a while. It was the question that he had been afraid to ask himself, but now that he was confronted with it, he allowed himself to sift through all the years that they spent in the military and at NASA. The friends that they had made along the way and all the experiences that they had—both together and separately. Frank knew that their faith in God taught them everything happens for a reason, and that Susan felt the same way. Almost immediately he felt a weight lift off of him. He finally looked up.

"Yes," he said. "Yes, I know she did, and I don't believe that she would change anything about our life, either."

"I was hoping that you would come to that conclusion," Dr. Brown said. "So now I'm going to suggest that you stop feeling so guilty about it and start figuring out how to make Susan feel more a part of your next mission—whatever that is going to be."

Frank was silent for a few more moments. "I can do that," he finally said with the same determination that got him to the Moon. "I'll do anything to make sure that she never feels ignored or overlooked again."

When he got back home to Miami, Frank threw himself back into solving the problems at Eastern but returned to Hartford every weekend to spend time with Susan. They would go for long walks on the grounds and make plans—talking and *communicating*—like they never had before.

In a way, it was a renewal of their wedding vows, and unbeknownst to Susan, Frank made a few extra vows of his own. He would always work hard, but vowed never to let Susan feel like her thoughts and opinions didn't matter. He would make time and communication with her a priority. Listening was a skill that he hadn't put much value in until now.

After returning from the institute the following weekend, Frank was invited to give a speech at the annual convention of military flight surgeons. It was composed of doctors from every branch of military service. Frank warned the convention representative that he had a lot to say and wouldn't be pulling any punches.

When he got up to the podium to deliver his speech, he took a moment to look at everyone in the room. He didn't have notes—he didn't need any.

"I want to tell you something," he began. "This isn't just about my wife and family, but it goes for every military wife and child whose feelings and issues have been ignored since the military began. The whole country has ignored them for too damn long. We have so much to say about the sacrifices that military men make, but how about their families? Why do they always get overlooked? What have you doctors done to find out about the lonely and scared wives of test pilots or SAC [Strategic Air Command] crews? What have you done for astronauts' wives or the wives of submariners who are alone for months at a time wondering if they will ever hear from their husbands again? I'll tell you what you have done—absolutely nothing. They need support, counseling, and help. They need to know that they are not alone. We are good at training our military personnel to do their jobs, but we don't help any of the extended families with the stresses of being married to the military. We don't do anything to help them cope."

When he was finished, Frank realized that he probably didn't do much more than make the room full of flight surgeons think a little. He hoped that they would start to see something beyond just treating the trained men in the military at that time. He was speaking on behalf of Susan and every other woman and child that had suffered because their husband or father did a job that was considered more important than they were.

He knew—especially in light of Susan's illness—that there were way too many assumptions made about how the families of military officers handled their lives. These were dangerous assumptions. Often military marriages did not have a happy ending. Frank knew that he was one of the lucky ones. Not only did his marriage survive what Susan was going through, but it was becoming stronger every time they really talked to each other. It was something they both learned was absolutely necessary moving forward. In a way, her breakdown was the very thing that brought them closer together and reminded them both of how much they loved each other and were committed not only to their marriage but to their family.

It would end up being a huge blessing, instead of an event that Susan would forever be ashamed of. Every person needs a safe place to really look at the pain that gets accumulated over the course of a lifetime, and that was what the Institute of Living was for her. Susan found the courage to face everything head-on, which may be one of the most difficult things a human being will ever do. As much as Frank had always been proud to be married to this amazing woman, he had never been more humbled or impressed as he was witnessing the bravery that she had dealing with one painful thing after another.

My Dearest Frank,

I found this poem on a card that someone left behind here, and it says everything that I want to say to you. I can't believe that I have been in Hartford almost four months. I have one more week and then I will get to come home to you, darling. I can't put into words what this time here has meant to me, and how much I needed it. I wish I could find words that are sacred and special to be used in only the most important circumstances. I am not that eloquent, so I am sending you this poem instead. I cannot wait to see you, my love . . .

"Your friendship and love, and all of the wonderful things that they bring to my life, are like nothing else that I have ever known. Our love grows more beautiful with each passing day. Moments of success may come and go, and material things bring us momentary joy. But you are with me always . . . in a smile, a touch, a memory, or a moment we share. People enter our lives, some only for a short time, but what we share is deep and secure. Even if everyone else abandoned me, I know that I would still have you. We pass through different phases of life with all of its problems and challenges, and one day turns into another. Through it all, our love is constant. You lend me strength when I need it most, and give me a precious gift each day by loving me just the way I am. I don't know

how you keep doing it, but in your own special way you fill my life and heart with joy that is always present. You make my life complete, and I will always love you."

—Linda Sackett-Morrison

Always now and forever my precious love and best friend, Su Su

When Susan left the institute, she had been there just over four months, and as she walked through the doors into Frank's arms, she had a deep compassion for herself and anyone else who had walked a similar road. She informed Frank that she would be taking her friend Amy under her wing. She would make sure that Amy knew she wasn't alone and that she had someone to turn to.

Susan helped Amy find an apartment as soon as they got back to Miami and also helped her find a job. She kept checking on her weekly so that she would be able to navigate her sobriety in the world outside of the institute. It was the beginning of Susan Borman's new mission—to help anyone dealing with addiction who needed to be understood instead of condemned. Frank Borman wasn't the only warrior in the family.

Frank had no idea how much he would need Susan at her best for the next challenge in his life. Not long after she got home, he was promoted to president of Eastern Airlines, and they were about to be in for a lot of turbulence.

22

THE NEXT MISSION

EASTERN AIRLINES HAD BEEN BLEEDING MONEY SINCE way before Frank had come on board. He didn't realize to what extent until he became president in May 1975. By that time, he was not only accepted but actually quite beloved by many of Eastern's employees, partly because of the crash of Flight 401 and how it had affected the company as a whole.

No job was beneath Frank, and he could be found doing everything from unloading baggage to checking engine parts on the tarmac. He didn't believe that he was better than anyone else who worked for him, and even though his salary had definitely improved since he was in the military, he still drove his old worn-out Chevy to work every day. He was completely hands-on and never hesitated to help in any way that was needed.

One of the first things that Frank did when he became president was to implement a rehabilitation and counseling program for employees with alcohol and drug problems. He was so committed to offering something that would be beneficial and actually work that it became known as one of the best programs in the industry of drug and alcohol rehab. He asked Susan to weigh in on everything. She was delighted to be able to contribute.

It was his way of showing Susan how proud he was of what she conquered, and instead of sweeping it under the rug, he bragged to anyone that would listen about her recovery. He talked about how much he admired her transparency and authenticity. Only he knew how hard she had fought, and there was absolutely no way that he would ever allow her to feel anything but self-respect in what she went through and overcame.

She wasn't afraid anymore, but if any of the old fears were triggered, Frank knew what to say: "How can I help you with this? Let's talk about it. I don't want you to ignore how you feel about something ever again. I want you to always know that you can talk to me about anything."

Frank had to start dealing with the failing company he was now in charge of by taking on the responsibility of leaning it out. That is when he created the variable earnings plan, or VEP. It was as much a philosophy as a financial experiment. Frank knew that his biggest challenge was to get the exorbitant labor costs down, so he created a new profit-sharing plan to offset the wage freeze that had to be enforced within Eastern.

The difference with the VEP was that the employees would not only share in the profits but would also share in the losses the company incurred. This was a family that he was fighting to keep together.

Each employee received 96.5 percent of his or her base pay, and Eastern held back 3.5 percent. Management had to contribute 5 percent of their wages, and Frank contributed 7 percent of his. If profits failed to meet the company's projected earnings, the funds that were withheld would go toward bringing them back up. If they met their projected revenues or exceeded them, the employees would get the withheld funds back, plus a bonus. It was a great deal for both the company and the employees. They realized that they had as much to lose or gain as Eastern did as a whole, and it was reflected in their job performance.

Eastern's board trusted Frank and stood by his decisions. He had proven himself countless times and was known to the board as an unpretentious man who didn't expect the perks that usually came with being the president of a major corporation.

But he also got accused of hiring "token" numbers of minorities, a charge that disgusted him. The message that he was trying to send and that he stood by was: "We want *anyone* that can do the job well, and it doesn't matter if the person is male, female, White, Black, or any other skin color. As long as they do a good job and take pride in their work, Eastern wants them."

He approached these problems and accusations like everything else that he experienced in his life in the military: "If you don't like what I am doing . . . then get the hell out of my way because it needs to be done."

Meanwhile, behind the scenes, Susan was launching her own campaign to help her husband. It was more honey, less vinegar. She organized and was the chairwoman of a ball for the Public Broadcasting Service in Miami to start connecting with the "who's who" in the area.

She also insisted on getting involved with employee relations at Eastern. "Frank, I want to start building a relationship with the wives of Eastern employees. They hold the purse strings at home and influence their husbands. Help me figure out a way to connect with them."

Frank thought it was a great idea but told her that the company couldn't pay for fancy cocktail parties or luncheons. Susan brilliantly came up with a "dutch treat" concept where the wives would pay for half the cost of lunch at a hotel, and they would use one of the boardrooms to meet in. It was an inexpensive and informal way to get to know these women and let them know what

Eastern was trying to do for the company as a whole. She became Frank's and Eastern's best ambassador, and the women naturally responded to her charisma and honesty. She spoke to them as a wife and mother and was able to get them to open up about their concerns. She would always end each luncheon the same way.

"Thank you for coming and talking to me. Through me, I want you to get to know Frank and what he is trying to accomplish at the airline."

The luncheons were a hit. Even when the unions started causing problems for Eastern and tried to make the husbands tell their wives to boycott them, and union officials themselves told their own wives they couldn't go to "Susan Borman's luncheon," the women went anyway. They trusted and confided in her, and she started hearing more and more about their personal lives.

One woman from the Eastern office in St. Louis told Susan that her husband was dying of terminal cancer and that it would mean a lot to him to hear from the top boss. Susan called Frank immediately and told him to do something for this man. Frank called him directly and let him know that he was not to worry about any medical bills—Eastern would take care of them and his family.

On Christmas Day Susan would organize and arrange for both her and Frank to leave their family for a couple of hours and go to the system control center at Eastern to bring lunch to everyone who had to remain on duty for the holiday. She also worked with a designer to decorate all the Eastern lounges for the holidays.

She was a big hit, and everyone adored her. She would pay close attention to anything that employees told her and then relay it to Frank when it was important.

"Frank, I need to tell you something, and I need you to fix it," she said on a call one day from Cleveland, where she was having a meeting with the Eastern wives. "You have people here that are madder than hell at you because their husbands' winter company jackets haven't arrived, and it is freezing here." Frank had no idea, and thanks to Susan the jackets were on a flight from Miami that day. Even the men who worked at Eastern across the country realized that the fastest way to get to Frank was through Susan.

Frank was ridiculed for this grassroots approach to reaching his employees, and the unions went out of their way to mock it and call it company propaganda. But when Ambassador Susan started rolling, all the doubts and criticism stopped, because it was working. It kept Frank in touch with the people on the ground who were doing most of the work.

Susan entertained Lawrence and Mary Rockefeller—major stockholders in Eastern—in their Miami home. She was the consummate hostess and never worried about people's status or the size of their bank account. The Bormans also entertained the heads of the unions that were causing problems for the airline and anyone one else that Frank was trying to bring on board to help save the company.

Susan was well versed in all the issues between the unions and what Eastern was trying to accomplish. Frank knew how much could be worked through and resolved at these innocuous dinners as opposed to countless meetings in a boardroom. He had a partner—and he needed her more than he ever had.

Susan started taking trips to visit her father's grave in New Jersey. He had wanted to be buried where he was born and grew up, and even though he died in Arizona, that wasn't home. She would jump on an Eastern flight from Miami periodically to go to the cemetery. The bond that they had was something that she would never forget, and she would always honor the place that he had in her life. Standing in front of her father's tombstone by herself with a bouquet of flowers, she told him again how much that she missed him.

"Daddy, thank you for being the only person in my young life that showed me what love was. I wish that you could know Frank and my amazing boys—you would be so proud. I know that I am . . ."

Between 1976 and 1980 Eastern enjoyed the most lucrative four-year period since it became an airline. These were the most peaceful years in Eastern's history and the culmination of everything Frank and Susan worked so hard for.

Because of the airline's unexpected success, Frank started getting approached to run for the US Senate, which he was always quick to discourage. When a reporter asked him if he would ever be interested in running for political office, he replied in the same way that he did every time the subject was brought up: "The answer is a firm no," he said. "And that comes from Susan Borman as well."

He was first approached to leave Eastern at the annual dinner of the Alfalfa Club in 1977. Frank was the president of the club that year. A few hours before the dinner was to begin, Frank got a phone call from the White House while in his hotel room. "President Carter wants to see you," the White House operator told him.

Frank was somewhat perplexed but made his way over to 1600 Pennsylvania Avenue—a place that was once quite familiar but hadn't been for about seven years. He was taken immediately to the Oval Office, where President Jimmy Carter and his top aide were waiting for him.

After the greetings were dispensed, the president wasted no time and got to the point. "Colonel Borman, we would like you to come and work for us. We think that you would make an excellent addition to this administration."

"What did you have in mind, sir?" Frank asked, trying not to sound shocked.

"It would be a cabinet-level position, but I can't tell you which one unless you agree to take the job."

Frank immediately thought back to working with Nixon, someone he not only respected but considered a friend. He remembered all the disillusionment, the sense of betrayal, and as politely as possible declined. "I'm completely committed to Eastern Airlines at the moment, Mr. President. We are working very hard to rebuild the airline, and I can't leave them right now."

President Carter implored Frank to reconsider, but Frank hadn't yet finished what he wanted to at Eastern and refused. As he walked out of the Oval Office, he shook his head and thought, *I just turned down the president of the United States.*

Three years later, Frank was approached by the newly elected president, just before Ronald Reagan's inauguration, to consider being the secretary of defense. He refused yet again. The airline was struggling once more, and Frank was trying to keep the company from going bankrupt.

He bowed out as gracefully as he could: "Thank you for the opportunity, but I can't leave right now—I'm guessing that the last thing a new president would want is to see a major US airline fail."

———

Susan and Frank were on a flight one weekend from New York back home to Miami when a flight attendant came up to them and tapped Frank on the shoulder looking very troubled. "Mr. Borman, can you please come to the cockpit with me?" she asked.

Frank's instincts sharpened immediately. "Is anything wrong?"

"Yes," she whispered. "But I would rather speak to you privately about it." She kept looking over her shoulder to the rear of the plane.

Frank turned to Susan and squeezed her hand. "I'll be right back."

As soon as they wedged themselves into the tiny cockpit, the flight attendant started speaking in haste. "We have what I believe is a crazy man in the rear section of the plane, Mr. Borman, and he knows who you and Mrs. Borman are. He's demanding to talk to you, but I really feel that you shouldn't. I think that he is dangerous."

Frank went into military mode. "I will go and talk to him."

"Please don't, sir. I think he means you harm."

Frank opened the door to the cockpit and watched in horror as the man in question came down the aisle and took his seat beside his wife. Another flight attendant came over immediately to help, and Susan waved them off. She glanced up at Frank with a look that said, "I've got this."

She proceeded to listen to the disturbed man ramble on about how he had been screwed over by Eastern and how unhappy he was. His intention was to set off a bomb when they landed so that no one would ever ignore him again. Susan was very calm and patient, and once he was done talking, she looked at him and said, "I understand what you are trying to tell me. If you will just go quietly back to your seat, I will have a news crew meet us when we land, and you can have a press conference about everything you just told me."

The man looked shocked and calmed down immediately. He mumbled a thank-you and docilely returned to his seat.

Frank had already alerted the police, and they were waiting at the airport in Miami when the plane landed. They escorted the man away and he went willingly but looked back at Susan with something close to gratitude. Susan understood that most people just need someone to listen to them and by doing that, she prevented what could have been a horrible tragedy. Frank looked at her as the man was being taken away and thought, *Quite a gal, my wife.*

In the early 1980s, Miami became known as the cocaine capital of America and was experiencing a literal drug war. The city was one of the principal points of entry for cocaine from Bolivia, Colombia, and Peru. With the drugs came a flood of illegal money and criminal activity, and higher murder rates than any other city in the world. So many bodies filled the morgue that it ran out of places to store them. This notoriety is what inspired the television series *Miami Vice.*

Susan was more than inspired to get involved with addressing the drug problems in Miami. She was especially concerned with how it was affecting young people. She started meeting with other women—mostly mothers—who were as concerned as she was, and they formed a group called Informed Families.

They wanted to target the youth of Miami, to help them understand just how detrimental drug use would be to their future. Susan not only became the chief fundraiser but also their main spokesperson. She arranged a meeting in Washington, DC, to speak with Vice President George H. W. Bush and First Lady Nancy Reagan in an effort to get their support to highlight the overwhelming problems that Miami was experiencing with the drug trade. Bush told Susan that he would increase the US Coast Guard's presence in Miami to try and discourage drugs coming in via water vessels.

Unfortunately, the First Lady's response was to come up with her own campaign to discourage drug use, which was ineffective to say the least. She turned a serious social problem into a contest, asking university students across the country to come up with a slogan. The winner was the simplistic motto "Just Say No."

This and Nancy Reagan's related efforts, like Drug Abuse Resistance Education (DARE), drew a lot of criticism, which Susan firmly believed they deserved. Susan was extremely disappointed that Nancy Reagan didn't seem to understand the problem at all, nor did she really try to. Instead of listening to her—a woman who had gone through hell to overcome her own addiction—the First Lady chose to use a platform that was neither helpful nor compassionate in any way. But Susan refused to quit and continued to campaign for Informed Families for the duration of the time that she and Frank were in Miami.

Frank got Eastern Airlines back in the black again and morale was high, but there were dark clouds on the horizon. The storm of airline deregulation was coming, when government legislation and laws in a particular market removed barriers to competition. Frank was working like a madman to prepare for it because when it came, Eastern would be the most vulnerable.

As a result of the company's prohibitive labor costs and debt, if and when deregulation happened, it would be something it might not recover from. Unfortunately, no one else at Eastern thought it would actually happen, so Frank was put in the category of "Chicken Little" and got scarcely any support.

Frank started doing whatever he could to cut costs. He ordered that lights be turned off in buildings when no one was in them, shut off the water to the Memorial Fountain outside its headquarters at the end of every day—anything to save money.

But the biggest challenges of all came in dealing with the unions and their labor agreements. They absolutely refused to budge on any contract that they had won, even if it hurt the entire company, which meant hurting the employees that they were supposed to represent.

When the airline industry was finally forced into deregulation, it happened almost overnight. If it had happened gradually, it would have benefited the industry as a whole, but because it didn't, it spelled disaster.

Frank believed Eastern could have actually survived the deregulation process but not the union's demands to keep the labor costs exorbitant in what was now a free market. Frank tried four different times to merge with another airline to save the company and to save everyone's jobs—to no avail.

He didn't realize that he had an enemy within, until Susan warned him about Charlie Bryan. He was the head of the International Association of Machinists and Aerospace Workers Union—IAM—which was one of Eastern's biggest unions.

Frank and Susan were at IAM's annual dinner in Las Vegas, and Susan was seated next to Bryan. He wouldn't stop pestering Susan about Apollo 8, and at first Susan thought he was just interested in the mission. She listened to him go on and finally had to stop him by saying, "Charlie, Apollo 8 is just a part of history. It's in the past. Frank is at Eastern now, and that is his purpose. NASA is a closed chapter in our lives."

He wouldn't stop asking about the Apollo mission until Susan shook her head and told him bluntly, "Charlie, I really would prefer to talk about something else."

He grinned slightly and looked at her. "Frank Borman had his moment of glory with Apollo 8. Now it's my turn—I'm going to have mine." Susan was chilled not only by his tone but by the dark determination that she saw in his eyes.

When they returned to their hotel room that night, Frank asked her how she got along with Charlie Bryan. She repeated what he had said to her. "Frank," she said gravely, "you are going to have a serious problem with this man."

Frank laughed it off as he pulled off his tie. "Susan, I think you're reading into this. He always seems like a nice enough guy every time I talk to him."

"You're wrong, Frank. He's obsessed with your fame and he wants to be known to the world like you are. He doesn't give a damn about Eastern or what is best for the people there."

As usual, Susan was right. Frank was going to learn the hard way that Charlie Bryan cared more about internal politics than the real economic issues; playing at politics is what kept the union IAM in power.

In one of the first conversations that Frank had with him after the dinner in Vegas, Charlie was just about to walk away and then turned back to Frank and said offhandedly, "You know, I feel I have a special calling with my union. When I appear at the meetings and explain the issues to my people, they all look to me for salvation. I feel like Jesus and they're reaching out to touch me."

Frank was resolute in trying to build some kind of working relationship with Charlie and invited him to their vacation home in Key Largo. Even though Susan had serious misgivings about him, she was gracious and welcoming. Frank tried to impress upon him the importance of working together for the good of the company as a whole. Charlie seemed to agree and always presented himself as a reasonable man, but Susan saw right through it—she knew that he had his own agenda, and no one was going to get in the way of it.

Frank had other massive problems to deal with besides the unions. He procured the routes to South America, which were helping bring money into Eastern, but they were also responsible for smuggling a lot of drugs into Miami. He sent drug-sniffing dogs to the airport in Bogotá, Colombia, to smell bags and passengers, and within one week all the dogs had been poisoned and killed. No matter what precautions were taken, the drugs kept coming in.

Frank finally had to acknowledge the fact that there were Eastern employees involved and on the take. Between 1981 and 1985, an Eastern Airlines employee smuggling ring brought in between 5,400 and 16,200 pounds of cocaine with a street value of $250,000 a pound.

Frank asked Charlie Bryan and his IAM union to help with the investigation, and their response was "It's your problem. We won't help you solve it."

In the end the DEA and the FBI arrested over fifty people—all employees at Miami International Airport. Twenty-two Eastern baggage handlers and low-level supervisors were indicted, and another fifty who weren't indictable were fired.

In 1983 things got progressively worse. Eastern was bleeding money, and Charlie was demanding a 30 percent pay hike for IAM union members. No matter who showed him the books with proof that Eastern could not afford that, he wouldn't listen.

He was also a darling of the press who seemed reasonable when interviewed and came off like he was a team player. It was almost impossible for Eastern to refute his comments, and no matter what Frank or anyone at Eastern said, it was put in the category of "company propaganda."

In order to push the wage hike, Charlie Bryan set a strike date for March 13 of that year. As the deadline approached, Frank got a call from a valued Eastern passenger that had used the airline so often he was known by his first name, Mike, to everyone at Miami headquarters. He was quite charming and the flight attendants would argue over who would take care of him on a flight. It also might have had something to do with the fact that the wealthy man kept tipping everyone, even though Frank had asked him repeatedly to stop—tipping Eastern employees was against regulations. Mike didn't care. Regardless, Frank enjoyed talking to this enigmatic man who went out of his way to get to know him.

One day as Frank was finishing up some paperwork in his office, his secretary came in and told him he had an urgent phone call.

"Frank, it's Mike," the voice on the phone said without any preamble. Mike was normally gregarious and constantly cracking jokes, but now he was serious. "There has been a death threat made against you, and my intel is that someone attached to the unions has taken out a contract on your life. I want to send you a couple of my guys to protect you for a while. You can trust them."

Frank was completely shocked and took a moment before answering. "Mike, I have no idea how you know this, but I'm pretty sure that this is just an intimidation tactic by the unions."

"That may be, Colonel, but you need to take it very seriously, and that means you need to have a protection detail. You should put one on your wife as well."

That got Frank's attention. "Is my wife in danger?"

"I wouldn't take any chances," Mike answered. "You need to trust me on this—it's a real threat."

Frank realized in frustration that he shouldn't ignore it, and the thought of Susan being in any danger made his blood run cold. "Thank you," Frank said. "Can I phone you back? I need to take care of a couple of things."

"Of course," Mike said. "But I am sending my son over anyway to look after your security."

Frank had just hung up the phone when his secretary burst in looking frazzled. "Frank, your wife is on the other line and she is frantic. She just got a phone call telling her that you have been kidnapped and are being held for ransom."

Frank picked up the phone immediately. "Susan, honey, it's OK, I'm OK." All he heard was a woman trying to get herself together on the other end. He went from worried to furious in seconds. *Those bastards.* It was one thing to come after him, but to terrorize his wife was totally unacceptable.

"Frank," Susan said. "They said that they had you. I didn't know if you had been hurt . . ." She couldn't finish. She was taking deep breaths trying to get herself under control.

Frank attempted to sound calm even though he was seething. "Susan, I need to call the FBI and get to the bottom of this. I don't think that this is anything but the unions trying to intimidate us, and they know that using you is the best way to get to me. We aren't going to give them the satisfaction, are we?"

Frank waited for Susan to reply. "No, Frank. There is no damn way that they will get anything from us," she said.

"I love you. Everything is going to be OK," he said.

"I love you, too," she said. "Be careful."

Frank hung up and called the FBI and demanded to talk to someone high up.

"This is Colonel Frank Borman. I am the president of Eastern Airlines and I was told by one of our best clients that there has been a contract taken out on me. Those sons of bitches just contacted my wife," he said with barely controlled fury. "They can come at me all day long, but she is off limits."

The agent told Frank that the threat was real and that they knew who warned him. Mike's wife was from the Genovese family, some of whom were part of the biggest mob organization in the United States. If Mike and his wife had heard that the Bormans were in trouble, they were, and needed protection.

For the next few weeks, Frank had to wear a bulletproof vest and carry a gun everywhere he went, day or night, and he had Mike's son as his personal security detail with him around the clock.

Susan was guarded by a deputy sheriff as well. Whether she was taking a trip to the grocery store or watching her grandchildren, she needed protection. As a precaution, a security detail was also assigned to Frank's son Fred, who now lived in Miami with his wife, Donna, and their children. It was like something out of an over-the-top gangster movie, except that it was real.

Two Eastern employees that spoke out against IAM were targeted, too. One had his home shot up with bullets; the other lost most of his hand after being fired at. Some of the Eastern planes were being tampered with, but there was never enough proof to charge anyone. Frank believed Charlie Bryan was sending a message: he would use whatever means necessary to win. And if his union won, the whole company would lose. The strike would mean almost certain death for Eastern Airlines.

Frank tried everything humanly possible to save Eastern as a last-ditch effort. He took multiple pay cuts. He begged and pleaded with anyone who would listen. He didn't want to fail the people that he had been working with for over a decade.

Over ten thousand pilots and flight attendants as well eighteen thousand nonunion employees signed a petition to cross the picket lines when the strike happened. They knew that IAM was going to take the whole company down. Travel agents called and offered to work for free. Everyone but the union was behind Frank and what he was trying to do, and they wanted to fight beside him. In the end it didn't matter. He had to give in to the union's demands and knew that it would destroy everything he had worked so hard for.

The same tenacity that got Frank in the air after being told he would never fly, and then on to being the commander of the most important mission to the Moon, helped him hang on at Eastern for three more years. He did it for the forty thousand employees who had become his extended family.

On February 23, 1986, for the last time, Frank made the same drive that he had made for nearly sixteen years, from his home in Coral Gables to Miami International. Charlie Bryan had done all the damage he could, and Frank and the board of directors were running out of options.

Frank stood in the lobby of Building 16, reminiscing before the board of directors arrived. He was lost in thought when he heard someone behind him.

Charlie had sent his lawyer, who was dressed in alligator shoes and red suspenders, to approach Frank: "My client wants you to quit. If you quit, he will back off."

Frank stared at him, appalled. "I already said that I would resign if that will help the company!"

The lawyer looked back at him with a mixture of pity and contempt. "He wants to humiliate you. That's all he cares about."

Frank shook his head but didn't respond. He then turned around and walked away.

Just a few hours later, Colonel Frank Borman—president and caretaker of Eastern Airlines—had to stand up in an auditorium and tell all those familiar faces that the company had been sold and he was no longer in charge. He barely got through his speech, then made a quick exit out a side door.

Frank drove home in a fog of bitterness and frustration. For the first time in his life he had failed to complete the mission. He tried to tell Susan what had happened but couldn't do it.

She had been pacing around the house most of the day, waiting for him to return, knowing what this meant to him. Knowing how heartbroken he was. She held him for a moment, then led him over to the couch.

Frank couldn't seem to get any words out and just looked at her with tortured eyes—the tough-as-nails air force pilot and NASA astronaut who helped save the lunar program and commanded the first mission to the Moon, the man who had been sought out by world leaders on multiple diplomatic missions overseas, the man who had been offered high-ranking cabinet-level jobs by three presidents and had addressed Congress on more than one occasion . . .

This man now put his head on his wife's lap, and wept.

EPILOGUE

It was July 1986, and Frank and Susan were about to celebrate their thirty-sixth wedding anniversary. Miami didn't feel
like home anymore—there were too many bad memories.

They had taken a trip to Tucson just a few months prior, with
the idea of moving back. It was where they had both been raised,
met, and fell in love, and seemed like the place to come back to.
But when they got there, it wasn't anything like they remembered.
Tucson had grown into a bustling, metropolitan city and didn't
feel at all like the quiet area where they imagined retiring.

The one thing Frank and Susan made sure to do before leaving
their hometown was to go back to the restaurant where they dined
on the night they got engaged. It had been closed for years, but
they walked around the now run-down property, holding hands
and marveling at how quickly time had flown by.

They were both lost in thought when an older man approached
them demanding to know what the hell they were doing there.

Frank told him right away why they had come, and the caretaker changed his tune immediately. He was touched that they
came back to the place where their love story began again. He
asked them if they wanted a tour, and Frank and Susan gave him
an enthusiastic "Yes!" He took them through and around the
dilapidated building while regaling them with the tale of how
the restaurant had been secretly owned by mobsters from Detroit

who bought the place as a hideout when things got too hot at home. The college kids from Tucson in 1950 thought it was just an out-of-the-way restaurant to drive to and be alone with their dates, but it was really a getaway for criminals. Another reminder of how things are never what they appear on the surface.

Not exactly romantic but such a great story. Frank and Susan left laughing. Their trip down memory lane had taken an unexpected turn. They left Tucson with no idea where they would end up moving but knew that they needed to get out of Florida.

Their son Fred, his wife Donna, and their two children had been living in Miami as well, after a spinal injury had forced Fred to leave the army. They managed a car dealership there but ended up leaving because Miami just wasn't the place where Fred and Donna Borman wanted to raise their family. They ended up relocating to a charming little city in New Mexico called Las Cruces and bought a Honda dealership.

Frank remembered flying a T-38 between Houston and California while he was with NASA, and looking down as he flew over Las Cruces, he had thought, *That would be a great place to live one day.*

It ended up being a premonition. After visiting their son, Frank and Susan realized that this beautiful area was a mirror image of the Tucson that they remembered from their youth. They packed everything up as soon as they got back to Miami, sold their condo, and moved to Las Cruces.

The Bormans were just getting settled in New Mexico when Susan found a lump in her breast. They went to the doctor in Las Cruces right away, and the doctor there agreed that the lump needed to be removed as soon as possible. He strongly suggested that Frank take Susan to a specialist in Houston to get a second opinion. The specialist in Houston confirmed that the lump was cancerous and was very concerned that the cancer would show up in the other breast. His recommendation was a double mastectomy.

Susan looked at the doctor and nodded. "All right, Doctor," she said. "Let's get on with it."

Frank and Susan still kept in close touch with their friends in Houston—the Elkins—and stayed with them after the surgery. Susan never complained or gave an indication of fear while going through the procedure and recovery process. In fact, even years later, no one had any idea that she ever had breast cancer until one of her girlfriends got it and Susan became an invaluable source of support.

Once Susan recovered from the surgery and they finally arrived back home in Las Cruces, she stopped and grabbed Frank's arm as they were about to walk through the door. "Let's live, Frank," she said. "I'm here, you're here. We have survived so much. Let's just live now."

Frank turned and squeezed her hand and couldn't answer right away. How was he the hero? This woman would always be his.

Susan's new lease on life inspired her to do something that she had always wanted to do. She bought an old adobe building on a plaza in the small town of Mesilla, a suburb of Las Cruces, and opened a gift and decor shop. She took on a very talented interior decorator as a partner. She would travel to Juárez to buy Mexican art and anything else that suited the store. It was such a success that she had to hire another employee, because not only was she the owner-operator of what was turning into a very popular tourist destination, she was also designing her and Frank's dream home.

Susan had looked at a few pieces of property but fell in love with ten acres in the desert foothills overlooking the Rio Grande Valley. When she took Frank out to show him, she was beside herself. This was home.

"Frank, can you feel it?" she said, barely containing her excitement. "This is where we are supposed to live."

Frank just smiled. It was her time now. She had stood by him through so many things. Hard things. "Su Su," he said, "if this is where you want to live, I'm in. Home is where you are, so this works for me."

Frank was keeping himself occupied with a business restoring vintage warplanes, called Picacho Aviation, that he'd started with a fellow ex–air force buddy. He was also on multiple corporate boards across the country. He would get asked to do air shows in his beloved P-51 Mustang airplane, and Susan insisted on coming with him. It was originally designed as a single-seat fighter plane, but Frank modified it so that his favorite copilot could fly with him.

The Bormans went everywhere in that plane. From Maine to San Diego, Florida to Alaska. He mentioned one day to her that if they ever had an emergency and needed to jump from the plane, he hoped that she would be able to handle a parachute.

Which is how seventy-year-old Susan Borman ended up at a skydiving lesson that she booked herself and proceeded to jump out of a perfectly good airplane to prove that she could handle whatever else life would throw at her. She wanted to do it again, but Frank convinced her that once was enough.

Frank and Susan were at an air show in Nebraska for their fiftieth wedding anniversary and celebrated that remarkable milestone at a simple buffalo barbecue in North Platte. All that either of them cared about was being together.

Susan designed their dream house in the Rio Grande Valley, and Frank helped build it. It was a spectacular home that combined the Southwest look that she had loved since childhood and the New Mexico flavor that reflected her store and her collection of indigenous art. It was one of the best periods of their lives.

They took a trip to Europe right after their fiftieth anniversary with nothing but a couple of pairs of Levi's in backpacks and two rail passes. Frank was able to show Susan all the places that he went to as a cadet in 1949.

—————————

As good as things were for the Bormans, between building the house and running the store, something was making itself known. Susan started struggling more and more with deep depression and anxiety attacks, which were becoming more difficult to hide. It was a precursor to what was later to come.

One day while at home, Frank and Susan got a phone call from their sons. They were hunting in Montana and thought that it would be a perfect spot for investing in some land to build a family vacation home. Susan and Frank jumped into the P-51 and flew north to check things out. They got a Realtor almost immediately and ended up buying a ranch an hour northeast of Billings.

Susan sold her gift shop in New Mexico, which broke her heart, but it had become too much to manage. They ended up building two homes on the forty-thousand-acre Montana ranch that Susan designed and decorated as well.

The larger house was big and open in bright, cheery colors for their kids and grandkids, and the smaller guesthouse was good for the two of them when the big house was full. They hosted weekend parties there regularly, and Frank would pick up friends from all over the country in his airplane to bring them there.

In 2008, the Lovells and the Anderses traveled to the Bormans' Circle B Ranch to celebrate the fortieth anniversary of Apollo 8. The fact that after six decades of marriage the three couples were still together was just as impressive as the first flight to the Moon.

They started to spend more time in Montana, and one day Susan turned to Frank and said, "Darling, we need to decide where we are living, Las Cruces or Montana. I feel like a boat without an anchor and want to stay put." Fred and Donna had already left Las Cruces to go to the eastern part of the country. There wasn't really anything keeping them in New Mexico anymore.

After living in Las Cruces for twelve years, the Bormans let the kids take whatever they wanted from their beautiful home on the Rio Grande and sold or donated the rest. They headed to Montana with hardly anything but a few pieces of art that Susan refused to part with and their beloved bichon dog.

Looking back, Frank wished that he had said something, had told Susan that he didn't really want to leave. Her anxiety and mood swings were getting worse, and at that point he would have done anything to alleviate her pain. He thought that if she were surrounded by family in a peaceful place it would help, but instead she felt extremely isolated at the ranch.

Finally, in desperation, Frank took her to the Mayo Clinic. They kept her for two weeks to help her with the severe anxiety attacks. The doctor recommended electroshock therapy, and Frank reluctantly agreed. It actually helped a great deal, and he was able to take her home to Montana. Things seemed to be going better for Susan when they got home, and Fred and Donna eventually moved there to start ranching in earnest.

Frank and Susan made themselves available to get anything the kids needed to get started on their new enterprise, but much to the family's worst fears, Susan started to decline again. She was finally diagnosed with Alzheimer's disease.

Although the majority of people with Alzheimer's aren't diagnosed until after age sixty-five, the disease can begin in the brain years before that. Multiple studies have seen a link between anxiety, depression, and Alzheimer's. This horrifying and irreversible disease, which slowly steals a person away before the body is ready to go, is one of the most agonizing things to watch a loved one go through.

The next worst day of Frank Borman's life was when Susan had to enter a long-term care facility in 2012. Frank was eighty-four years old and had to accept that he just couldn't give her the care that she needed anymore. She could no longer walk on her own, couldn't feed herself, and basically had stopped speaking except for an occasional "Yes" or "No."

Frank took her a big bouquet of flowers not long after she had been moved to the Canyon Creek Memory Care facility. It was their sixty-sixth wedding anniversary. He leaned down to kiss her, and she looked at him with confusion. She didn't recognize the man that had been by her side for all these years. Frank sat with her all day, and when he got up to leave, her vision cleared briefly. He knew that for a few moments she recognized who he was. She put a trembling hand on his cheek as he leaned over to hear what she wanted to say.

"I'm so sorry, darling," she said. "I'm so sorry that I did this to you . . . that you have to go through this." That was his Susan. She was slowly dying—but was more concerned with how it was affecting her soul mate.

In the fall of 2019, shortly after the Bormans' sixty-ninth wedding anniversary, Frank sold his house, packed his flight suit, and moved into a seniors' home across the park from Susan's care facility. Despite all his remarkable achievements, the only mementos displayed on the walls of his small apartment are pictures of Susan and two cards she wrote him. One is a framed anniversary card that hangs where Frank can always see it: "*You promised me the moon Frank, and you delivered . . . your one and only, Susan.*" His other most prized possession is a Christmas card written by Susan shortly after she was diagnosed with Alzheimer's. The intimate note is stored safely in the top drawer of his desk, out of view.

Most days Frank still meets someone eager to chat about his epic life. While always gracious, he thinks about his time at Eastern Airlines, NASA, and his voyage to the Moon like contrails behind his airplane. The awards and personal mementos collected during those years have been distributed among his children, grandchildren, and a few close friends, and what was left he donated to the EAA Aviation Museum in Oshkosh, Wisconsin, in 2018.

For the fighter pilot who commanded the first manned mission to the Moon and seemed to have an almost mythological life, Frank Borman's most cherished possessions are ones he keeps close to himself. Along with the memories of his and Susan's life together are countless photos, love letters, and cards from Susan he stores safely in a small watertight container.

———

In that still and settled place, there's nobody but you.
You're where I breathe my oxygen, you're where I see my
    view.
When the world feels full of noise, my heart knows what
    to do.
It finds that still and settled place and dances there with you.

—Edward Monkton

It is 4 AM in Billings, Montana, and Frank Borman is getting up to go to the gym so that he can stay as healthy as possible. From there he will stop at his favorite coffee shop, read the paper, and wait. He is waiting until Susan wakes up at the care facility that she has been living at for a few years now. When the unpredictable weather in Big Sky Country cooperates, Frank flies his T-34 over to Bighorn to check the ranch and reminisce about his life with Susan. *Su Su IV* is a bright yellow 1954 air force trainer and, like all the planes he's owned, named for his girl.

By all accounts Frank is the oldest licensed pilot in the state of Montana. "I may still be the best pilot in the world," the ninety-two-year-old chuckles.

Susan doesn't recognize who Frank is anymore and can barely speak, but is anxious every morning when she wakes up and doesn't know where she is.

Frank makes sure that he is there beside her to reassure her, to comfort her. He lets her know that she is his beautiful wife and that he will sit with her all day so that she is never alone. Besides the staff at the home, he has hired caregivers for her, named Brenda and Tonya, and night caregivers named Jessica and Loni, who love Susan and are treated like family. One of them is always with her when he finally leaves to go to his small apartment across the street to heat up a microwave dinner and sleep. It's very important to him that she is never alone. He takes her to get her hair done a couple of times a week and makes sure she is always wearing something nice, because that was important to her.

He does this every day. Every day. And he will continue to do it every day until he has to say good-bye to the love of his life.

Even though her body and mind have nearly stopped working, Susan still seems to sense how much Frank needs her, needs to have this one last mission to watch over her. It's his only reason to get out of bed every day. Their deep bond is why she won't let go and neither will he.

A love like that is a powerful force all its own. It may not be a fairy-tale ending, but it is so much better. Because it's real. It's messy. It's beautiful and raw. It's full of all that life can give two people—and they continue to face it together.

It is *the* definition of true love.

As on that Christmas Eve in 1968 when he flew around the far side of the Moon and out of communication with the rest of humanity, Frank is quick to remind us when it comes to a love like his and Susan's, regardless of time and space, loss of signal is only temporary.

"I don't know about having more than one lifetime," Frank says as he looks over at Susan. "But I have always been with her, and I always will be."

ACKNOWLEDGMENTS

I F IT WAS UP TO ME, I would have included every astronaut wife in this book that I was able to talk to during this process because they were all truly an inspiration. These are women who were put in extraordinary circumstances and just simply rose to the occasion. They were thrust into the spotlight overnight, and they handled it with grace and dignity. Most were in their twenties and thirties raising children within a system that didn't really care about them, and yet they exuded incredible strength and fortitude.

It has been my privilege and my honor to be able to talk to these women. They have become my heroes, and it is why I was so compelled to write Susan's story. All of these women should be acknowledged for their courage and commitment to their country just as their iconic husbands were. So, thank you to Marilyn Lovell, Harriet Eisele, Beth Williams, and the astronauts' personal nurse Dee O'Hara for your honesty and candor. Your love for Susan was evident in all our conversations.

Thank you to Michael Collins of Apollo 11 for reading the book and the wonderful quote you provided. Thank you to Kate Collins and Ann Collins Starr, daughters of Michael and Pat, for your insight into the lives that you led. Thank you to Apollo 15 commander Dave Scott, and Apollo 16 lunar module pilot Charlie Duke and his wife, Dotty.

Thank you to photojournalist Larry Mayer, and to Jerry Strutz of the Tucson High Badger Foundation.

Thank you to Fred and Donna Borman, and Edwin and Barbara Borman, for your insights about your beloved mother.

Thank you to Susan's close friends, Bev Sargent, Audrey Ray, Vivian McCarthy, and Miliana Drachman Kelly. You helped to paint a picture of Susan's childhood and her years after NASA.

Thank you to Susan's caregivers Tonya Benjamin and Brenda Vidrine for your candid interviews about Susan. Your affection for her was very evident. Many thanks to Stephanie Castillo and Laura Rochon from NASA, who have been an invaluable resource on several projects I've been associated with.

Thank you to Eric Anderson, Morgan Maxwell, Jim Tolley, and Russ Ray for sharing your memories of Frank and Susan. Jerome Pohlen of Chicago Review Press, thank you for your faith in this book and your support.

And to Frank Borman, whose devotion to this extraordinary woman will never cease to inspire me: your honesty and willingness to acknowledge the painful things that both of you went through reminds us of the meaning of unconditional love.

And finally, to my amazing husband, Michael. You are my hero and story archaeologist, who has always believed that story is the the most powerful cultural force on the planet.

NOTES

2. Duty Calls

"beautiful—with poise": Robert Kurson, *Rocket Men: The Daring Odyssey of Apollo 8 and the Astronauts Who Made Man's First Journey to the Moon* (New York: Random House, 2018), 58.

8. "You Gave Your Ass to the Air Force"

"Anybody who would spend $40 billion": Douglas Brinkley, *American Moonshot* (New York: HarperCollins, 2019), 260.

9. The New Nine

"Being an astronaut's wife means": Eugene Cernan and Don Davis, *The Last Man on the Moon* (New York: St. Martin's Press, 1999), 176.

"You can only do this if you believe": Cernan and Davis, 176.

"My name is not going to be in the history books": Cernan and Davis, 344.

"Frank thought that their time": John W. Young with James R. Hansen, *Forever Young* (Gainesville: University Press of Florida, 2012), 74.

"The egos of Grissom and Borman": Cernan and Davis, *The Last Man on the Moon*, 66.

"Jim got along with everybody": Donald K. Slayton with Michael Cassutt, *Deke!* (New York: Forge, 1994), 161.

"For heaven's sake, wipe your tears": Kurson, *Rocket Men*, 67.

"These past weeks I have worn": Kurson, 67.

11. "There's More to Life than Living"

"aggressive and capable": Michael Collins, *Carrying the Fire* (New York: Far-
rar, Straus and Giroux, 1974), 59.

"I was always the impatient": Borman with Serling, *Countdown*, 124.

"A good move, given Frank's independence": Tom Stafford with Michael Cassutt, *We Have Capture* (Washington, DC: Smithsonian, 2002), 105.

"She just worked at being Ed's wife": Lily Koppel, *The Astronaut Wives Club*
(New York: Grand Central, 2013), 170.

"If you think going to the Moon is hard": Cernan and Davis, *The Last Man on
the Moon*, 254.

"We in the space program had overlooked": Borman with Serling, *Countdown*.

"Stop the witch hunt": Borman with Serling, *Countdown*, 180.

"He handled himself with professional assurance": Walter Cunningham, *The
All-American Boys* (New York: MacMillan, 1977), 14.

"I'm not going to make it back": Craig Nelson, *Rocket Men: The Epic Story of
the First Men on the Moon* (New York: Penguin, 2009), 192.

12. 50/50

"We knew that the Russians were hell bent": *Earthrise: The First Lunar Voyage*,
directed by Kevin Michael Kertscher (Indigo Studios and WWCI, 2005,
2013), via SpaceRip, YouTube, December 22, 2015, https://youtu.be
/xfmtFO2eAag?t=64.

"People in our country assumed": Stafford with Cassutt, *We Have Capture*, 117.

"It's insane!": Kurson, *Rocket Men*, 45.

"Of course there are risks": Borman with Serling, *Countdown*, 191.

13. Mission vs. Family

"Susan and Marilyn did more socializing": Borman with Serling, *Countdown*, 122.

"Once he got a whiff of that moon": Collins, *Carrying the Fire*, 297.

"I was wrong about some things": Borman with Serling, *Countdown*, 192.

The NASA "squawk box": "NASA Wives and Families," *American Experience* official website, accessed June 9, 2021, https://www.pbs.org/wgbh
/americanexperience/features/moon-nasa-wives-and-families/.

"I felt like a rat": Kurson, *Rocket Men*, 153.

Make a congenial home: Quoted in Kurson, 128–129.

14. Loss of Signal

"It really was a miracle": Borman with Serling, *Countdown*, 225.

"Start at the beginning": Robert Zimmerman, *Genesis: The Story of Apollo 8* (New York: Four Walls Eight Windows, 1998), 236.

"I think it gave a lot of people hope": *Earthrise: The Story of the Photo That Changed the World*, directed by Emmanuel Vaughan-Lee (Go Project Films, 2018), via National Geographic Short Film Showcase, YouTube, December 24, 2018, https://youtu.be/BsShNeDvccc?t=1710.

"the most influential": Kluger, *Apollo 8*, 288.

"It was one of the most traumatic": *Chasing the Moon*, PBS documentary, 2019.

15. Moral Compass

"I don't think you could find": Borman with Serling, *Countdown*, 225.

"My hope is that space exploration": Borman with Serling, *Countdown*, 224.

19. "It's Time for a Reckoning"

"Recovery is a process": "Mission & Values," Institute of Living official website, accessed June 9, 2021, https://instituteofliving.org/about-us/mission-values.

22. The Next Mission

higher murder rates than any other city: Robert Sherrill, "Can Miami Save Itself: A City Beset by Drugs and Violence," *New York Times Magazine*, July 19, 1987.

INDEX

314INDEX